Promoting Healthy Living in Latin America and the Caribbean

DIRECTIONS IN DEVELOPMENT
Human Development

Promoting Healthy Living in Latin America and the Caribbean

Governance of Multisectoral Activities to Prevent Risk Factors for Noncommunicable Diseases

María Eugenia Bonilla-Chacín, Editor

THE WORLD BANK
Washington, D.C.

Contents

Box

Figures

Tables

Acknowledgments

This report was prepared by a World Bank technical team led by María Eugenia Bonilla-Chacín, Senior Economist, LCSHH. The rest of the team included Edmundo Murrugarra, Senior Economist, LCSHS, and consultants Claudia Trezza, Public Health Specialist; Luis Marcano Vázquez, Economist; Kimie Tanabe, Economist; Ricardo Sierra, Economist; Barbara Koeppel, editor; Cecilia Parker, editor; with logistic and administrative support from Isadora Nouel, Program Assistant and Evelyn Rodriguez-Quevedo, consultant, LCSHH. The work was conducted under the guidance of Joana Godinho, Sector Manager. Edmundo Murrugarra was responsible for the section on labor market impact on NCDs; this section benefited from the financial support of the Disability Trust Fund and conversations with Alexandra Posarac.

The document, particularly in its first three chapters, draws from commissioned background papers that were prepared by the following people: Luis Marcano Vázquez, consultant, Inter-American Development Bank; Claudia Trezza, senior researcher, The George Washington University; Kimie Tanabe, consultant, World Bank; and Rocardo Sierra, consultant, Inter-American Development Bank. Those responsible for the country case studies were María Eugenia Barbieri for Argentina's National Ministry of Health for the two Argentina case studies; Olga Sarmiento, Adriana Díaz del Castillo, and Ethel Segura for the Bogotá, Colombia, case study; Evelyne Rodriguez for the Mexico case study; and Amanda Sica, Franco González Mora, and Winston Abascal and Ana Lorenzo from Uruguay's National Program for Tobacco Control for the Ministry of Public Health for the Uruguay case study.

This report benefited from comments received from Michael Engelgau, Margaret Grosh, Son-Nam Nguyen, and Patricio Márquez, as well as additional comments from Amparo Gordillo, Montserrat Meiro-Lorenzo, Joy de Beyer, Luis Orlando Perez, and Fernando Lavadenz.

An important part of this work would not have been possible without the support and participation of the Argentinean Ministry of Health, the Uruguayan Ministry of Public Health, and the support of different health officials from both countries including Dr. Máximo Diosque, Dr. Marina Kosacoff, Dr. Sebastián Laspiur, Dr. Mario Virgolini, and Dr. Jonatan Konfino in Argentina and Dr. Jorge Venegas and Dr. Clara Niz in Uruguay. The team also acknowledges and thanks the support received from Mexico's Secretariat of Health, particularly from Dr. Mauricio Hernández Ávila, Dr. Ricardo Pérez Cuevas, Dr. Pablo Kuri Morales, and Dr. Eduardo Jaramillo, and Colombia's Ministry of Health and Department of National Planning.

This work was possible thanks to the financial support of the Spanish Fund for Latin America and the Caribbean (SFLAC).

About the Authors

María Eugenia Bonilla-Chacín is a senior economist working on the Health, Nutrition and Population unit of the Latin America and the Caribbean region at the World Bank. She has also worked on human development issues in the Africa region of the World Bank. Her areas of interest are human development policies, particularly health policies, and poverty. She has led and participated in several analytical pieces supporting operational work and country dialogue. These efforts have included work on health policy, health financing, governance, and service delivery, work on multisectoral approaches to prevent noncommunicable diseases, and work on public expenditure management in both health and education sectors. María Eugenia earned a PhD in economics (applied microeconomics) from The Johns Hopkins University. She also has a master's degree in development economics from Vanderbilt University. She earned a bachelor's degree in international relations at the Universidad Central de Venezuela in Caracas, República Bolivariana de Venezuela.

Edmundo Murrugarra is a senior economist with the Human Development Department in the Latin America and the Caribbean region at the World Bank. His areas of interest are labor markets, social protection policies, and poverty. He has recently worked on the policy design and implementation of interaction between labor markets and social protection programs in marginal urban areas, involving a multisectoral team including health and urban development. He previously worked on the links between poverty, health status, and health care utilization; social assistance programs; migration; and vulnerability and poverty in several regions including Europe and Central Asia, Middle East, North Africa, and Latin America. He has taught at the Pontificia Universidad Católica del Perú and the Central Reserve Bank of Peru, Lima. He earned a bachelor's degree in economics from the Pontificia Universidad Católica del Perú and a master's degree and PhD in economics from the University of California, Los Angeles.

Claudia Trezza has a master's degree in global public health from New York University. She has worked for the New York Academy of Medicine, the World Bank, and other international organizations. She is currently a senior researcher at the Department of Epidemiology and Biostatistics at The George Washington University's School of Public Health and Health Services.

María Eugenia Barbieri has a bachelor's and a master's degree in economics from the University of Buenos Aires. She was a researcher at the Center for the Study of the State and Society (CEDES), Department of Economics (2002–07) and has been a researcher at the Epidemiological Research Institute, National Academy of Medicine (IIE-ANM), since 2007. María was a fellow of the multicentric study "Methodologies to Set Research Priorities in Health 2006–2007" and a principal researcher in 2008. She received the National Academy of Medicine Award 2009 for the research "Family, Social and Economic Impact of Injuries. An Interdisciplinary Approach." María was a consultant for various international organizations (e.g., Inter-American Development Bank, United Nations Children's Fund, Pan American Health Organization), social security institutions in Argentina, and the National Ministries of Economics and Health in topics related to public health, health economics, and public policies. She has been a professor of public and private universities.

Adriana Díaz del Castillo Hernández is an independent researcher and consultant. She holds a master's degree in medical anthropology from the University of Amsterdam and a medical degree from the Universidad Nacional de Colombia. She has worked with public and private institutions in Colombia and abroad. Her field of study involves the interplay between health and society. Specifically, she is interested in the study of urban infrastructures as spaces with the potential to construct equality and well-being and shape people's experiences in cities. She has participated in studies and publications about Bogotá's Ciclovía and other programs and infrastructures that promote physical activity and quality of life.

Ethel Segura Duran is an architect who graduated from the Universidad de Los Andes in Colombia in 2003. She is specialist in planning for regional development. She obtained a master's degree in governance in 2011 from the Universidad de los Andes. She has developed studies in urban management and urban legislation, support systems for spatial decisions at the ITC–Netherlands, and in project management at the School of Business in Los Andes. She has worked as a functionary at the planning office for the District of Bogotá in the Territorial Plan since 1999 in urban normative and the interinstitutional coordination of digital cartographic information for the evaluation of the plan in 2003.

Olga L. Sarmiento is an Associate Professor of the Department of Public Health at the School of Medicine at Universidad de los Andes (Bogotá, Colombia). She holds an M.D. from the Universidad Javeriana (Bogotá), an M.P.H., and a Ph.D. from the Department of Epidemiology at the School of Public Health at the University of North Carolina at Chapel Hill. Currently she is the director of the Group of Epidemiology at the Universidad de los Andes. She is a board member of the International Society of Physical Activity and Health and the Global Advocacy for Physical Activity (GAPA) council. In 2011 she received the Honorary Distinction from The National Institute of Sports in Colombia (Coldeportes Nacional) for the academic work towards promoting healthy behaviors in Colombia. Her current research interests include physical activity, nutrition and built environment among the populations of children and adults in Latin America. She is currently working in the IPEN Network (International Physical Activity, and Environment Network), the evaluation of the effectiveness of the Recreovia Program for the promotion of physical activity in community settings, the Challenge Score for evaluating the Ciclovías Recreativas of the Americas and The International Study of Childhood Obesity, Lifestyle and the Environment (ISCOLE). Her work has been published in prestigious journals including the Lancet, The American Journal of Public Health and Social Science and Medicine.

Evelyne Rodriguez has a bachelor's degree in economics from the Instituto Tecnológico de México (ITAM). She has a master's degree in Public Policy from the J. F. Kennedy School of Government at Harvard University. From 1988 to 2005, she held a number of positions in Mexico's government, including director for economic and social benefits at the Mexican Social Security Institute; treasurer of Mexico; general director of planning and budget for agriculture, social development and environment at the Ministry of Finance; and general director for economic studies in the deregulation program at the Ministry of Trade. Ms. Rodriguez has played a significant role in the structural reform of key sectors in the design, implementation and evaluation of public expenditure policies, poverty alleviation and rural development programs, including the creation and implementation of *Progresa-Oportunidades*. She is the author of numerous articles and coauthored a book with Santiago Levy (IDB), entitled *Sin Herencia de Pobreza*. She currently heads the Department for Research in Health Policies at the Center for Economic and Social Studies of Mexico's Children's Hospital Federico Gomez and does consulting for international organizations in different countries.

Amanda Sica holds a Diploma in Social Psychologist (ICI - Buenos Aires - Argentina) 1991. Since 1993 she has been the Technical Deputy of the Technical Training and Vocational Area of the Honorary Commission to Fight Cancer (Montevideo, Uruguay). She has developed, coordinated, and lectured courses on Tobacco Control in public and private institutions since 1999. She was the Official Delegate to the Intergovernmental Authority on the WHO Framework Convention on Tobacco Control (INB4) in 2002. Member of research groups and official advisory committees on Tobacco Control from 2005 to date. She was awarded the National Grand Prize of the Academy of Medicine 2012, as coauthor of the study "Impact of tobacco control policies in Uruguay, 2006-2009".

Ana Lorenzo she is the Assistant to the Director of the National Program for Tobacco Control of Ministry of Public Health of Uruguay. Alternate Member of the Intergovernmental Commission on Tobacco Control of MERCOSUR and Associated States. Representative of Uruguay in the Working Group for the development of the Guidelines of Article 14 of the WHO Framework Convention on Tobacco Control. Representative of Uruguay in the Working Group on "Sustainable Measures to strengthen the implementation of the Framework Convention on tobacco Control".

Franco González Mora holds a degree in sociology and master's degree in Demography and Population Studies. He currently serves as a teacher and researcher in the Department of Preventive and Social Medicine, Faculty of Medicine, University of Uruguay, Montevideo. He is a consultant at the Educational Research and Statistics Department of the National Public Education Administration (ANEP). He is a researcher at the Department of Sociology, Faculty of Social Sciences, University of Uruguay, Montevideo.

Winston Abascal is the Director of the National Program for Tobacco Control at the Ministry of Public Health of Uruguay. Representative of Uruguay to the Intergovernmental Committee for the Tobacco Control of MERCOSUR and Associated States. Representative of Uruguay to the Conference of the Parties to the WHO Framework Convention on tobacco Control.

Abbreviations

ADL	activities of daily living
ALAD	Latin American Diabetes Association
ALIAR	Alianza Libre de Humo—Argentina (Smoke-free Partnership—Argentina)
ANCT	Alianza Nacional para el Control del Tabaco (National Alliance for Tobacco Control), Uruguay
ANMAT	Administración Nacional de Medicamentos, Alimentos y Tecnología Médica (National Administration of Drugs, Food, and Medical Technology), Argentina
ANSA	Acuerdo Nacional para la Salud Alimentaria (National Agreement on Food Health), Mexico
ASAGA	Asociación Argentina de Grasas y Aceites (Argentine Fats and Oils Association)
AsAT	Asociación Argentina de Tabacología (Argentine Tobacco Association)
BAC	blood alcohol concentration
BAT	British American Tobacco
BMI	body mass index
BRT	bus rapid transit
CAMDI	Central American Diabetes Initiative
CANACINTRA	Cámara Nacional de la Industria de la Transformación (National Chamber for the Transformation Industry), Mexico
CASEN	Encuesta de Caracterización Socioeconómica Nacional (National Socioeconomic Survey), Chile
CATCH	The Child and Adolescent Trial for Cardiovascular Health
CATU	Comisión Antitabáquica del Uruguay (Uruguayan Anti-Tobacco Commission)
CCE	Consejo Coordinador Empresarial (Business Coordination Council), Mexico
CDC	Centers for Disease Control and Prevention, U.S.
CHD	coronary heart disease

CHLCC	Comisión Honoraria de Lucha contra el Cáncer (Honorary Commission to Fight Cancer), Uruguay
CIC	Comisión de Investigación Científica (Scientific Research Commission), Buenos Aires, Argentina
CIET	Smoking Epidemic Research Center
CLACCTA	Comité Latinoamericano Coordinador para el Control del Tabaquismo (Latin American Coordinating Committee on Tobacco Control)
CONADE	Comisión Nacional de Cultura Física y Deporte (National Commission of Physical Culture and Sport), Mexico
COFEMER	Comisión Federal de la Mejora Regulatoria (Federal Commission for Regulatory Improvement), Mexico
CONAGUA	Comisión Nacional del Agua (National Water Commission), Mexico
CONAL	Comisión Nacional de Alimentos (National Food Commission), Argentina
CONCAMIN	Confederación de Cámaras Industriales (Confederation of Chambers of Industry), Mexico
CONMEXICO	Consejo Mexicano de la Industria de Productos de Consumo (Mexican Council of Consumer Products Industries)
CONPES	Consejo Nacional de Política Económica y Social (National Council for Economic and Social Policy), Colombia
COPAL	Coordinadora de las Industrias de Productos Alimenticios (Coordinator of Food Product Industries), Argentina
COPD	chronic obstructive pulmonary disease
CSO	civil society organization
CVD	cardiovascular disease
DALYs	disability-adjusted life years
DBP	diastolic blood pressure
DHS	demographic and health survey
DIGESA	Dirección General de Salud (Directorate General of Health), Uruguay
DOT	Department of Transportation
DOTA	Declaration of the Americas on Diabetes
EAAB	Empresa de Acueducto y Acantarillado de Bogotá (Bogotá Water Supply and Sewage Company)
ECV	Encuesta de Condiciones de Vida (Quality of Life Survey), Colombia
EHPM	Encuesta de Hogares de Propósitos Múltiples (Multiple Purpose Household Surveys), El Salvador

EMNV	(Encuesta de Hogares sobre Medición de Nivel de Vida (National Standard of Living Survey), Nicaragua
ENCOVI	National Quality of Life Survey (Encuesta Nacional de Condiciones de Vida), Guatemala
ENSANUT	Encuesta Nacional de Nutrición y Salud (National Health and Nutrition Survey), Mexico
EPODE	Ensemble Prevenons l'Obesite Des Enfants (Together Let's Prevent Childhood Obesity)
ETB	Empresa de Telecomunicaciones de Bogotá (Bogotá Telephone Company)
FAIPA	Federación Argentina de la Industria del Pan y Afines (Argentine Federation of Baked Products Industry)
FAO	Food and Agriculture Organization
FBS	food balance sheet
FCND	Food Consumption and Nutrition Division
FCTC	Framework Convention on Tobacco Control
FDA	Food and Drug Administration, United States
FENALCO	Federación Nacional de Comerciantes (National Federation of Businessmen)
FET	Fondo Especial del Tabaco (Special Tobacco Fund), Argentina
FIC Argentina	Inter-American Heart Foundation—Argentina
GATS	Global Adult Tobacco Survey
GDP	gross domestic product
GUIA	Guide for Useful Interventions for Physical Activity
HIV	human immunodeficiency virus
HSS	Health and Human Services
ICSID	International Centre for Settlement of Investment Disputes
IDF	International Diabetes Federation
IDRD	Instituto Distrital de Recreación y Deportes (District Recreation and Sports Institute), Colombia
IDS	individual survey
IDU	Instituto de Desarrollo Urbano (Urban Development Insitute), Colombia
IFPRI	International Food Policy Research Institute
IMESI	tobacco excise tax, Uruguay
IMSS	Mexican Social Security Institute (Instituto Mexicano del Seguro Social)
INAL	Instituto Nacional de Alimentos (National Food Institute), Argentina

INCA	National Institute of Cancer
INEC	National Institute of Statistics and Census (Encuesta de Hogares de Propósitos Múltiples)
INNSZ	Salvador Zubirán National Institute of Medical Sciences and Nutrition
INSP	Instituto Nacional de Salud Pública (National Institute of Public Health), Mexico
INTI	Instituto Nacional de Tecnología Industrial (National Institute of Industrial Technology), Argentina
IP-TFA	industrially produced partially hydrogenated fat
ISSSTE	Instituto de Seguridad y Servicios Sociales de los Trabajadores del Estado (Institute for Social Security and Social Services for State Workers), Mexico
JICA	Japanese International Cooperation Agency
L&M	low- and middle-income
LAC	Latin America and the Caribbean
LUVEC	Liga Uruguaya de Vooulntarios de Educación para la Prevención y Control del Cáncer (Uruguayan League of Education Volunteers for Cancer Prevention and Control)
MADD	Mothers Against Drunk Driving
MERCOSUR	Mercado Común del Sur (Common Market of the South)
MET	1 kcal/kg/hour
MHAS	Mexican Health and Aging Study
MLDA	minimum legal drinking age
MoALF	Ministry of Agriculture, Livestock, and Fisheries
MOH	Ministerio de Salud (Ministry of Health)
MSP	Ministerio de Salud Pública (Ministry of Public Health)
MxFLS	Mexican Family Life Survey
NCD	noncommunicable disease
NCD/D	noncommunicable disease and disability
NCHS	National Center for Health Statistics
NGO	nongovernmental organization
NYSRA	New York State Restaurant Association
OECD	Organisation for Economic Co-operation and Development
OOP	out-of-pocket expenditure
PA	physical activity
PAHO	Pan American Health Organization
PEMEX	Mexican Petroleum

PMC	Plan Maestro de CicloRutas (CicloRutas Master Plan), Bogotá, Colombia
PNAD	Pesquisa Nacional por Mostra de Domicilios (National Household Sampling Survey), Brazil
POT	Plan de Ordenamiento Territorial
PROFECO	Federal Consumer Protection Agency
PROPIA	Programa de Prevención del Infarto en Argentina (Program to Prevent Heart Attacks in Argentina)
PSA	public service announcement
R&D	research and development
RENALOA	Red Nacional de Laboratorios Oficiales de Análisis de Alimentos (National Network of Official Laboratories for Food Protection), Argentina
RENAPRA	Red Nacional de Protección Alimentaria (National Food Protection Network), Argentina
S/.	Peruvian nuevos soles
SAGARPA	Secretaría de Agricultura, Ganadería, Desarrollo Rural, Pesca y Alimentación (Secretariat of Agriculture, Livestock, Rural Development, Fisheries, and Nutrition), Mexico
SBP	systolic blood pressure
SE	Secretaría de Economía (Secretariat of Economy), Mexico
SEDENA	Secretaría de la Defensa Nacional (Secretariat of National Defense), Mexico
SEDESOL	Secretaría de Desarrollo Social (Secretariat of Social Development), Mexico
SEMAR	Secretaría de Marina (Secretariat of the Navy), Mexico
SEP	Secretaría de Educación Pública (Secretariat of Public Education), Mexico
SFLAC	Spanish Fund for Latin America and the Caribbean
SHCP	Secretaría de Hacienda y Crédito Público (Secretariat of Finance and Public Credit), Mexico
SMU	Sindicato Médico del Uruguay (Uruguayan Medical Union)
SNDIF	Sistema Nacional para el Desarrollo Integral de la Familia (National System for Comprehensive Family Development), Mexico
STPS	Secretaría del Trabajo y Previsión Social (Secretariat of Labor and Social Welfare), Mexico
SUMEFA	Uruguayan Society of Family Physicians
SUT	Uruguayan Tobaccology Society
TB	tuberculosis

TFC	transnational food companies
TFR	total fertility rate
TLS	traffic light system
TM	TransMilenio, Bogotá, Colombia, bus rapid transit system
TTC	transnational tobacco companies
UATA	Unión Antitabáquica Argentina (Argentine Anti-Smoking Union)
UNLP	Universidad Nacional de la Plata (National University of La Plata), Argentina
USAID	United States Agency for International Development
USDA	United States Department of Agriculture
VAT	value added tax
VIGI+A	Health Surveillance and Disease Control
WHO	World Health Organization

Overview

María Eugenia Bonilla-Chacín

The purpose of this report is to contribute to the design and implementation of policies that promote healthy living in Latin America and the Caribbean (LAC), thus effectively preventing premature mortality from noncommunicable diseases (NCDs) in the region. It examines the health and economic impact of NCDs in the region and the governance challenges in the design and implementation of multisectoral policies to prevent these conditions, including polices to improve diet, increase physical activity, and reduce tobacco use and alcohol abuse. The study focuses on how policy decisions involving multisectoral interventions to prevent health risk factors are taken, which stakeholders directly or indirectly participate in those decisions, which incentives they experience, and what strategies they use in these processes.

The document is based on desk reviews, an analysis of existing databases, and commissioned case studies. In analyzing the health and economic burden of NCDs and their risk factors, this study incorporates new detailed analysis of dietary patterns in selected countries in LAC. It also includes new analyses of household surveys that explore the potential impact of NCDs on labor markets and on households' health expenditures in the region. Finally, for the analysis of the governance challenges involved in the design and implementation of selected multisectoral policies in LAC, country case studies were commissioned. These case studies were mainly based on interviews with key stakeholders that participated in these processes.

The Health and Economic Burden of NCDs in LAC

The Latin American and Caribbean region has been experiencing a rapid demographic and epidemiological transition. Not only is the region's population aging fast, it is also experiencing major lifestyle changes, including dietary alterations and more sedentary ways of life. These changes, in turn, have led to shifts in LAC's disease and mortality profiles, which have translated into a greater proportion of NCDs within the overall burden of disease.

NCDs such as heart disease, stroke, cancer, and diabetes are the main causes of death and disability in the region. In addition, NCD death rates in LAC (adjusted by age) are higher than those prevalent in higher income countries; in fact, the region has some of the highest diabetes death rates in the world. And not only are death rates higher in LAC than in higher income countries, people in the region are also dying from these conditions at younger ages. NCDs affect everyone in the region, rich and poor, urban and rural residents, men and women.

NCDs also represent an increasing economic and development threat to households, health systems, and economies in the region. NCDs require continuous contact with the health system for long periods of time and, if not controlled, can result in costly hospitalization. Moreover, out-of-pocket payments for health services, particularly for drugs, can impoverish households that have members with these conditions. Data from Colombia, Jamaica, Nicaragua, and Peru show that out-of-pocket expenditures in households that include someone with a chronic condition are more than double those of households that do not; the greatest difference is in expenditures on drugs. In Colombia and Nicaragua, households with a chronic disease patient are also more likely to have catastrophic health expenditures. NCDs also generate a large negative impact on the labor market, particularly in countries where most workers are in the formal sector. Evidence from Brazil, Chile, Colombia, El Salvador, and Honduras suggests that NCDs have a greater negative impact (5 percent or higher) on labor market participation in more formal economies such as Chile's or Brazil's. The combination of NCDs' effect on labor participation, hours worked, and productivity suggests that in these countries these diseases could have a negative impact of about 0.25 percent of gross domestic product (GDP), which could increase to 0.40 percent once the effect of related disability is included.

Much of this health and economic burden can be avoided, however, since an important share of NCDs is due to exposure to preventable risk factors, such as an unhealthy diet, a sedentary lifestyle, tobacco use, and alcohol abuse (WHO 2005). Indeed, there are cost-effective, population-based interventions designed to reduce exposure to these risk factors (WHO 2011a).[1] Many of these interventions require the active participation of several sectors outside of the health sector, although the health sector's involvement is key to ensure that these needed interventions actually occur.

Risk Factors for NCDs in LAC

An unhealthy diet represents an important health risk for the LAC population. Diets in several countries in the region are dense in energy and high in sodium, refined sugar, and fats. An analysis of household surveys from Bolivia, Costa Rica, Ecuador, Guatemala, Honduras, Nicaragua, and Panama shows that, on average, the consumption of added sugar and fat in these countries' diets is higher than WHO's recommended levels. Moreover, estimates from all these countries indicate that caloric intake in a large share of households is higher than necessary to maintain a healthy weight. Average sodium intake is also higher than recommended levels, while the intake of fruits and vegetables is lower. These dietary patterns are likely to increase the risk of developing NCDs.

Energy-dense diets, and diets rich in salt, sugars, and fats and poor in fruits and vegetables increase the risk for cardiovascular diseases, diabetes mellitus, certain cancers, dental caries, and osteoporosis (WHO 2003).

Energy-dense diets, combined with a sedentary lifestyle, are responsible for the large percentage of overweight and obese adults in the region, particularly among women. According to WHO data, half of adult men and two-thirds of adult women in the region are overweight or obese, greatly exceeding the average rate in the Organisation for Economic Co-operation and Development (OECD) countries. Indeed, due to the disability-adjusted life years (DALYs) lost attributed to high body mass index (BMI), the Burden of Disease Study 2010 ranked high BMI as the first health risk factor in some Southern Cone countries (Argentina, Chile, and Uruguay); the second in the Caribbean and in Central America, Colombia, and República Bolivariana de Venezuela; and the third in the rest of the region (Lim and others 2012).

In several countries, high rates of overweight and obesity coexist with high rates of chronic malnutrition. Three of the four countries in the world with the highest percentage of overweight mothers and malnourished children are in LAC—Bolivia, Guatemala, and Nicaragua (Garret and Ruel 2003). Often, these conditions are related; for instance, low birthweight and child malnutrition have been associated with increases in the rates of hypertension, cardiovascular diseases, and diabetes in adults (WHO 2005).

Tobacco use remains among the first five health risk factors in the region, due to the DALYs lost attributed to it (Lim and others 2012). Nearly one in four adult men and one in seven adult women in the region smoke; smoking prevalence is also high among youth. Argentina, Bolivia, Chile, Cuba, Uruguay, and República Bolivariana de Venezuela are the countries in the region with the highest percentage of adults who are tobacco users (WHO 2011b).[2]

Alcohol abuse is the leading health risk factor in most Latin American and Caribbean countries. In fact, in 2010 alcohol use was estimated to be the leading health risk factor in all LAC subregions, with the exception of the Caribbean and of countries such as Argentina, Chile, and Uruguay, where alcohol ranked among the first five risk factors (Lim and others 2012). WHO ranked Belize, Ecuador, Guatemala, Mexico, Nicaragua, and Paraguay as the region's countries with the highest alcohol-related health risk. These countries have the highest consumption of alcohol per drinker and the largest percentage of drinkers reporting binge drinking (WHO 2011c). Alcohol abuse not only increases the risk of developing some NCDs, but it also increases the risk of injuries, including those related to traffic accidents and violence.

International Experience in Multisectoral Interventions to Prevent Health Risk Factors: Overcoming Governance Challenges Involved in Their Design and Implementation

These changes in lifestyle and in the disease profile in the region present important demands on policymakers. Many of the interventions needed to prevent some of the negative economic and health impacts of NCDs go beyond the health sector and beyond interventions that it traditionally delivers. Thus, health-sector policymakers not only must ensure that the prevention, control, and surveillance of these diseases take place within the sector but also must ensure that multisectoral preventive interventions are implemented. Improving diet, increasing physical activity, and reducing tobacco use and alcohol abuse require the concerted effort of various stakeholders working in multiple sectors (see table O.1). In addition to the public sector's participation, the private sector and civil society also must participate. Given the involvement of so many stakeholders, often holding opposing views, policymakers and other health advocates must cope with various challenges in the governance of the decision-making process of these interventions.

Despite these challenges, there are many promising or successful international experiences, including promising examples in LAC, such as are listed in table O.1. The table's second column classifies the different groups of interventions to improve nutrition, promote physical activity, and reduce tobacco use and alcohol abuse, according to their cost-effectiveness following WHO (2011a). Most interventions included in the table are those that WHO (2011a) considers as "best buys," in that they are "cost-effective, low cost, and can be implemented in low resource settings"; the majority of these aim at controlling tobacco use and alcohol abuse, but some target improving diet. Other cost-effective interventions, as well as effective interventions whose cost-effectiveness evidence remains limited, are also listed in the table.

In order to learn from these successful or promising international examples, it is important to understand the processes whereby they were developed and implemented. To that end, it is important to examine the major stakeholders who influenced and shaped policy decisions, their positions, incentives faced, and strategies used; the institutional arrangements that framed the decision-making process; public perception of the policies; interaction between different stakeholders during the decision-making and implementation process; and lessons learned from these experiences. Table O.2 maps the main stakeholders, their position and strategies, and the results obtained for some of the policies reviewed.

Main Stakeholders

Many different stakeholders participate in the design and implementation of interventions aimed at improving diet, promoting physical activity, and reducing tobacco use and alcohol abuse (table O.1 and table O.2). In policies aimed at improving diet, many government actors outside the ministries of health or local health authorities have played important roles, such as ministries of agriculture, institutes of industrial technology, and consumer protection agencies (e.g., the United States Food and Drug Administration [FDA]). The food industry also has actively participated, sometimes opposing government actions, sometimes working with the government to advance public health goals. Restaurant associations and the advertising industry also have become involved. In many policies to promote physical activity, local authorities (e.g., cities, municipalities, and communities) had leading roles in their design and implementation, particularly

Table O.1 International Examples of Multisectoral Interventions Designed to Reduce Noncommunicable Disease Risk Factors

Risk factor	Cost-effectiveness	Intervention	Examples	Sectors involved
Unhealthy diet	Best buys[a]	Salt-reduction strategies	North Karelia, Finland, community program subsequently extended nationwide. Argentina, agreements with the food industry to reduce sodium in processed foods.	Agriculture, health, food industry, food retail industry, advertising industry, restaurant associations, city governments, the legislature, others.
		Replacing trans fats	New York City, ban on trans fats. Denmark, legislation regulating trans-fat levels in processed foods. Puerto Rico, ban on trans fats. Argentina, reform of the Food Code to regulate amount of trans fats in processed foods.	
	Other cost-effective[b]	Regulating advertising on marketing of foods and beverages high in salt, fat, and sugar, especially to children	United Kingdom, statutory regulation on advertising	
		Taxes and subsidies to promote healthy diets	Poland, elimination of butter and lard subsidies.	
Physical inactivity	Effective with insufficient evidence on its cost-effectiveness.[c]	Modifying the built environment to increase physical activity	New York City, bike lanes and bike paths. Bogotá, Colombia, sustainable public transportation, Ciclovía, CicloRutas, and outdoor gyms.	City governments, urban planning, transport, health, civil society organizations (CSOs), and the media.

table continues next page

Table O.1 International Examples of Multisectoral Interventions Designed to Reduce Noncommunicable Disease Risk Factors *(continued)*

Risk factor	Cost-effectiveness	Intervention	Examples	Sectors involved
Community-based programs to improve nutrition and increase physical activity	Effective with insufficient evidence on its cost-effectiveness.[c]	Work-based programs	United States, "Treatwell 5-a-Day" program to increase fruit and vegetable consumption.	Agriculture, health, food industry, food retail industry, schools, work places, food retailers, others.
		School-based programs	United States, Child and Adolescent Trial for Cardiovascular Health (CATCH). United States, Pathways (randomized control study among Native American schoolchildren).	
		Other community-based programs	North Karelia, Finland, decreasing salt and fat consumption and increasing fruit and vegetable consumption. Europe, EPODE.	
Tobacco use	Best buys[a]	Fiscal Measures Banning smoking in public places. Raising awareness and increasing knowledge about dangers of tobacco use. Enforcing bans on tobacco advertising, promotion and sponsorship.	Several successful examples worldwide. Uruguay, tobacco-control policy is one of LAC's most successful efforts in this regard.	Finance, health, agriculture, legislature, international organizations, tobacco industry, farmers, CSOs.

table continues next page

Table O.1 International Examples of Multisectoral Interventions Designed to Reduce Noncommunicable Disease Risk Factors (continued)

Risk factor	Cost-effectiveness	Intervention	Examples	Sectors involved
Alcohol abuse	Best buys[a]	Fiscal policies	USSR, Gorbachev anti-alcohol legislation.	Federal and state governments, city governments, health sector, police, agriculture, alcoholic-beverage industry, and CSO.
		Restrictions on availability and access to alcohol	Sweden, state monopoly on alcohol sale (*Systembolaget*).	
			Various U.S. states' alcohol licensing systems	
		Limiting the hours of alcohol sales	Australia, Halls Creek Aboriginal town limit of alcohol sales.	
			New Zealand, liquor bans and limitations on alcohol-sale hours.	
			Brazil, city of Diadema alcohol-sale restrictions.	
		Age restrictions on alcohol purchase and sale	United States, raising the Minimum Legal Drinking Age (MLDA).	
	Other cost-effective efforts[b]	BAC[d]	United States, "Checkpoint Tennessee" program to decrease drunk driving.	

Source: Author, based on data from chapter 4 of this publication.

Note: The table includes most of the programs reviewed for this study. The cost-effectiveness classification in the second column of the table refers to the intervention in general (in the abstract) as per WHO (2011a). It does not necessarily refers to each particular example provided of each intervention.

EPODE = Ensemble Prevenons l'Obesite Des Enfants (Together Let's Prevent Childhood Obesity); LAC = Latin America and the Caribbean.

a. "Best buys" are interventions that WHO (2011a) considers as "cost-effective, low cost, and can be implemented in low resource settings."

b. These are other cost-effective interventions that are not among WHO's "best buys."

c. These are effective interventions for which there is insufficient evidence on their cost-effectiveness.

d. Blood alcohol concentration.

Table O.2 Design and Implementation of Population-Based Preventive Polices, by Risk Factor

Intervention	Key stakeholders	Positions	Strategies	Outputs or outcomes
An unhealthy diet				
Salt and saturated fat reduction strategies in North Karelia, Finland. (This community-based program aimed at reducing risks for cardiovascular disease and included a component aimed at decreasing tobacco use and promoting vegetable and fruits intake.)	Local government, health services, schools, social services, nongovernmental organizations (NGOs), supermarkets, food industry, community leaders, and media. Ministries of Agriculture and of Commerce National Nutrition Council	**The government:** reducing salt intake benefits the population's health. **The food industry:** salt is an inexpensive way to add taste and to preserve food. **Ministries of Agriculture and of Commerce:** support to farmers and businesses affected by the change in consumption patterns. **Dairy farmers:** reduction of dairy consumption has negative economic effect.	**The government:** (1) informational and awareness campaign, which guaranteed consumer demand for less salty products; this pressured industry to lower sodium content. (2) Labeling regulations, which required listing sodium levels on prepackaged foods. **Ministries of Agriculture and of Commerce** financed a collaborative project between berry farmers, the berry industry, and commercial and health authorities to find innovative ways and new product development to promote berry consumption and help dairy farmers switch to berry production.	20 percent decrease in salt intake in 20 years. Decreased cardiovascular disease rates by 80 percent among men in North Karelia between 1969–71 and 2006 (Puska and others 2009).
Agreements with industry to reduce sodium in processed foods and to amend the Food Code to regulate trans fats in Argentina	Ministry of Health (MOH) National Food Institute (INAL) National Institute of Industrial Technology (INTI) Ministry of Agriculture, Livestock, and Fisheries (MoALF) COPAL (Coordinator of Food Product Industries), which included FAIPA (Argentine Federation of Baked Products Industries) and ASAGA (Argentine Fats and Oils Association)	**MOH:** protect the population against harmful effect of excessive sodium and trans fats. **INAL:** as part of the Ministry, held similar position. **INTI:** similar position to the Ministry, but with a few disagreements. **MoALF:** promote value added of healthy foods.	**MOH:** (1) Coordinated the process, (2) articulated actions with other public agencies, (3) negotiated actions with the private sector, and (4) disseminated information to consumers. **INAL:** Contributed regulatory, technological, and monitoring knowledge. With INTI, MoALF, and COPAL, it designed a manual to help small and medium enterprises to eliminate trans fats in their production processes.	8,000 bakeries have signed agreements to reduce salt in bread. In addition, more than 20 large companies signed agreements with the Government to reduce sodium in several processed foods in 2011 and more in 2012. *Outputs:* Currently about *Outcomes:* Both policies still need to be fully monitored and their impact evaluated.

table continues next page

Table O.2 Design and Implementation of Population-Based Preventive Polices, by Risk Factor *(continued)*

Intervention	Key stakeholders	Positions	Strategies	Outputs or outcomes
	COPAL/FAIPA/ASAGA: representing the industry wanted to avoid sudden implementation of policies that could be costly and respond to demands from public for healthier foods. In terms of trans fats, the industry had already started to eliminate them and there were technologies available. In terms of sodium, it was considered as an inexpensive way to add flavor and preserve foods and it has fewer replacements.	**INTI**: In terms of sodium, it provides training to bakeries. In the case of trans fats, it presents and disseminates evidence on the viability of replacing trans fats and sodium in food. **MoALF**: Contributed regulatory and technological knowledge. **COPAL/ASAGA**: Organized meetings with companies to agree on the terms and goals to be discussed with the MOH. Collected and delivered information on sodium content in food. Through ASAGA, it contributed technical know-how to replace trans fats and organized meetings with companies to agree on the terms and goals to be discussed with the MOH. It also helped design the manual for small and medium size enterprises with INTI and MoALF.	

table continues next page

Table O.2 Design and Implementation of Population-Based Preventive Polices, by Risk Factor *(continued)*

Intervention	Key stakeholders	Positions	Strategies	Outputs or outcomes
Replacing trans fats in restaurants in New York City, United States	New York City Board of Health New York State Restaurant Association (NYSRA)	**The government:** reducing trans-fat intake benefits the population's health. **NYSRA:** changing production processes is costly.	**Board of Health:** (1) first strategy was to convince restaurants to voluntarily reduce trans fats. City provided training for this. When this failed, strategy moved to ban trans fats. (2) To address restaurants concerns, the city gave an extension to reach goal of reducing trans-fat levels to 0.5 grams per serving. (3) Effective communication campaign linking trans fats to coronary heart disease	This regulation is enforced. The city has fines of up to US$2,000 for noncompliance.
Physical inactivity				
New York City bike lanes, United States	New York City Department of Transportation (NYC DOT) Neighbors for Better Bike Lanes Seniors for Safety Businesses The public	**NYC DOT:** bike lanes promote environmental sustainability, attract businesses and tourism, and increase physical activity. **Neighbors for Better Bike Lanes and Seniors for Safety:** Both sued NYC DOT, charging that DOT provided named information about the benefits of the bike lanes. **Businesses:** bike lanes would inconvenience city drivers, would limit parking for deliveries, and would hinder sales. **The public:** A poll showed a higher than 60 percent support for bike lanes	**NYC DOT** made all information available, showing that the increase in bike lanes actually reduced the number of pedestrian killed in pedestrian–bike accidents.	—

table continues next page

10

Table O.2 Design and Implementation of Population-Based Preventive Polices, by Risk Factor *(continued)*

Intervention	Key stakeholders	Positions	Strategies	Outputs or outcomes
Tobacco use				
Tobacco-control policies, Uruguay	The presidency MOH and, since 2005, the Tobacco Control Program National Alliance for Tobacco Control (ANCT), which includes the MOH, and several parastatals, international organizations, NGOs, CSOs, and others. The tobacco industry. Trade associations of bars, restaurants, casinos, and businesses. Bus-drivers union.	**The presidency**: Supported tobacco control **MOH**: Supported tobacco control **Alliance**: Strong advocate of tobacco-control policies **The tobacco industry**: tried to avoid these policies. **Trade associations of bars, restaurants, casinos, and businesses**: Originally opposed the smoke-free environments as they thought it would have negative economic impacts on them. They also wanted to ensure transparency in the implementation of penalties for noncompliance with smoke free environments. **Bus-drivers union**: opposed the smoke-free environment decree.	**The presidency**: Enacted several executive decrees to fast track tobacco-control policies. **The Alliance**: lobbied in Parliament for tobacco control; worked toward the ratification of the Framework Convention on Tobacco Control (FCTC); and provided lawmakers with scientific evidence on the extent of the tobacco problem. **MOH and National Tobacco Control Program**, since 2005: launched broad media campaign to ensure public support of the smoke-free environment decree; developed and launched the country's controls and, at the national level, coordinated its efforts with the other groups that were developing policies; and checks policy's compliance.	From 2006 to 2009 there was a 10 percentage point decline the prevalence of daily smokers among people 15–64 years old in urban centers (95 percent of population)

table continues next page

Table O.2 Design and Implementation of Population-Based Preventive Polices, by Risk Factor *(continued)*

Intervention	Key stakeholders	Positions	Strategies	Outputs or outcomes
			The tobacco industry: (1) When Uruguay became a smoke-free country in 2006, the industry claimed the controls limited "freedom" and smokers' "rights," (2) further, when parliament debated the tobacco law, it lobbied lawmakers to reject it; (3) finally, it used litigation at national and international levels. In 2008, it filed judicial and administrative lawsuits in the country against all the regulations. In 2012, it requested arbitration to the International Centre for Settlement of Investment Disputes (ICSID) (World Bank).	
New York City Smoke-free Air Act (the ban was combined with a tax increase).	NYC Board of Health Tobacco industry New York Nightlife Association. Empire State Restaurant and Tavern Association Public	**The New York City Board of Health**: measure would educe exposure to second-hand smoke. **The tobacco industry**: measure would lead to loss of revenues. **New York Nightlife Association and Empire State Restaurant and Tavern Association**: the ban would harm the city's economy by decreasing profits on the city's bars and restaurants. *The public*: poll showed a 59 percent approval rate of the ban among NYC residents.	**New York Nightlife Association and the Empire State Restaurant and Tavern Association**: A study prepared for the associations stated that, following the ban, staffing had been reduced by 16 percent in bars, hotels, and nightclubs, and that three-fourths of bars and restaurants had experienced a 30 percent decline in patronage (Ridgewood Economic Associates 2004). **The tobacco industry**: it financed the restaurant and bar associations' opposition to the ban.	After the ban and the tax increase, smoking decreased by 11 percent (from 21.6 percent to 19.2 percent) between 2002 and 2003, following the intervention. The decrease occurred in all five boroughs across all age groups, race/ethnicities, education levels, and gender. Almost half of all respondents attributed the air free act, and the decreased exposure to smoke, as the primary reason for the decrease in smoking (Frieden and others 2005).

table continues next page

Table O.2 Design and Implementation of Population-Based Preventive Polices, by Risk Factor *(continued)*

Intervention	Key stakeholders	Positions	Strategies	Outputs or outcomes
			The New York City Board of Health: sponsored an evaluation that contradicted the associations' findings. Its study found that, despite the smoking ban, the city had experienced increases in jobs, liquor licenses, and business tax payments since the law had taken effect. Moreover, data from the city's Department of Finance found that, from April 2003 to January 2004, city restaurant revenues had increased by about US$ 1.4 million, compared to the same period the year earlier (Elliott 2004).	
Alcohol abuse				
USSR, 1985 Gorbachev anti-alcohol legislation	Ministry of Finance Ministry of Trade Central Planning Commission Health authorities	**Ministries of Finance and of Trade and the Central Planning Commission:** Opposed the law because it drastically reduced revenues from alcohol sales of government distilleries and from excise taxes. **Health authorities:** wanted to reduce the burden of disease created by alcohol abuse.		Between 1985 and 1987, years when the anti-tobacco policy was in effect, male life expectancy in Russia increased from 61.7 to 64.9, and female life expectancy increased from 73 to 74.3. In contrast, from 1988 to 1994, after the legislation was rescinded, male life expectancy decreased to 57.6 and female life expectancy to 71 years (Leon and others 1997).

table continues next page

Table O.2 Design and Implementation of Population-Based Preventive Polices, by Risk Factor *(continued)*

Intervention	Key stakeholders	Positions	Strategies	Outputs or outcomes
U.S. National Minimum Drinking Age Act increased the MLDA to 21 years.	Advocacy groups such as Mothers Against Drunk Driving (MADD) Different Congress representative Alcohol industry President Public	**Advocacy groups:** wanted to increase the MLDA to reduce traffic accidents produce by drunk driving. **Congressional representatives:** Two house representatives introduced a bill to increase MLDA to 21; some senators opposed it, sustaining that it violated the Constitution, as it ran against principles of federalism; in their view this should be a responsibility of the states. **The alcohol industry:** opposed the measure, as it would reduce sales. **The president:** originally opposed the federal mandate, but eventually supported measures to increase MLDA. **The public:** strong support for the measure.	**Advocacy groups:** presented a large body of research showing the benefits of increasing MLDA, particularly in regard to the dramatic increase in fatal accidents following less restrictive alcohol policies.	

Note: — = not available.

14

local transportation, sports and recreation, and urban-planning agencies. In tobacco- and alcohol-control policies, various governmental agencies were important players, not just those within the health sector, but also agencies in agriculture, commerce, economy, and finance sectors, as well as the legislative branch of government. In tobacco- and alcohol-control policies, the role of civil society organizations has been particularly important and effective in advocating for and supporting control policies. In both alcohol- and tobacco-control policies, particularly in the case of tobacco control, industry and producers can become stakeholders who effectively oppose control efforts.

The mobilization toward a public health goal does not necessarily originate with the government, but can arise with external interest groups that advocate for reform. These groups can be provider groups, such as doctors or nurses; consumer groups; or groups advocating for specific issues, such as preventing underage drinking (the United States), reducing tobacco use (Uruguay and Argentina), or temporarily closing roads to motor vehicles for recreational activities (Bogotá, Colombia). These groups' legislative success depends on various factors, including their ability to convince and mobilize enough political players and to develop sound, evidenced-based solutions to public health challenges.

Governments and health advocates face no shortage of difficulties in promoting healthy living. On the one hand, companies and businesses tend to resist measures they view as overly intrusive or that could lower their profits; on the other, citizens may oppose the idea because they may feel that it infringes on their personal liberties or lifestyle, or that it tells them how to live. Some of these stakeholders can be very powerful in terms of the resources they can bring to bear in opposing these policies. This is particularly so regarding the transnational tobacco, alcohol, and food and beverage industries. Efforts to improve public health by reducing salt intake, eliminating trans fats from processed foods, levying taxes on alcohol, adding bike lanes, or banning smoking in public places, are far from immune to such opposition.

Governments also face internal hurdles. Often, policymakers have differing views on what public goals are valid and on how best to pursue them. For instance, in the case of tobacco control in producer countries, health ministries' views may differ from those held by agriculture and finance ministries. The development and later removal of the Gorbachev-era alcohol control policies in the USSR is a case in point of policies that faced strong opposition within the government. Legislative or regulatory success often hinges on the effectiveness of a government's strategy to align the interests of political parties and agencies, civil society groups, private businesses, and the public toward common public health goals.

Stakeholder Strategies

In the design and implementation of these policies, policymakers, politicians, and other health advocates have been able to overcome the different governance challenges. This has required, among other things, intense dialogue and negotiation with all parties involved, strong coordination mechanisms, the assessment and mobilization of public opinion, the use of information and research to steer public opinion and important stakeholders, strong leadership of politicians and policymakers, and taking advantage of favorable conditions for the design and implementation of these policies.

As a result of the government's initiating a dialogue, an industry may develop its own guidelines and standards to improve public health. Such was the case in the United Kingdom, when the food manufacturers developed their own nutritional labeling standards (Traffic Light System [TLS]).

Because these voluntary actions can be ineffective, policymakers have had to impose regulations to replace them. In Europe, Canada, and the United States, early voluntary nutrition labeling actions failed to meet government standards and expectations, leading governments to switch to mandatory guidelines. In New York City, encouraging restaurants to voluntarily provide customers with nutrition information in plain sight also proved ineffective, and the city mandated regulation. Industry-led initiatives to pursue public health goals and prevent NCDs also have proven to be less satisfactory in the case of food advertising. For example, industry guidelines restricting inappropriate advertising, such as promoting unhealthy foods to children, proved weak and resulted in low levels of adherence across the industry. This led the U. K. government to impose statutory regulations that restricted advertising for unhealthy foods by limiting the hours during which ads for foods high in fat, sugar, and salt could be aired on television (Hastings and Cairn 2010).

Sometimes the interplay between the government and the sector it seeks to regulate can be highly confrontational, and governments should be prepared for this. The regulation of the tobacco industry is one such example. Until recently, the tobacco industry was one of the most powerful industries in the consumer market. It is not a coincidence, then, that tobacco-control policies sometimes took decades to take effect and, in the success stories reviewed here, required the commitment of many political players. The steadfastness of policymakers, coupled with popular support, becomes even more critical in tobacco-producing countries such as Brazil and Argentina. But even those countries that have successfully reduced tobacco prevalence through strong control policies still face hurdles, as does Uruguay. In 2010, Phillip Morris International brought to the International Centre for Settlement of Investment Disputes (ICSID) an arbitration procedure against the Government of Uruguay for its tobacco-control policies, specifically for the requirement that 80 percent of the packages display health warnings and for the prohibition for companies to differentiate their brands across products.

Most successful efforts required strong coordination among the many participating stakeholders. Often, this coordination was made possible through the leadership of ministries of health and through institutional arrangements that favored such coordination. The role of the health sector has been key in many of the examples reviewed. Often it initiated the dialogue among relevant actors and ensured coordination among them. Such was the case in Argentina's agreements to reduce sodium and the revision of the country's Food Code to reduce trans fats in processed foods. To this end, a Ministry of Health (MOH) initiative created a National Commission to Eliminate Trans Fats and Reduce Salt that included several public and business organizations, scientific associations, and civil society groups. Similarly in Uruguay, at the request of the MOH, the National Alliance for Tobacco Control (ANCT) was established; this coordinating entity comprised government agencies, parastatal organizations, international organizations, academic institutions, and nongovernmental organizations (NGOs). Finally, in the case of the Ciclovía in Bogotá, Colombia, the creation early on of the Ciclovía multisectoral committee (composed of bicycle activists, the police, the Traffic and Transport Department, and the National Cycling Federation) bolstered its development.

Policymakers and health advocates in general often gauge and mobilize public opinion in support of health promotion policies and ensure their design and implementation. For instance, while the regulation to reduce trans fats was being discussed in New York City, the city government provided constant and persuasive messages to the public on the links between trans fats and coronary heart disease; this concerted information campaign contributed to garner public support for the regulation. The policy to promote smoke-free environments in Uruguay also was accompanied by strong communication campaigns to ensure public support. Similarly, in the city of Diadema, Brazil, through education campaigns and discussions with alcohol retailers, public opinion quickly turned favorable to alcohol restriction policies (Pacific Institute for Research and Evaluation 2004).

In many of these ventures, research played a critical role in the adoption of population-wide preventive interventions. Independent research institutions were fundamental in moving policies forward, and their participation often represented the turning point toward reform. A solid and convincing research base is indispensable for shaping public opinion and raising support for policies. In the United Kingdom, for example, the decision to create a statutory regulation on advertising foods to children was influenced by research that found an association between advertising and children's food preferences and by a study showing that a large percentage of the expenditure on food advertising during children's air time was for foods high in fat, sugar, and salt (Hastings, Stead, and McDermott 2003). In Brazil, the National Cancer Association organized meetings and conferences following the circulation of alarming data on the health consequences of tobacco consumption (Da Costa and Goldfarb 2003), but that research needs to be communicated effectively to policymakers and the public. Both in the United Kingdom and in Brazil, civil society groups played a crucial role in publicizing that data and raising awareness among the population.

Whether an initiative is community-based or national in scope, whether it tackles obesity, enforces alcohol restrictions, or limits tobacco use, the leadership and political commitment of a few key political figures has been at the heart of many of the successful cases. For example, Brazil and Uruguay are countries where a group of committed politicians and policymakers, supported by strong advocacy groups, effectively fought efforts from tobacco lobbyists and put in place comprehensive and effective tobacco-control policies. In Brazil, which is a major tobacco producer, the leadership and commitment of key political players, such as the director of the National Institute of Cancer, Marcos Moraes, and the then-Minister of Health, Jose Serra, were crucial in leading the country along the path of tobacco control. In Uruguay, President Tabaré Vasquez played an important role in moving policies forward. In Bogotá, Colombia, the continuous effort of two mayors, Antanas Mockus and Enrique Peñaloza, was behind the consolidation of the city's built environment. The leadership of New York City Mayor Michael Bloomberg also deserves mention as an important factor behind the healthy lifestyle initiatives in that city.

Often, policymakers' engagement is shaped by the advocacy and persuasion of civil society groups. Such was the case for policies involving the Minimum Legal Drinking Age (MLDA) in the United States. One organization in particular, Mothers Against Drunk Driving (MADD), founded by the mother of a victim of a repeat drunk driver, was fundamental in convincing politicians and policymakers, including then-President Ronald Reagan, to pass a bill that awarded highway funds to states with anti-drunk-driving measures in place (Grant 2011).

Taking advantage of favorable conditions or moments has also been key in the successful enactment and implementation of some of these policies. In the case of tobacco control, the international context created by the Framework Convention on Tobacco Control (FCTC) has facilitated the adoption of tobacco-control policies worldwide. The signing and ratification of the FCTC in Uruguay gave strong impetus to that country's tobacco-control policies. Similarly, Colombia's decentralization process made it possible for elected mayors to independently pursue policies that changed Bogotá's built environment.

Multisectoral Interventions to Prevent Health Risk Factors in LAC— The Unfinished Agenda

Given LAC's disease profile and the existing evidence on cost-effective interventions to prevent NCDs at the population level, it is important for the region's countries to strengthen their multisectoral efforts to reduce health risk factors, particularly those targeting tobacco use and alcohol abuse. Although there are several cost-effective interventions to decrease exposure to tobacco use and alcohol abuse, there are fewer measures intended to improve diet and promote physical activity, with the exception of interventions aimed at decreasing the intake of sodium and trans fats. Thus, controlling tobacco use and, particularly, alcohol abuse, the main health risk factors in most of the region, should be the main priority. That said, given the importance of overweight and obesity as a risk factor, the region's countries also should experiment with different programs and policies aimed at stopping the increase in BMI and even to reverse it.

The region has seen several examples of successful or promising interventions to promote healthy living, such as the agreements between the government and industry to reduce sodium and the reform of the Food Code to reduce trans fats in processed foods in Argentina; the establishment of a built environment that promotes physical activity in Bogotá, Colombia; the national agreement for food health in Mexico (Strategy against Overweight and Obesity); and tobacco-control policies in Uruguay (table O.1). And there are additional examples: at both the local and national levels, groups of motivated and deeply committed policymakers and health advocates have effectively countered opposition and been able to put in place effective and long-lasting policies to prevent NCDs.

Despite these successful and promising examples, however, there is scant evidence of ongoing activities to fight NCDs at the population level in LAC, with the exception of tobacco control. Much remains to be done in the region to improve diet, promote physical activity, and reduce tobacco use and alcohol abuse.

For example, even though Argentina, Brazil, Chile, Costa Rica, and Mexico are pursuing reductions in the intake of sodium and trans fats, these efforts are the exception, rather than the rule. Moreover, these measures have yet to be consolidated and evaluated. And the region is only starting to design and implement community-based interventions to prevent and control overweight and obesity. Although halting the increasing trend in the percentage of overweight and obese persons has proven difficult across the globe, there are some policies that have proven effective in improving diet and promoting physical activity. Since nutrition habits start very early on in life, and since a growing number of children in the region are overweight, interventions at the school level would be important to consider and evaluate.

An example worthy of closer examination was Mexico's National Agreement for Food Health, a promising blueprint for action in the fight against obesity. With high rates of obesity in the country, the government set up a comprehensive strategic plan that involved the collaboration of multiple actors, including different government agencies, the private sector, civil society, and academia. The government intended to reduce overweight and obesity by increasing opportunities for physical activity and improving the population's diet. According to the plan, increased physical activity was to be pursued throughout schools, workplaces, neighborhoods, and communities. The plan also sought to ban trans fats and to implement programs across different sectors of society to encourage a greater consumption of fruits, vegetables, and grains.

Some of the region's cities are implementing policies aimed at building environments that facilitate physical activity. For example, many cities in the region have Ciclovías,[3] sustainable public transportation systems, and/or bike routes. One of the best examples of this approach is in Bogotá, Colombia. Mostly, though, these efforts concentrate in large urban centers and in upper-middle-income countries. In the case of Ciclovías, for instance, although a majority of countries have at least one, most are in one or two large urban centers. Only Colombia, Brazil, Mexico, and Peru have several active ones.[4]

In terms of tobacco control, almost all the region's countries have ratified the FCTC and have passed laws and regulations accordingly. But often these laws are not fully enforced. Moreover, there is also much improvement to be done in terms of fiscal policies, since many countries still have room to increase taxes on tobacco products. In 2010, in only 4 out of 32 countries for which data was available, did taxes represent more than 70 percent of the price of the most frequently sold brand of cigarettes (WHO 2011b).

Most countries have in place some cost-effective interventions needed to control alcohol abuse, but often these are not adequately enforced either (WHO 2011b; Monteiro 2007). For instance, most countries in the region have laws on blood-alcohol concentration levels and restrictions on hours when alcohol can be sold, but their enforcement is inconsistent. In addition, because there are many gaps in these laws, particularly in terms of restricting alcohol sales, legislation needs to be strengthened. As mentioned earlier, alcohol abuse is the leading health risk factor in the region, as it increases the risk of injuries and of developing NCDs. Despite this, information about comprehensive strategies to control alcohol abuse in the region is scanty. In the literature review conducted for this study, only two good examples were found of comprehensive strategies, both at the local level: initiatives in the cities of Diadema and Paulina in Brazil.

Because some multisectoral interventions to prevent health risk factors are more effective at the regional level, it is important that regional and subregional approaches to promote healthy living be developed. This is true for fiscal policies, particularly tobacco and alcohol taxation policies. Further, harmonizing tobacco and alcohol pricing (through tax levels) at the regional level would reduce the incentive for smuggling. And harmonizing tobacco advertising bans and nutrition labels would also make these policies more effective. There are some subregional efforts under way in this regard, such as the work by Common Market of the South (MERCOSUR) countries in nutritional labeling and the work of the intergovernmental Commission for Tobacco Control, which also is part of MERCOSUR.

Strengthening the countries' surveillance systems should be part of any strategy to prevent and control NCDs. There is little information on some health risk factors and, when it is available, it is not standardized and thus is difficult to compare. This is particularly true for information on sedentary lifestyle, overweight and obesity, abnormal blood-glucose levels, high blood pressure, and high blood-lipid levels. Some countries do not even have available data on tobacco use and alcohol abuse. Information on the prevalence of NCDs, although available for most countries, is usually based on administrative data, which makes it very difficult to disaggregate by socioeconomic group, rural or urban residence, or level of education. This, in turn, makes it difficult to target interventions to groups that need it most.

Little research and evaluation has been conducted on existing policies and interventions in LAC countries. This is particularly important in the case of policies aimed at improving diet and promoting physical activity, as there is less international evidence on cost-effective interventions targeting these risk factors. Project Guide for Useful Interventions for Physical Activity (GUIA), an initiative funded by the U.S. Centers for Disease Control and Prevention (CDC), is attempting to fill this void for physical inactivity. Yet, as important as this project is in shedding light on current physical activity interventions in the region, it is not enough. In order for the region's governments to execute meaningful plans to reduce NCDs, it is crucial that they themselves establish an overview of the current situation, demonstrating the strengths and weaknesses of ongoing programs and identifying where more action is needed. In addition, international and regional experiences have shown the importance of research, not only for evidence-based policymaking, but also to enlist the public's support for health promotion policies.

Notes

1. There are also cost-effective clinical interventions to control some of the biological or intermediate risk factors. However, they are not the focus of this document.
2. Data comes from WHO's Global Health Observatory Data Repository on Tobacco Control, at http://apps.who.int/gho/data/node.main.Tobacco.
3. A ciclovía is a program that temporarily closes streets to motor vehicles and offers safe and free spaces for recreation and physical activity.
4. For additional information on Ciclovías, visit http://www.cicloviasrecreativas.org /en/map.

Bibliography

Da Costa, L. M., and S. Goldfarb. 2003. "Government Leadership in Tobacco Control: Brazil's Experience." In *Tobacco Control Policies: Strategies Successes and Setbacks*, edited by J. de Beyer and L. W. Bringden. Washington, DC: World Bank.

Elliott, A. 2004. "Bars and Restaurants Thrive Amid Smoking Bans, Study Says." *New York Times*, March 29.

Fletcher, J., D. Frisvold, and N. Tefft. 2010. "The Effect of Soft Drink Taxes on Child and Adolescent Consumption and Weight outcomes." *Journal of Public Economics* 94: 967–74.

Frieden, T. R., F. Mostashari, B. D. Kerker, N. Miller, A. Hajat, and M. Frankel. 2005. "Adult Tobacco Use Levels after Intensive Tobacco Control Measures: New York City, 2002–2003." *American Journal of Public Health* 95 (6): 1016–23.

Garret, J., and M. Ruel. 2003. "Stunted Child-Overweight Mother Pairs: An Emerging Policy Concern." FCND Discussion Paper 148, International Food Policy Research Institute, Washington, DC.

Grant, D. 2011. "Politics, Policy Analysis, and the Passage of the National Minimum Drinking Age Act of 1984." Working Paper 1103, Sam Houston State University, Department of Economics and International Business, Huntsville, AL.

Hastings, G., and G. Carins. 2010. "Food and Beverage Marketing to Children." In *Preventing Childhood Obesity. Evidence Policy and Practice*, edited by E. Waters, B. Swinburn, J. Seidell, and R. Uauy. Oxford, UK: Wiley-Blackwell.

Hastings, G., M. Stead, and L. McDermott. 2003. *Review of Research on the Effects of Food Promotion to Children*. Glasgow, Scotland: University of Stratchclyde.

Leon, D., L. Chenet, V. M. Shkolnikov, S. Zakharov, J. Shapiro, G. Rakhmanova, S. Vassin, and M. McKee. 1997. "Huge Variation in Russian Mortality Rates 1984–94: Artefact, Alcohol, or What?" *Lancet* 350: 384–88.

Lim, S. S., A. D. Lopez, C. J. L. Murray, M. Ezzati, T. Vos, A. D. Flaxman, G. Danaei, K. Shibuya, H. Adair-Rohani, M. Amann, H. Ross Anderson, K. G. Andrews, M. Aryee, C. Atkinson, L. J. Bacchus, A. Bahalim, et al. 2012. "A Comparative Risk Assessment of Burden of Disease and Injury Attributable to 67 Risk Factors and Risk Factor Clusters in 21 Regions, 1990–2010: A Systematic Analysis for the Global Burden of Disease Study 2010." *Lancet* 380: 2224–60.

Monteiro, M. 2007. *Alcohol and Public Health in the Americas. A Case for Action*. Washington, DC: PAHO.

Pacific Institute for Research and Evaluation. 2004. "Prevention of Murders in Diadema, Brazil. The Influence of New Alcohol Policies." http://resources.prev.org/resource _pub_brazil.pdf.

Puska, P., E. Vartiainen, T. Laatikaninen, P. Jousilahti, and M. Paavola, eds. 2009. *The North Karelia Project: From North Karelia to National Action*. Helsinki: Helsinki University Printing House.

Ridgewood Economic Associates. 2004. "The Economic Impact of the New York State Smoking Ban on New York's Bar." Prepared for the New York Nightlife Association and the Empire State Restaurant and Tavern Association, May 12.

Sturm, R., L. M. Powell, J. F. Chriqui, and F. J. Chaloupka. 2010. "Soda Taxes, Soft Drink Consumption, and Children's Body Mass Index." *Health Affairs* 29 (5): 1052–58.

WHO (World Health Organization). 2003. "Diet, Nutrition and the Prevention of Chronic Diseases: Report of a Joint FAO/WHO Expert Consultation." Technical Report Series 19, WHO, Geneva.

———. 2005. "Preventing Chronic Diseases. A Vital Investment." WHO Report, Geneva.

———. 2011a. *Global Status Report on Noncommunicable Diseases 2010*. Geneva: WHO.

———. 2011b. *WHO Report on the Global Tobacco Epidemic 2011*. Geneva: WHO.

———. 2011c. *Global Status Report on Alcohol and Health*. Geneva: WHO.

Introduction

Noncommunicable diseases (NCDs) represent an important and growing burden to the health and economies in Latin America and the Caribbean (LAC). Some of this burden can be prevented or controlled, however, through targeted clinical services and multisectoral activities aimed at improving diet, promoting physical activity, and reducing tobacco use and alcohol abuse. This study focuses on population-wide, multisectoral interventions to prevent risk factors for NCDs.

This report hopes to contribute to the design of policies that promote healthy living and effectively prevent NCDs in LAC. It examines the health and economic burden of NCDs in the region and the governance challenges countries face in designing and implementing population-wide, primary-prevention measures targeting NCDs.

More specifically, this publication seeks to answer the following questions: What is the health and economic burden of NCDs in the region? What are countries doing to promote healthy living and prevent risk factors for NCDs? What are the main governance challenges countries face in developing and implementing population-wide NCD prevention interventions, and which are the success stories? What else can the region do to reduce health risk factors and prevent the onset of NCDs?

This report uses the concept of governance posed by Plumptre and Graham (1999), whereby governance "involves the interactions among structures, processes and traditions that determine how power is exercised, how decisions are taken, and how citizens and other stakeholders have their say." It focuses on how policy decisions involving multisectoral interventions to prevent health risk factors are taken, which stakeholders directly or indirectly participate in these decisions, what incentives they face, what power they have to influence these decisions, and what strategies they use in these processes.

The document is based on desk reviews, on an analysis of existing databases, and on country case studies commissioned specifically for it. Because data on NCDs in the region are scarce and often are not standardized across countries, some analyzes were done only for some countries. The document uses information from WHO's Global Burden of Disease data from 2004 and 2008, as well as risk-factor data from the WHO's Global Data Repository. The document also analyzes information from living standard measurement surveys and income and expenditure surveys. The latter instruments provide information on household food consumption that was used to analyze dietary patterns. Some of these surveys also provide information on individual time use that was used to analyze physical activity. Finally, a few surveys provide information on self-reported prevalence of some chronic conditions and on household out-of-pocket expenditures on health and on individual labor market outcomes; this information was used to examine the economic effect of NCDs on households and labor markets.

The study's first part provides a snapshot of the main chronic conditions affecting the region and their risk factors, and how these vary across countries and across socioeconomic variables within countries. The control of NCDs and the care of persons suffering from them represent significant costs for the health systems, high out-of-pocket expenditures for patients, and significant productivity losses due to absenteeism, disability, and premature death. This first part also gives an overview of these economic costs.

The study's second part evaluates countries' responses to the NCD epidemic. Specifically, the study examines the process whereby public officials develop and implement primary-prevention policies and programs. This second part, which is mainly based on a literature review and on commissioned case studies, illustrates the incentives involved in the passage and implementation of policies and programs. Some of the interventions examined in this section have proven to be among the most cost-effective in reducing exposure to an unhealthy diet, a sedentary lifestyle, and tobacco use and alcohol abuse. Most are multisectoral and are often conducted outside the health system. Nonetheless, the role of health sector stakeholders, particularly of the ministries of health, is often essential to make these policies happen. The case studies presented in this report pay particular attention to the ministries of health's role in the decision-making process.

The report's second section seeks to answer the following questions:

- What incentives did public officials face when designing and implementing policies and programs to prevent NCD-related risk factors (e.g., an unhealthy diet, a sedentary lifestyle, and tobacco use and alcohol abuse)?
- Which stakeholders (e.g., industry, the ministry of health, the ministry of finance, civil society groups) influenced the public officials that developed the policies? How much power did these stakeholders, particularly the ministries of health, have and what specific role did they play in the policy-making process (e.g., providing information for decision-making, leading or participating in the process, implementing and evaluating the policy or program)? What was the source of their power? What were their strategies?
- Were there any interactions with players or processes at the global level that helped shape these policies?[1]
- What was the public's perception of these policies, and how was this perception shaped during the process?
- What lessons can be drawn from these processes? What were the successes and setbacks?

Health policies are shaped not just by public officials, but also by wider and contextual social and political processes (Roberts and others 2008). In population-wide interventions, these processes tend to be complex. In contrast to secondary-prevention and curative interventions that take place within the health system, population-based interventions involve a multitude of actors and opposing forces within and outside government. Through in-depth overviews of case studies, this report provides a glimpse into the types of opposing interests and power games involved in proposing, passing, and implementing successful population-based health interventions in LAC and other countries, particularly those in the Organisation for Economic Co-operation and Development (OECD). The aim is to provide information on the struggles and challenges involved in the design and implementation of policies, presenting an array of possible instruments and models that could be useful and adaptable to specific scenarios.

To study how successful policies and programs intended to prevent risk factors for NCDs were developed and implemented, this study uses the framework detailed in the work by Roberts and others (2008), which was used to explain the political economy of tobacco control in low- and middle-income countries in Bump and others (2009). This framework explains the politics of any health reform and, in doing so, shows how health policies are shaped by the interaction of four factors: players, each player's relative power, the position taken by the players, and the public perception of the reform. The interplay between the different stakeholders, their power to shape policies, and the strategies they use inevitably affects the short- and long-term outcomes of any population-based reform (Roberts and others 2008). According to this framework, the above-mentioned four factors are not fixed and can be influenced through political strategies that the players adopt.

Note

1. For example, in tobacco-control efforts, the existence of the Framework Convention on Tobacco Control (FCTC) and/or having different taxation policies in neighboring countries could affect the decision-making process.

Bibliography

Bump, J. B., M. R. Reich, O. Adeyi, and S. Khetrapal. 2009. "Towards a Political Economy of Tobacco in Low and Middle Income Countries." HNP Working Papers, World Bank, Washington, DC.

Plumptre, T., and J. Graham. 1999. "Governance and Good Governance: International and Aboriginal Perspectives, Institute on Governance." Unpublished paper, Ottawa. http://www.iog.ca.

Roberts, M., W. Hsiao, P. Berman, and M. Reich. 2008. *Getting Health Reform Right: A Guide to Improving Performance and Equity*. New York: Oxford University Press.

CHAPTER 1

Noncommunicable Diseases in Latin America and the Caribbean

María Eugenia Bonilla-Chacín

Noncommunicable diseases (NCDs) such as heart disease, stroke, cancer, and diabetes represent a large share of the burden of disease of Latin America and the Caribbean (LAC). They account for three of every four deaths and for two of every three disability-adjusted life years (DALYs) lost in the region. The burden of disease from NCDs in LAC is slightly lower than it is in higher-income Organisation for Economic Co-operation and Development (OECD) countries, but this difference is quickly narrowing (figure 1.1). The impact of these conditions on health will likely continue to increase as the population ages and as it increasingly becomes exposed to health risk factors such as an unhealthy diet, a sedentary lifestyle, tobacco use, and alcohol abuse.

Figure 1.1 Age-Standardized Death Rates (Estimates for 2004 and 2008) and DALYs Lost (Estimates for 2004), Latin America and the Caribbean and OECD

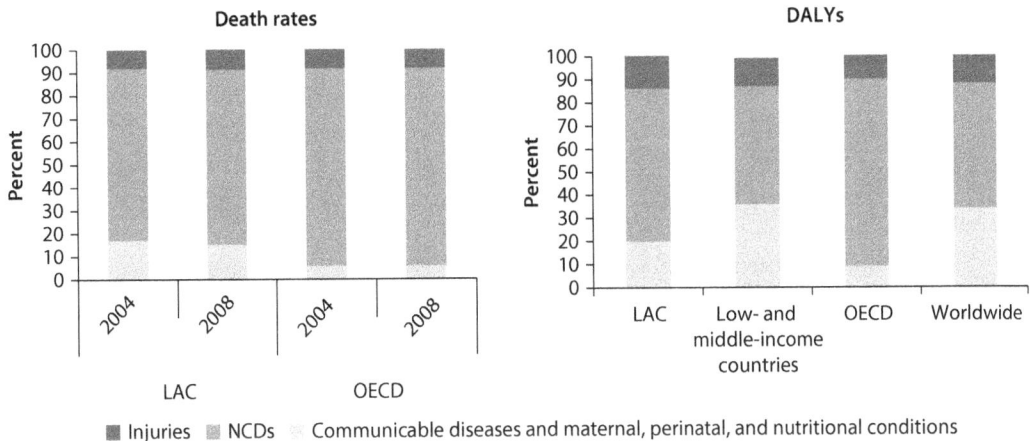

Source: Estimates based on WHO 2004 and 2008 data from the Global Burden of Disease. http://www.who.int/healthinfo/global_burden_disease /estimates_country/en/index.html.
Note: Regional estimates are population weighted. DALY = disability-adjusted life year; LAC = Latin America and the Caribbean; NCD = noncommunicable disease; OECD = Organisation for Economic Co-operation and Development.

Figure 1.2 Age-Standardized DALYs from NCDs, Communicable Diseases, and Injuries, Selected Latin American and Caribbean Countries, Estimates for 2004

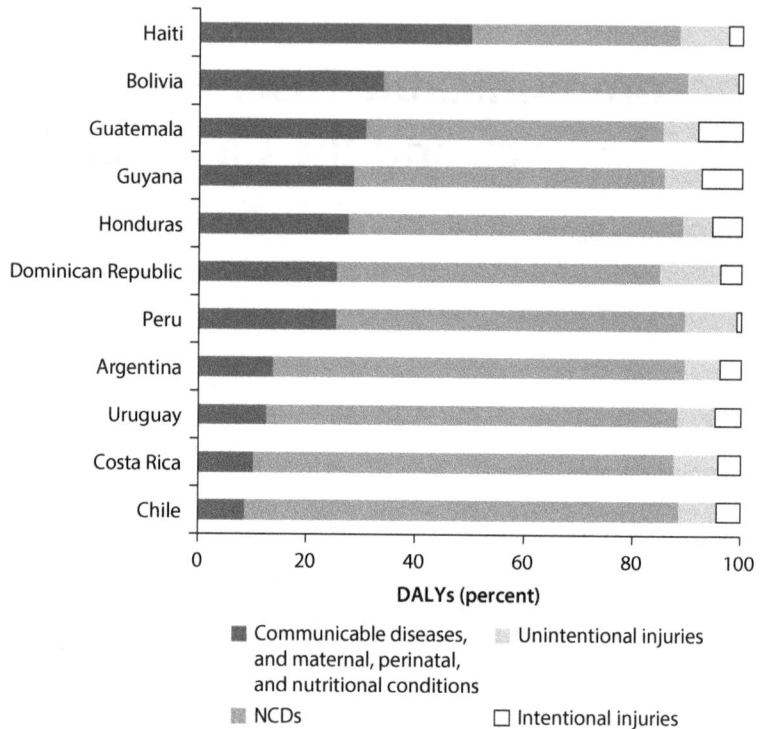

DALYs (percent)

■ Communicable diseases,   ▨ Unintentional injuries
  and maternal, perinatal,
  and nutritional conditions
  ▨ NCDs   □ Intentional injuries

Source: Estimates based on WHO 2004 and 2008 data from the Global Burden of Disease. http://www.who
.int/healthinfo/global_burden_disease/estimates_country/en/index.html.
Note: DALY = disability-adjusted life year; NCD = noncommunicable disease.

Some of the region's countries face a double burden of disease, with both communicable and noncommunicable diseases causing many deaths and much disability. Thanks to advances in the control of infectious diseases and improvements in maternal and child health, the burden of disease due to communicable diseases and to maternal and child conditions has decreased significantly in the region. But in some countries, particularly Bolivia, Guatemala, Guyana, Haiti, and Honduras, communicable diseases are still responsible for much death and disability; in some cases, these conditions may account for one-quarter or more of healthy years of life lost. In contrast, in Argentina, Chile, Costa Rica, Cuba, and Uruguay, communicable diseases account for less than 15 percent of DALYs lost (figure 1.2). Injuries also pose a significant burden in the region, and some countries face a triple burden of disease, given the large share of deaths and disability due to injuries.

Cardiovascular diseases (CVDs) and cancer are the leading causes of death in the region (figure 1.3); in a few countries, diabetes also accounts for an important share of death and disability. In many countries, deaths due to CVDs (heart disease and stroke) are twice as high as those due to malignant neoplasms, which is the second cause of death in the region.[1] In 2008,

Figure 1.3 Percentage of Age-Standardized Deaths, by Disease Groups, Latin America and the Caribbean, 2008

Percent

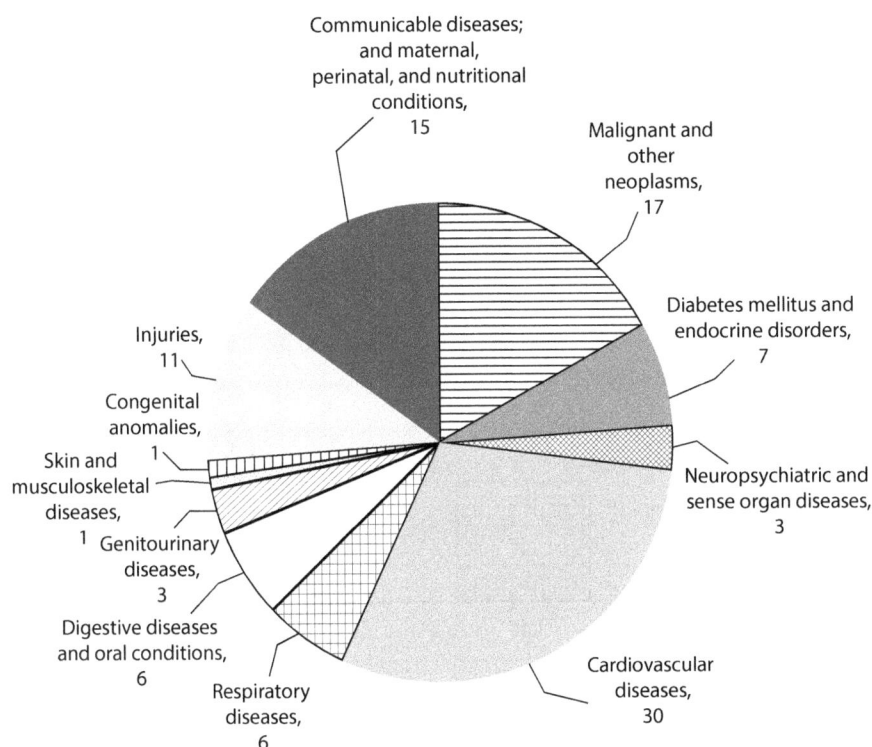

Source: Estimates based on WHO 2008 data on the Global Burden of Disease. http://www.who.int/healthinfo/global _burden_disease/estimates_country/en/index.html.

diabetes was the second cause of death after CVDs in Mexico and Trinidad and Tobago. In most Caribbean countries and in Nicaragua, Paraguay, and República Bolivariana de Venezuela, diabetes was the third leading cause of death. The main causes of DALYs lost in the region as a whole in 2004 were neuropsychiatric disorders,[2] but those conditions are outside the scope of this report. In 2010 the main cause of DALYs lost in the region was ischemic heart disease (IHME and World Bank 2013).

NCD death rates in the region are significantly higher than they are in high-income OECD countries. The age-standardized NCD death rate in LAC is 23 percent higher than that in OECD countries (figure 1.4). The gap is wide for most conditions, particularly for diabetes. The diabetes-related death rate in LAC is more than twice that in OECD countries.

Although more research is needed to understand the determinants of higher death rates from these diseases in the region, the following consider-ations may partially explain this: (a) persons in LAC are more exposed to certain health risk factors than are people in wealthier countries, particularly

Figure 1.4 Age-Standardized Mortality Rates from Specific NCDs, Latin American and Caribbean and OECD Countries, 2008

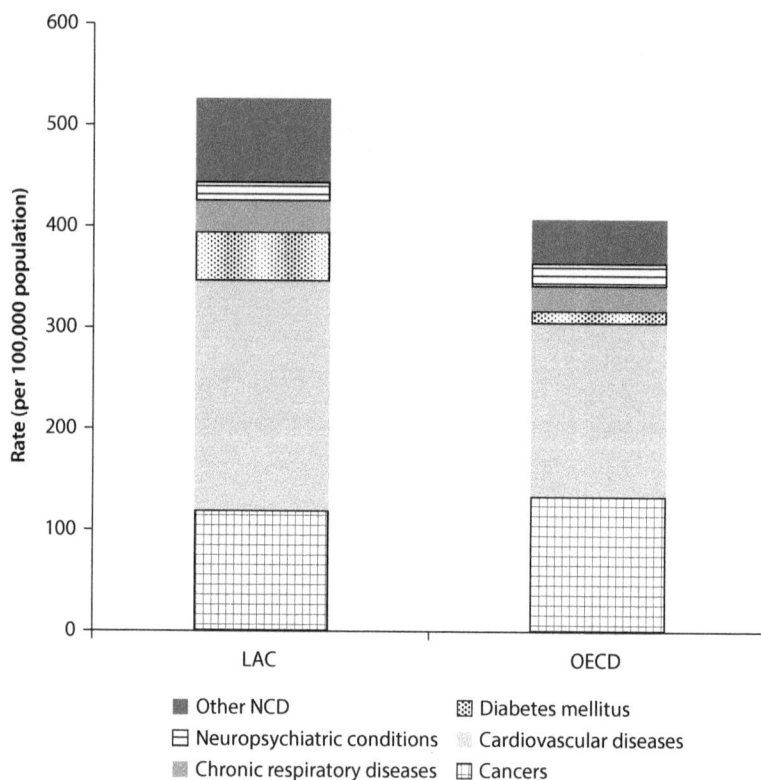

Source: Estimates based on WHO 2004 and 2008 data on the Global Burden of Disease. http://www.who.int /healthinfo/global_burden_disease/estimates_country/en/index.html.

in terms of an unhealthy diet; (b) many of those with chronic conditions in the region are unaware that they have them and, thus, do not control them (table 1.1), leading to complications and premature death; and (c) persons in the region may have lower access to quality health services.

Some Caribbean countries present the highest NCD death rates in the region. For example, diabetes mortality rates in this subregion rank among the highest in the world, and CVD death rates are the highest in the region. As seen in figure 1.5, several Caribbean countries have estimates for diabetes death rates higher than 60 per 100,000 population in 2008; a few have rates higher than 80 per 100,000. A few countries in Mesoamerica, including Belize, Honduras, and Mexico, also had high diabetes death rates. Five out of the six LAC countries with CVD death rates higher than 300 per 100,000 are in the Caribbean, including the Dominican Republic, Guyana, Haiti, Suriname, and Trinidad and Tobago (figure 1.6). The only non-Caribbean country with such high estimates of diabetes death rates is Honduras.

Table 1.1 Prevalence (%) of Adults 20 Years and Older with Existing and Newly Diagnosed Diabetes Mellitus and Hypertension, Selected Central American Cities, 2003–06

	Belize City	San José	San Salvador	Guatemala City	Tegucigalpa	Managua
Diabetes mellitus						
Previously known	7.6	6.3	5.4	4.3	2.5	5.3
Newly diagnosed	5.3	2.5	2.2	2.9	2.9	4.5
Hypertension[a]						
Stage 2	2.9	2.3	0.7	1.2	2.7	2.8
Stage 1	9.6	7.7	3	5.1	8.3	7.5
Prehypertension	22.8	26.7	17.5	26.6	25.1	33.2
Previously known	18.8	15.3	16.4	11.2	11.8	18.6

Source: PAHO 2010.
a. Hypertension stage 1 corresponds to systolic blood pressure between 140 and 159 and stage 2, ≥160.

Figure 1.5 Age-Standardized Mortality Rates from Diabetes, Selected Latin American and Caribbean Countries and Regional Average, 2008

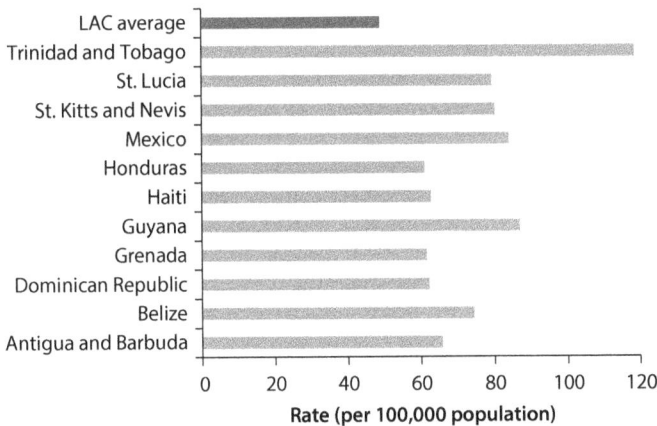

Source: Estimates based on WHO 2008 data on the Global Burden of Disease. http://www.who.int/ healthinfo /global_burden_disease/estimates_country/en/index.html.
Note: LAC = Latin America and the Caribbean.

Age-adjusted NCD death rates are not only higher in LAC countries than in high-income countries, they also occur at younger ages. In low- and middle-income countries, almost one-third of deaths occur among adults aged 15–59 years, whereas in OECD countries, most deaths occur among those 60 years old and older. Table 1.2 shows that the percentage of deaths among persons younger than 60 years old in LAC nearly doubles those seen in OECD countries. The implications are significant: since NCD-related deaths and disability in low- and middle-income countries occur at younger ages, in the region these diseases tend to affect people in their most productive years, leading to significant productivity losses, as detailed in Chapter 3.

Figure 1.6 Age-Standardized Death Rates from Specific Cardiovascular Diseases, Selected Latin American and Caribbean Countries and Regional, OECD, and Worldwide Averages, 2008

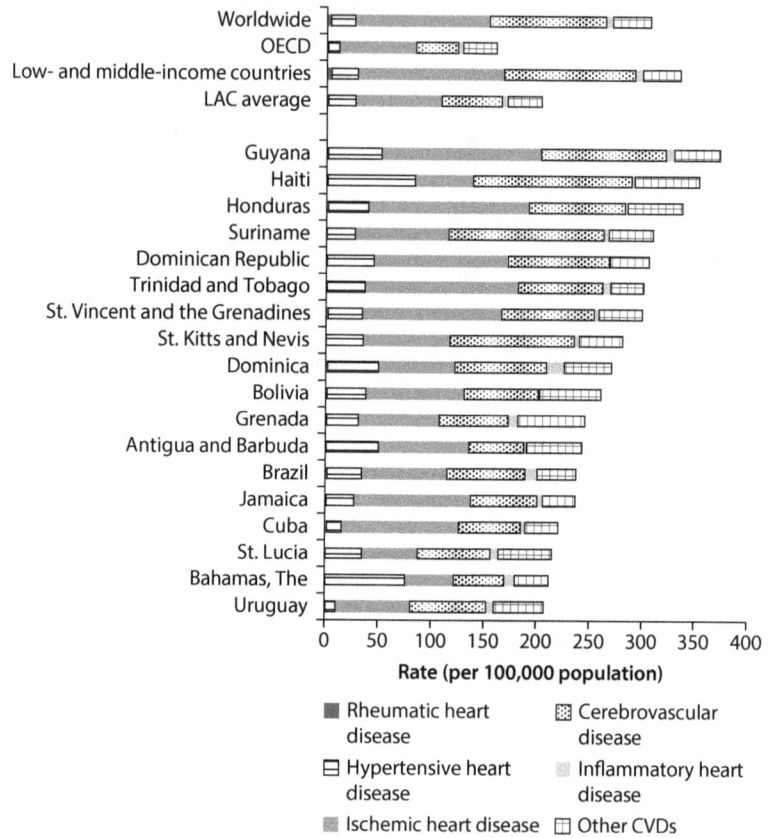

Source: Estimates based on WHO Global Burden of Disease data for 2008. http://www.who.int/healthinfo /global_burden_disease/estimates_country/en/index.html.
Note: CVD = cardiovascular disease.

Table 1.2 Percentage of Deaths from All Causes, Communicable Diseases, Noncommunicable Diseases, and Injuries, by Age Group, Latin America and the Caribbean, Lower- and Middle-Income Countries, OECD, and Worldwide, 2008

	Latin America and the Caribbean (age group)			Low- and middle-income countries (age group)			OECD (age group)			Worldwide (age group)		
	0–14	15–59	60 and +	0–14	15–59	60 and +	0–14	15–59	60 and +	0–14	15–59	60 and +
All causes	8.7	29.7	61.6	20.8	27.8	51.4	1.7	15.9	82.4	16.9	27.6	55.5
Communicable diseases	34.7	24.4	40.9	54.4	24.4	21.2	11.9	11.9	76.1	52.0	26.8	21.2
Noncommunicable diseases	3.0	23.6	73.4	2.9	24.4	72.7	0.7	13.4	85.9	2.3	23.0	74.7
Injuries	7.2	75.2	17.6	12.5	63.7	23.8	3.2	55.1	41.7	12.2	63.2	24.6

Source: Estimates based on WHO Global Burden of Disease Data for 2008.
Note: OECD = Organisation for Economic Co-operation and Development.

Who Is Most Affected?

NCDs affect everyone in the region: men and women, rich and poor, rural and urban residents, and people with different educational levels. Figure 1.7 shows the distribution of people who reported a chronic condition, by several demographic and socioeconomic factors, in five countries in the region. While these numbers are not comparable because different countries use different survey instruments (see appendix A), they do provide an overall view of the burden that these conditions pose for each country. For the countries shown in figure 1.7, roughly 10 percent or more of the population at different consumption quintiles report having a chronic condition; in Brazil, more than 20 percent report an NCD in every income quintile. Similar results were found in Jamaica, where persons at different socioeconomic levels reported having asthma (4.34 percent), diabetes (4.8 percent), and hypertension (9.97 percent) (Shao, Carpio, and de Gent 2010). In addition, an important percentage of rural and urban residents reported having a chronic condition; differences between the two areas are small in all countries with available data. Similarly, a large share of people at different levels of education reported a chronic condition; the pattern varies by country, but, in general, people without any formal education are more likely to report a chronic condition. Data limitations

Figure 1.7 Prevalence of NCDs, by Rural and Urban Areas, Sex, Age, and Educational Subgroups and Income Levels

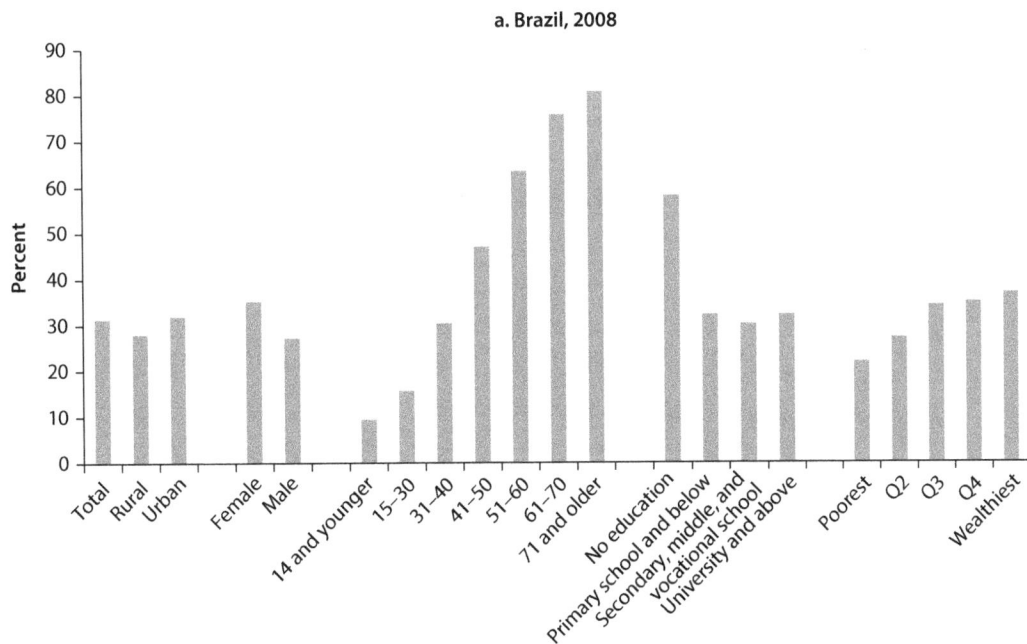

a. Brazil, 2008

figure continues next page

Figure 1.7 Prevalence of NCDs, by Rural and Urban Areas, Sex, Age, and Educational Subgroups and Income Levels *(continued)*

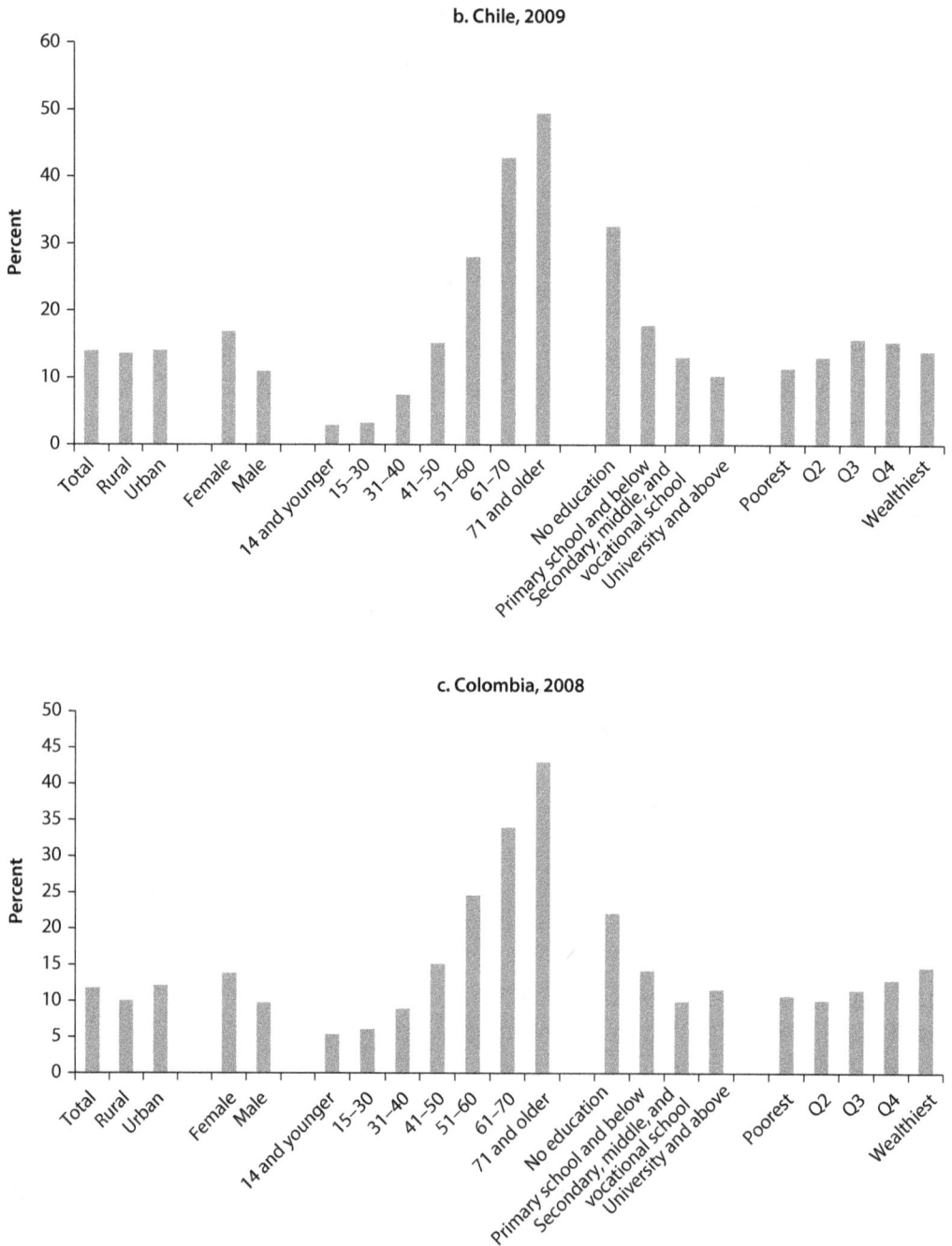

b. Chile, 2009

c. Colombia, 2008

figure continues next page

Figure 1.7 Prevalence of NCDs, by Rural and Urban Areas, Sex, Age, and Educational Subgroups and Income Levels *(continued)*

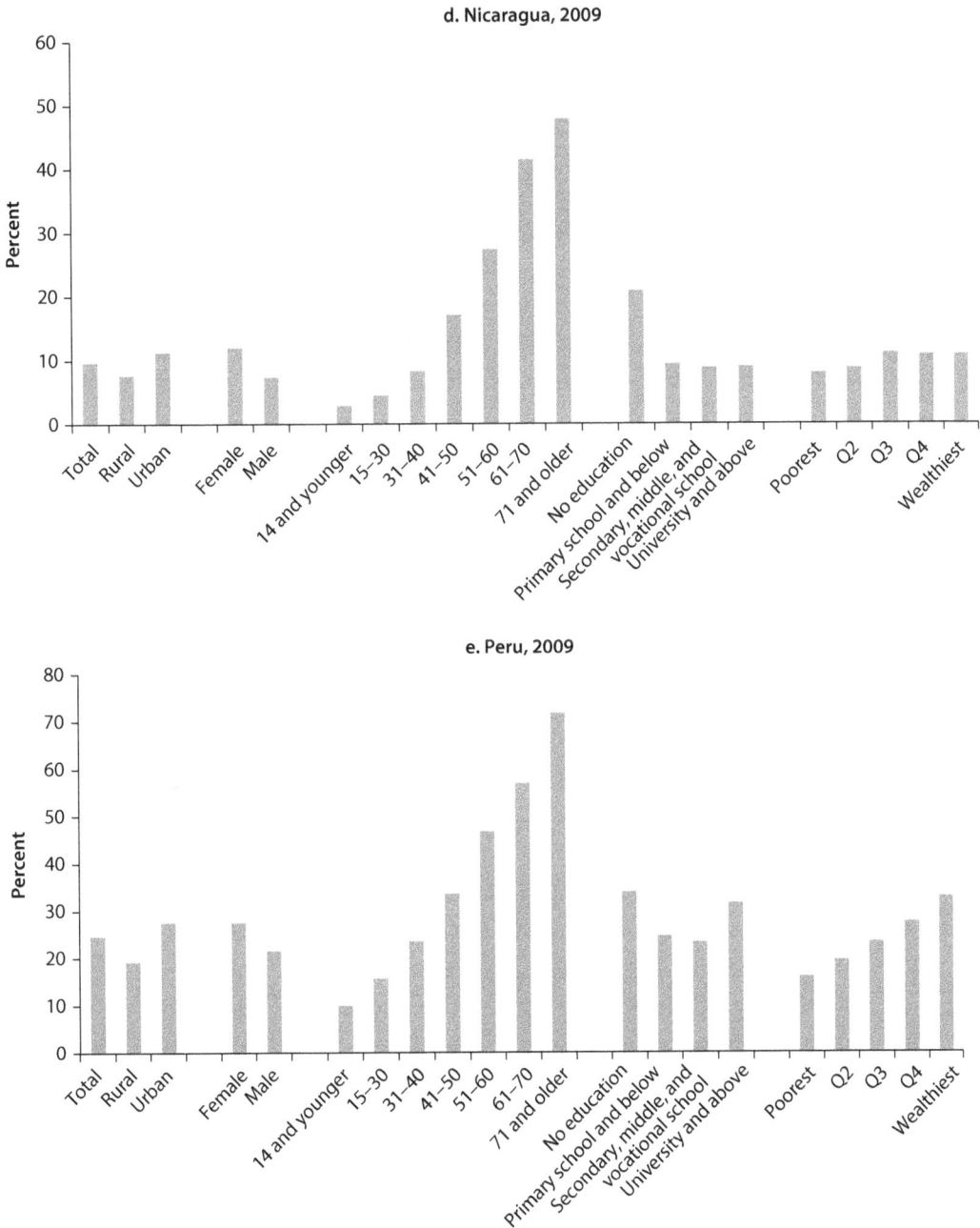

d. Nicaragua, 2009

e. Peru, 2009

Sources: Estimates from Brazil, Pesquisa Nacional Por Amostra de Domicilios (PNAD 2008); Chile, Encuesta de Caracterización Socioeconómica Nacional (CASEN 2009); Colombia, Encuesta de Calidad de Vida, 2008; Nicaragua, Encuesta de Hogares sobre Medición de Nivel de Vida (EMNV 2009); Peru, Encuesta Nacional de Hogares 2008.

Note: NCD = noncommunicable disease, Q2 = second quintile, Q3 = third quintile, and Q4 = fourth quintile.

make it impossible to determine who is most affected or to make reliable country comparisons.[3]

Although data are not fully comparable across countries, information from Colombia, Chile, and Nicaragua seems to show the smallest socioeconomic gradient among people reporting a chronic condition, while Peru's shows one with the highest. In fact, in analyzing the variables associated with reporting a chronic condition, income quintiles are not among the statistically significant variables in Colombia, but they are in Peru. The reasons behind this difference are unknown, but it is possible that screening services in Chile and Colombia are more accessible than those in Peru. As detailed in Chapter 3, income quintile is not significantly associated with health care utilization in Colombia, but it is in Peru.[4]

An important percentage of the working-age population in the five countries shown in figure 1.7 reported having an NCD. In Chile, Colombia, and Nicaragua about 15 percent of adults 41–50 years old have a chronic condition; in Peru, one-third do; and in Brazil, one-half do. Among those 51–60 years old, one-quarter of adults in the first three countries have a chronic condition; in Peru, one-half do, and in Brazil, more than 60 percent do.

Diabetes, hypertension, and asthma are the most frequently reported conditions. In Chile in 2009, for example, about 7 percent of persons reported having hypertension; 3 percent, diabetes; and 1 percent, asthma. In Brazil, 14 percent reported hypertension; 5 percent, asthma; and 3.6 percent, diabetes (Shao, Carpio, and de Gent 2010).[5] Although there is little information on co-morbidities in household surveys, 2009 data from Brazil show that about 13 percent of the population reported having more than one chronic condition, about 41 percent of those reporting NCDs.[6]

Differences in NCD Death Rates by Sex

The differences in NCD rates by sex are significant regionwide. Although more women than men report having an NCD (figure 1.7), except in the Dominican Republic and Jamaica, the overall death rate due to NCDs across the region is higher in men than in women, with some variation seen across diseases. In most of the region's countries, women have higher death rates due to diabetes and musculoskeletal disorders, but men have higher death rates for all other NCDs, particularly for neuropsychiatric disorders, respiratory diseases, and digestive diseases.

Sex differences also vary from country to country. Overall, diabetes affects more women than men in LAC, but there are exceptions (figure 1.8). In Argentina, for example, age-adjusted death rates due to diabetes are 60 percent higher among men than among women. In Uruguay, death rates are equal among men and women, and in Chile and Trinidad and Tobago, they are 40 percent higher among men (WHO 2008).

Figure 1.8 Age-Standardized Death Rates from Diabetes, by Sex, Selected Latin American and Caribbean Countries, 2008

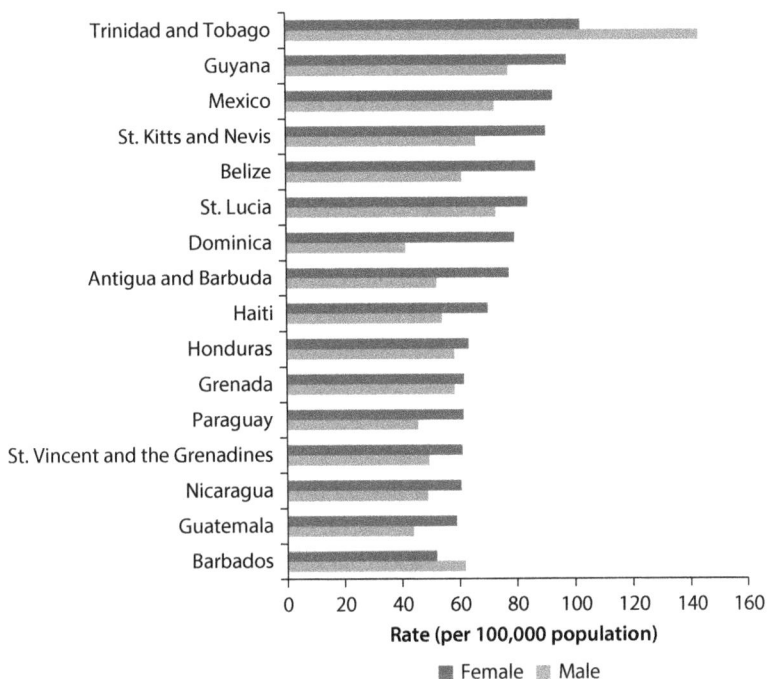

Source: WHO 2008 Global Burden of Disease Data.

Notes

1. Data for 2008 comes from WHO's Global Repository. For more information, visit: http://www.who.int/gho/mortality_burden_disease/global_burden_disease_death _estimates_sex_2008.xls.

2. See WHO Global Health Observatory Data Repository, DALYs, WHO Regions. Data available at: http://apps.who.int/gho/data/node.main.923?lang=en.

3. Very few countries have information on the distribution of NCDs across socioeconomic conditions or even across educational levels or between urban and rural residence in LAC. What little information is available (as it is for the countries shown in figure 1.7), is often self-reported and, thus, likely to be biased, since many people with an NCD are unaware that they have one. Those with better access to health services, such as better-educated urban dwellers and the wealthy, might be more likely to be aware of their condition. In three of the five surveys analyzed in the figure, Colombia's, Nicaragua's, and Peru's questions about chronic conditions included chronic communicable diseases such as HIV/AIDS and tuberculosis. Colombia's survey did not give examples of chronic conditions, but Peru's did, and included information on HIV/AIDS and tuberculosis (for a more detailed analysis of data limitations see the section on the labor market impact of NCDs in chapter 3 of this publication).

4. This analysis was not done for Chile or Nicaragua.

5. In addition to figures from Shao, Carpio, and de Gent 2010, these numbers come from estimates from Chile's CASEN 2009 and Brazil's PNAD 2008 surveys.

6. Figures come from Brazil's PNAD 2008 National Household Survey.

Bibliography

Departamento Administrativo Nacional de Estadística, Dirección de Metodología y Producción Estadística y Dirección de Metodología y Producción Estadística. 2008. *Encuesta Nacional de Calidad de Vida*. Bogota, Colombia.

IHME (Institute for Health Metrics and Evaluation), and World Bank. 2013. *The Global Burden of Disease: Generating Evidence, Guiding Policy—Latin America and Caribbean Regional Edition*. Seattle, WA: IHME.

Instituto Brasileiro de Geografia e Estatística. 2008. *Pesquisa Nacional Por Amostra de Domicilios* (PNAD 2008).

Instituto Nacional de Estadística e Informática. 2008. *Encuesta Nacional de Hogares sobre Condiciones de Vida en el Perú*. Lima, Peru.

Instituto Nacional de Información de Desarrollo. 2009. *Encuesta de Medición del Nivel de Vida 2009*. Managua, Nicaragua.

Ministerio de Desarrollo Social. 2009. *Encuesta de Caracterización Socioeconómica Nacional*. Santiago, Chile.

Ministerio de Economía y Finanzas y el Instituto Nacional de Estadísticas y Censos de la Contraloría General de la República. 2008. *Encuesta de Niveles de Vida ENV 2008*. Panama, Panamá.

PAHO (Pan American Health Organization). 2010. *The Central American Diabetes Initiative (CAMDI). Survey of Diabetes, Hypertension, and Chronic Disease Risk Factors. Belize, San José, San Salvador, Guatemala City, Managua, and Tegucigalpa*. Washington, DC: PAHO.

Shao S., C. Carpio, and W. de Gent. 2010. *The Burden of NCDs in Jamaica*. Washington, DC: World Bank.

WHO (World Health Organization). 2008. *The Global Burden of Disease: 2004 Update*. Geneva: WHO.

CHAPTER 2

Risk Factors for NCDs in Latin America and the Caribbean

María Eugenia Bonilla-Chacín

Despite the grim situation presented in Chapter 1, a large share of noncommunicable diseases (NCDs) are preventable, because they result from known determinants that can be modified through public policy (figure 2.1). Cardiovascular diseases, cancer, chronic respiratory conditions, and diabetes share several intermediate risk factors such as high blood pressure, high blood glucose, abnormal blood lipids, and overweight and obesity. These intermediate factors, in turn, are the result of shared and modifiable risk factors, such as an unhealthy diet (e.g., high in energy-dense food; low in vegetables and fruits; and high in sugar, fat, or salt), a sedentary lifestyle, tobacco use, and harmful use of alcohol. These common factors are affected by underlying socioeconomic, cultural, and environmental determinants, such as population aging, rapid urbanization, globalization, income disparities, and education-level differences (figure 2.1). The following sections examine some of the risk factors that can lead to NCDs and how they affect Latin America and the Caribbean (LAC).

Underlying Factors

Population Aging

The growing burden of NCDs in the region can be partly explained by an aging population. The region has been experiencing a rapid "demographic transition," shifting from high to low levels of fertility and mortality and, thus, to a higher life expectancy. This transition has been coupled with an epidemiological transition characterized by a shift in the leading causes of death from communicable diseases and perinatal and maternal conditions to chronic noncommunicable diseases, conditions that are more prevalent among older adults.

Lower mortality rates, particularly lower child mortality rates, have ushered an increase in life expectancy in the region. Since the 1950s, life expectancy at birth has increased by 22 years (Cotlear 2010). On average, life expectancy at birth in

Figure 2.1 Determinants of and Risk Factors for Chronic, Noncommunicable Diseases

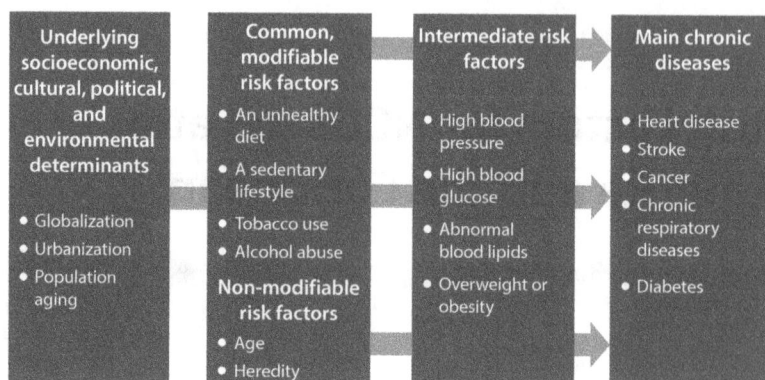

Underlying socioeconomic, cultural, political, and environmental determinants	Common, modifiable risk factors	Intermediate risk factors	Main chronic diseases
• Globalization • Urbanization • Population aging	• An unhealthy diet • A sedentary lifestyle • Tobacco use • Alcohol abuse **Non-modifiable risk factors** • Age • Heredity	• High blood pressure • High blood glucose • Abnormal blood lipids • Overweight or obesity	• Heart disease • Stroke • Cancer • Chronic respiratory diseases • Diabetes

Source: WHO 2005; the framework was modified to include alcohol abuse.

the region is only about 1.2 years lower than the average in Europe. But while Chile, Costa Rica, and Cuba have the highest life expectancy at birth in LAC at more than 78 years, Bolivia and Haiti, have the lowest, at 66 and 61 years, respectively. These changes in life expectancy are mainly due to improvements in the population's health, as both infant and maternal mortality have been quickly decreasing over the years (Saad 2010).

In addition to those overall improvements in the population's health, the total fertility rate in the region has also decreased significantly in the last decades—from 5.9 children per women during 1950–55, to 2.4 in 2005–10 (Cotlear 2010). Currently some countries in the region have total fertility rates that are at or lower than the replacement rate of 2.1 children per women. Such is the case of Barbados, Brazil, Costa Rica, Cuba, Chile, Uruguay, Puerto Rico, and Trinidad and Tobago. Barbados and Cuba have the lowest total fertility rates in the region, about 1.5 children per woman. In contrast, Bolivia, Guatemala, Haiti, and Honduras have the highest total rates in the region, at more than 3 children per woman (Saad 2010).

These changes in the total fertility rate, coupled with increases in life expectancy, have resulted in dramatic changes in the region's population structure. The percentage of people older than 60 years is increasing, and increasing fast. While between 1950 and 2000 this percentage increased from 5.5 to 8.8 percent, over the subsequent 50 years it will rise from 8.8 to 23.6 percent (Saad 2010). And, although this process varies considerably from country to country, as the population ages, the likelihood of developing an NCD increases regionwide.

Rapid Urbanization and Globalization

As the demographic and epidemiologic transitions progress, a rapid urbanization and the globalization process are changing the way people live, creating additional risks for NCDs. The percentage of the population living in urban areas has been increasing rapidly—while in 1960 only 49 percent of people in LAC lived in urban areas, by 2010, 79 percent did.[1]

Urbanization brings about major lifestyle changes that affect health. Evidence from various countries shows that rapid urbanization has significantly changed food-consumption and physical-activity patterns. Urbanization has been associated with higher caloric intake and the consumption of more sweeteners, more fats and oils, and more animal protein from meats and dairy products (Kearney 2010; Thow and Hawkes 2009). These dietary changes are combined with lower energy expenditure in urban jobs compared with rural work, and less physical activity during leisure time.

Globalization is yet another driver of lifestyle changes, mainly on the population's diet and physical activity patterns. Reductions in trade barriers, the spread of transnational food companies, foreign direct investment, and liberalization of the media are thought to be some of the channels through which globalization affects healthy behaviors (Thow and Hawkes 2009). Income growth, urbanization, and lifestyle changes have been linked to increased consumption of fats and sweeteners (Drewnowski and Popkin 1997; Popkin 2006) and higher body mass indexes (BMIs). At the same time, the growth of transnational food companies has made processed and fast foods much more available, and they have been made more desirable to consumers thanks to their advertising and promotion. One of the most visible effects of the growing presence of transnational food companies and of the changing nature of the food industry and food behavior in Latin America has been the rapid replacement of local food stores with supermarkets. Supermarkets control 50–60 percent of the food retail sector in the region (Hawkes 2007). This dramatic dietary transition due to globalization is evident in Central America. A descriptive study on the effects that reductions in trade barriers have had on the diet in this subregion concluded that trade liberalization there has contributed to an increase in the availability of animal products and processed foods (Thow and Hawkes 2009). This increase in such food's availability in the subregion, along with social and demographic changes, has facilitated a shift toward increased consumption of meat, dairy products, and processed foods.

Modifiable Behavioral Risk Factors

An Unhealthy Diet

As they are in higher income countries, diets in the region tend to be energy-dense.[2] As seen in table 2.1, adults in some countries in the region have, on average, daily calorie intakes that are similar to those seen in adults in Canada, Poland, and Spain during the early 1990s. More recent data from an individual nutrition survey from the United States, the National Health and Nutrition Examination Survey 2007–08, also show similar levels of consumption: 2,504 calories for adult men and 1,771 calories for adult women (Wright and Wang 2010). All these comparison countries have relatively large percentages of

Table 2.1 Average Calorie Intake per Adult Equivalent,[a]
Selected Latin American and OECD Countries, Various Years

Country and survey year	Average intake	(95% confidence interval)	
Bolivia, 2009	2,341	2,253	2,430
Costa Rica, 2004	1,908	1,904	1,911
Ecuador, 2006	1,955	1,915	1,994
Guatemala, 2006	2,594	2,590	2,598
Honduras, 2004	1,801	1,799	1,802
Nicaragua, 2009	2,185	2,183	2,187
Panama, 2008	2,450	2,411	2,490
Canada, 1990–92	2,115	—	—
Poland, 1990–92	2,629	—	—
Spain, 1990–92	2,634	—	—

Sources: For LAC, for OECD countries, Bonilla-Chacin and others 2013.
Notes: — = not available; LAC = Latin America and the Caribbean;
OECD = Organisation for Economic Co-operation and Development.
a. Adult equivalent is a measure of per capita consumption that takes into account the
heterogeneity of household composition. (See appendix B for methodological details.)

overweight and obese people, although not as high as at the time of the surveys (except for the United States), many of which date from the early 1990s. Although these estimates are not fully comparable across countries, particularly the ones from the United States since they are based on an individual rather than a household survey, they nonetheless provide an idea about differences in dietary patterns between and within countries (see appendix B for methodological details).

Data from some of the region's countries show that food consumption in many households is higher than needed to maintain a healthy weight. Although the needed calorie intake for an individual varies by sex, age, and level of physical activity, estimates from household surveys found that many households exceeded 2,755 calories per adult equivalent (table 2.2). As a comparison, according to the U.S. Dietary Guidelines (USDA and HSS 2010), an adult male with a moderate level of physical activity only needs about 2,600 calories per day to maintain a healthy weight.

The average calorie intake increases with socioeconomic level and tends to be higher in urban areas. As seen in table 2.3, calorie intake per adult equivalent in households in the wealthiest consumption quintile is significantly higher than in households in the poorest quintile. Calorie intake per adult equivalent also tends to be higher in urban areas than in rural ones, with some exceptions. In Bolivia and Ecuador for the years shown, there were no statistically significant differences in consumption by residence; in Costa Rica, however, calorie intake per adult equivalent was higher in rural areas than in urban ones.

In countries with available data, the main sources of calorie intake are grains, followed by meat, foods with added sugar, and oils (figure 2.2). In wealthier countries (Costa Rica and Panama), an important share of total calorie intake

Table 2.2 Daily Calorie Intake (Percentage) per Adult Equivalent,[a] Selected Central American Countries, Various Years

Calories	Guatemala	Honduras	Nicaragua	Panama
0–1,165	12.2	28.8	29.5	27.6
1,165–2,755	49.2	54.5	57.1	55.7
2,755–4,132	26.7	15.4	11.1	11.4
4,133–5,510	8.1	1.2	1.9	3.0
5,510 and over	3.8	0.1	0.4	2.4

Source: Bonilla-Chacin and Marcano-Vázquez 2010.
a. Adult equivalent is a measure of per capita consumption that takes into account the heterogeneity of household composition. (See appendix B for methodological details.)

Table 2.3 Average Daily Calorie Intake per Adult Equivalent,[a] by Urban and Rural Residence and by Consumption Quintile, Selected Latin American Countries, Various Years

Country and year	Residence			Consumption quintiles				
	Total	Urban	Rural	Poorest	II	III	IV	Wealthiest
Bolivia, 2009	2,341	2,303	2,417	1,583	2,150	2,393	2,685	2,898
Costa Rica, 2004	1,908	1,900	1,920	1,289	1,664	1,889	2,197	2,479
Ecuador, 2006	1,955	1,971	1,922	1,346	1,773	2,013	2,250	2,391
Guatemala, 2006	2,594	1,871	2,419	2,632	2,488	2,619	2,599	2,594
Honduras, 2004	1,801	2,089	1,496	1,278	1,641	1,948	2,077	2,095
Nicaragua, 2009	2,185	2,310	1,993	1,159	1,682	2,040	2,387	2,969
Panama, 2008	2,450	2,648	2,052	1,225	1,738	1,993	2,561	3,636

Source: Bonilla-Chacin and others 2013.
a. Adult equivalent is a measure of per capita consumption that takes into account the heterogeneity of household composition (see appendix B for methodological details).

comes from animal protein (beef, chicken, fish, and others). A worrisome pattern in all these countries is the high share of total calorie intake that comes from oils (vegetable oil, margarine, etc.) and from added refined sugar. Following WHO/FAO dietary guidelines, added sugars should represent no more than 10 percent of the total calorie intake (WHO 2003). Diets that are energy-dense and poor in micronutrients, usually diets high in fat and added sugar such as sweetened beverages, tend to promote weight gain (WHO 2003); in addition, sugars produce dental caries.

The consumption of fruits and vegetables in the region tends to be lower than recommended to maintain a healthy life. Because a diet high in fiber, mainly from fruits, vegetables, and whole grains, promotes weight loss and can protect against coronary heart disease, WHO and Food and Agriculture Organization (FAO) have recommended that more than 400 g of fruits and vegetables per person per day be consumed (WHO 2003). As seen in table 2.4, on average, the

Figure 2.2 Calorie Sources in the Diet, Selected Central American Countries, Various Years
Percent

a. Costa Rica, 2004

b. Guatemala, 2006

c. Honduras, 2004

d. Nicaragua, 2009

e. Panama, 2008

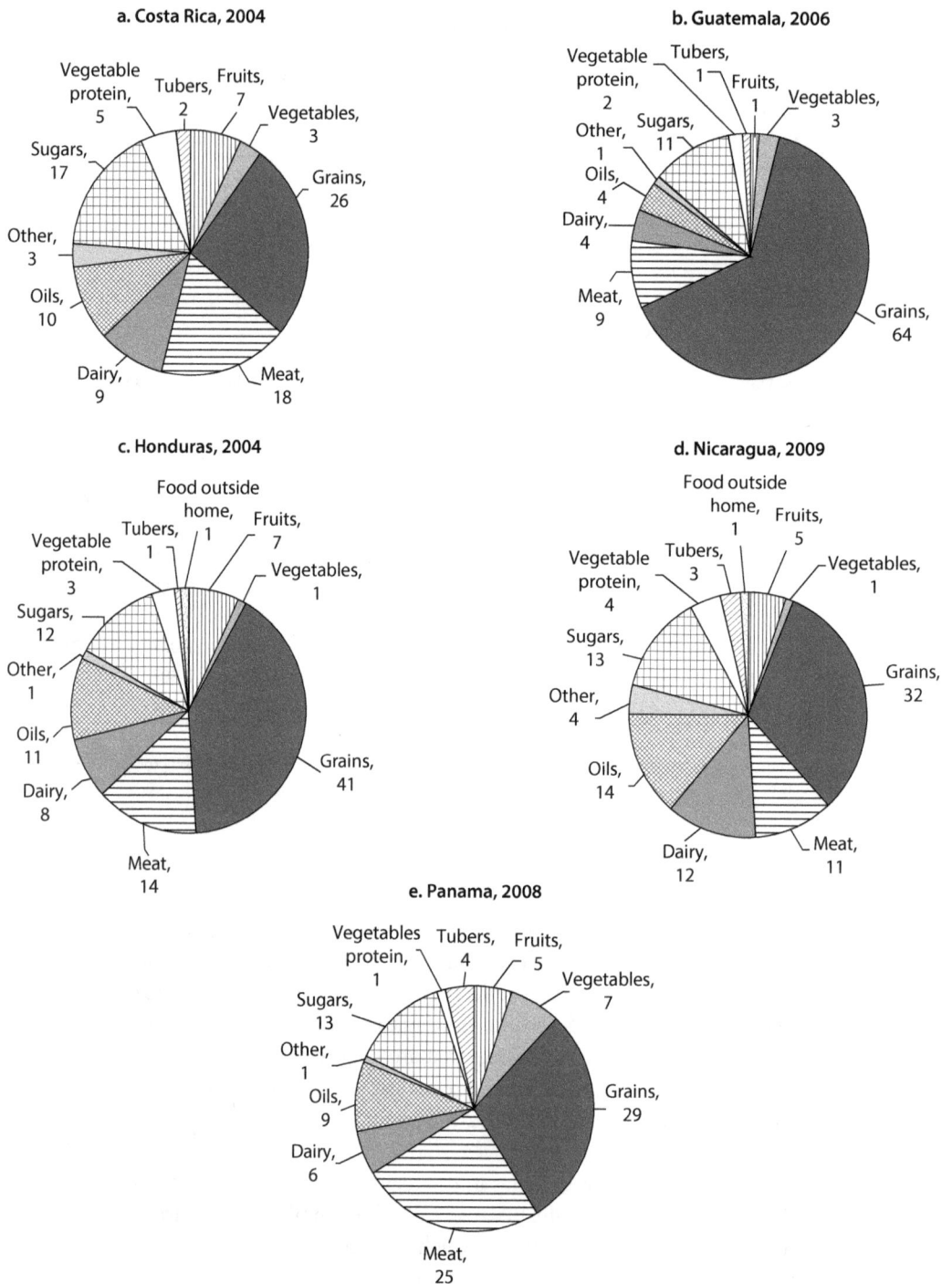

Sources: Bonilla-Chacin and others 2013, using the following household surveys: living conditions surveys for Guatemala, 2006; Nicaragua, 2009; Panama, 2008; Costa Rica, income and expenditure survey, 2004.

Table 2.4 Average Adult Equivalent[a] Consumption of Fruits and Vegetables (in grams), by Urban and Rural Residence and Consumption Quintile, Selected Latin American Countries, Various Years

Country and year		Total	Urban	Rural	Consumption quintiles				
					Poorest	II	III	IV	Wealthiest
Costa Rica, 2004	Fruits	143	167	104	67	80	142	176	247
	Vegetables	100	111	83	51	73	96	121	160
	Vegetable protein	35	29	43	32	37	35	35	34
	Fruits	127	154	96	84	90	113	147	202
Guatemala, 2006	Vegetables	329	364	287	240	272	309	380	443
	Vegetable protein	195	171	224	169	206	203	203	194
	Fruits	176	257	91	59	106	173	237	314
Honduras, 2004	Vegetables	77	105	47	31	51	75	101	130
	Vegetable protein	47	49	44	43	48	50	49	43
	Fruits	195	194	196	126	136	167	193	290
Nicaragua, 2005	Vegetables	83	103	52	20	43	62	88	150
	Vegetable protein	68	54	88	75	71	70	67	61
	Fruits	91	87	100	60	65	64	93	138
Panama, 2008	Vegetables	207	180	261	287	140	150	190	262
	Vegetable protein	53	60	39	21	34	36	42	100

Source: Bonilla-Chacin and others 2013.

Notes: According to the World Health Organization and the Food and Agricultural Organization categories, tubers such as potatoes and yuca were not included as vegetables; vegetable proteins refers to beans and seeds.

a. Adult equivalent is a measure of per capita consumption that takes into account the heterogeneity of household composition. (See appendix B for methodological details.)

consumption of fruits and vegetables in all the countries analyzed is lower than this recommended threshold.

Diets in the region are also high in sodium. Figure 2.3 shows two Central American countries with one-third or more of households consuming sodium at levels that are significantly higher than the 2.3 g per day threshold recommended by the U.S. Dietary Guidelines (USDA and HSS 2010) (WHO recommends a threshold of 2 g of sodium or 5 g of salt per person per day). These graphs show the result of two estimates, one that considers only sodium intake from foods consumed and another that also includes sodium from salt bought separately. The first, more conservative estimate is shown to the right; the second estimate may overestimate sodium consumption. In Guatemala, about 80 percent of households have sodium intakes higher than recommended thresholds. Similar patterns are found in other countries in the region. For instance, as discussed in chapter 5, Argentines on average consume 12 g of salt daily (Ferrante and others 2011).

Energy-dense diets and diets high in sugar, salt, and fat also increase the risk of developing NCDs, in that they raise the risk of high blood pressure, high blood glucose, abnormal lipids in the blood, and overweight and obesity. Such diets also increase the risk for cardiovascular diseases, diabetes mellitus, certain cancers, dental caries, and osteoporosis (WHO 2004).

More specifically, high-sodium diets are associated with high blood pressure (Brown and others 2009). Diets rich in animal fats, such as meat, eggs, and dairy products, increase the blood's cholesterol level, thus also raising the risk of cardiovascular diseases.[3] Eliminating saturated fats and trans fats from foods and substituting them with monounsaturated and polyunsaturated fats not only decreases the risk of coronary heart disease, but it also reduces the risk of type 2 diabetes, which is directly associated with the consumption of

Figure 2.3 Levels of Sodium Consumption (Total Intake and Intake from Food Only) Per Adult Equivalent[a]

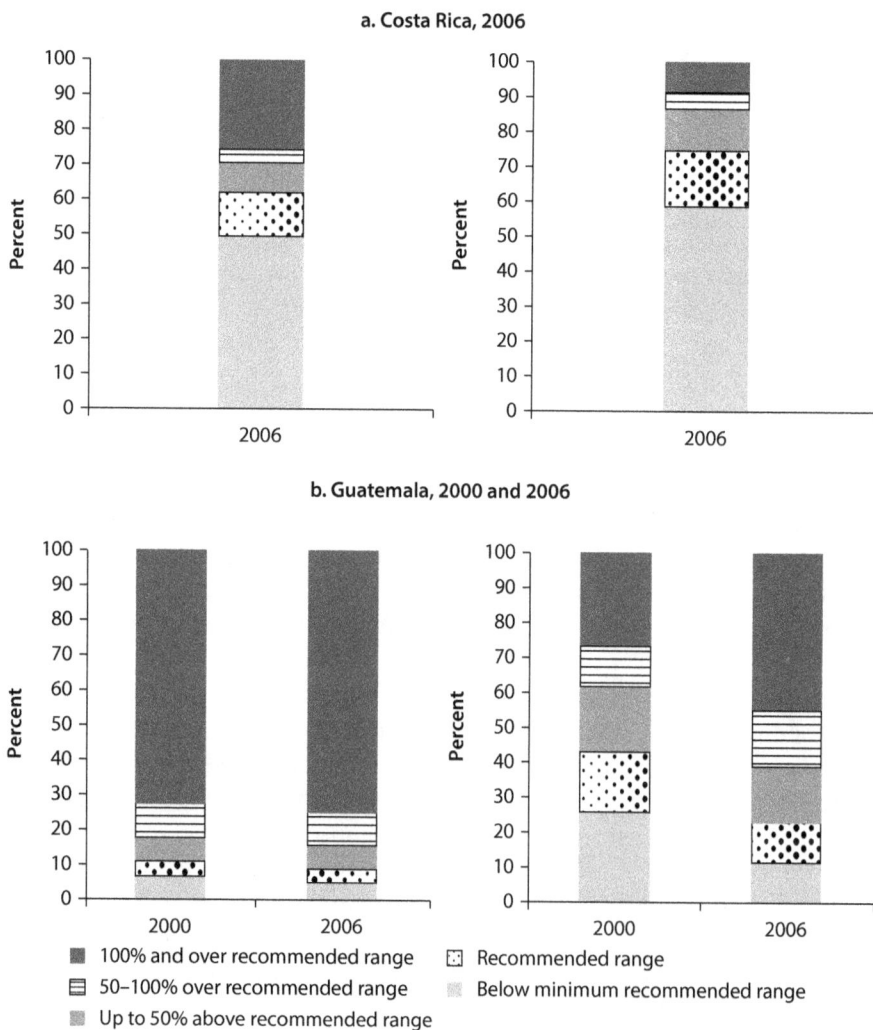

a. Costa Rica, 2006

b. Guatemala, 2000 and 2006

■ 100% and over recommended range ⬚ Recommended range
▤ 50–100% over recommended range ▨ Below minimum recommended range
▨ Up to 50% above recommended range

Source: Bonilla-Chacin and others 2013.
a. Adult equivalent is a measure of per capita consumption that takes into account the heterogeneity of household composition. (See appendix B for methodological details.)

saturated fats and trans fats and inversely associated with the consumption of polyunsaturated fat from vegetable sources (Hu and Willet 2002).

Physical Inactivity

There is little information on the level of physical activity in the region, but what little information is available shows high levels of inactivity. In Mexico, for instance, 37 percent of men and 38 percent of women do not meet WHO's recommended threshold for physical activity (WHO 2011a).[4] According to Uruguay's first National Survey on Risk Factors, 2009, 35 percent of the country's population is sedentary (table 2.5). High levels of physical inactivity are also found in Guatemala (figure 2.4, right), Costa Rica (figure 2.5), and Argentina,

Table 2.5 Activity Level (Percentage), by Age and Sex, Uruguay, 2009

| Age group | Activity level | | | | | | | | |
| | Low (<600 MET-min/week) | | | Moderate (600 MET-min/week and <3,000) | | | High (3,000 MET-min/week) | | |
	Men	Women	Both	Men	Women	Both	Men	Women	Both
25–34	17.3	36.3	27.1	24.7	33.5	29.2	58.0	30.2	43.7
35–44	34.8	40.4	37.8	16.5	27.5	22.2	48.6	32.1	40.0
45–54	33.1	41.0	37.3	23.9	26.5	25.3	42.9	32.5	37.4
55–64	33.1	47.5	40.9	27.5	31.4	29.6	39.4	21.2	29.4
Total	29.0	40.7	35.1	22.8	29.8	26.5	48.2	29.5	38.4

Source: Uruguay National Survey on Risk Factors 2009.
Note: MET = 1 kcal/kg/hour (corresponds to the amount of energy consumed while seated).

Figure 2.4 Percentage of the Population that Falls below the Recommended Level of Physical Activity, by Age, Sex, and Income Quintile, Guatemala, 2006

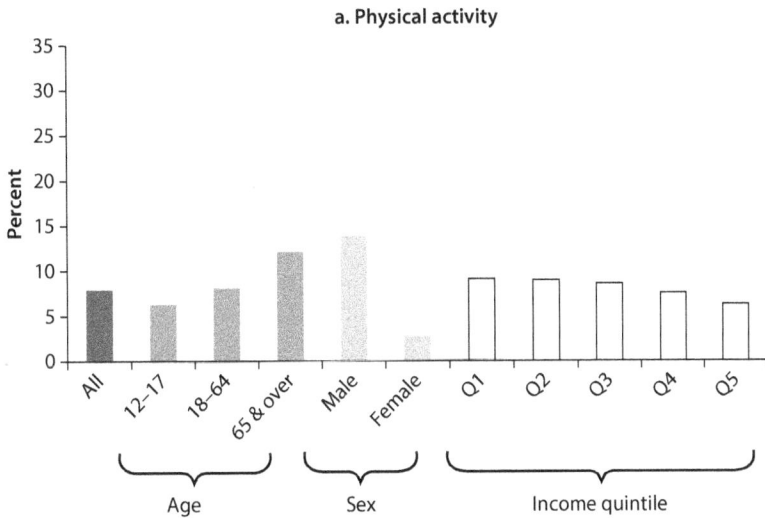

a. Physical activity

figure continues next page

Figure 2.4 Percentage of the Population that Falls below the Recommended Level of Physical Activity, by Age, Sex, and Income Quintile, Guatemala, 2006 *(continued)*

b. Lack of excercise

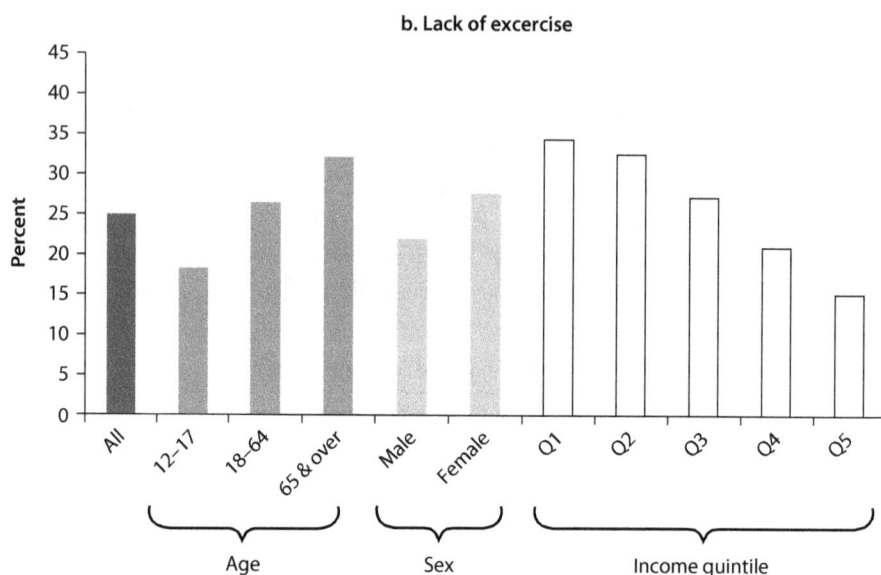

Source: National survey of living conditions, 2006 (Encuesta Nacional de Condiciones de Vida [ENCOVI] 2006).
Note: The physical-activity graph includes the following: livestock raising, house repairs, throwing out the garbage, childcare, ironing and washing clothing, cutting wood, sports, cultural activities, recreation. The lack-of-exercise graph only includes sports and cultural and recreational activities.

(according to the 2005 and 2009 National Risk Factor Surveys), where physical inactivity increased from 46.2 percent in 2005 to 54.9 percent in 2009. Physical activity reduces the risk of hypertension, coronary heart disease, stroke, diabetes, breast and colon cancer, depression, and falls; it also improves bone and functional health, and reduces the risk of becoming overweight.[5]

Overall, men exercise more than women, but women tend to engage in more physical activity doing household chores. In Costa Rica, for example, adult men and youth are most likely to engage in exercise; but if other chores that imply bodily activity are considered, these groups are the least likely to be physically active. Although adult men and teenagers are more likely to engage in exercise than are women and working age adults, on average, they are less likely to meet the recommended threshold for physical activity, because they do not engage in other activities as much. In contrast, while women tend to engage less in exercise, they are more physically active, mainly by doing household chores.[6] In Guatemala, when only sports and recreational activities are taken into account as physical activities, women tend to be more physically inactive than men (see the lack-of-exercise graph in figure 2.4).[7]

At higher income levels more people engage in the expected amount of physical activity. In Costa Rica in 2004, for example, about 17 percent of persons older than 12 years did not meet the recommended threshold of physical activity.[8] However, as seen in the exercise-only graph in figure 2.5, the higher the income level, the higher the percentage of persons that met the threshold for physical

Figure 2.5 Percentage of the Population that Falls below the Recommended Level of Physical Activity, by Age, Sex, and Income Quintile, Costa Rica, 2004

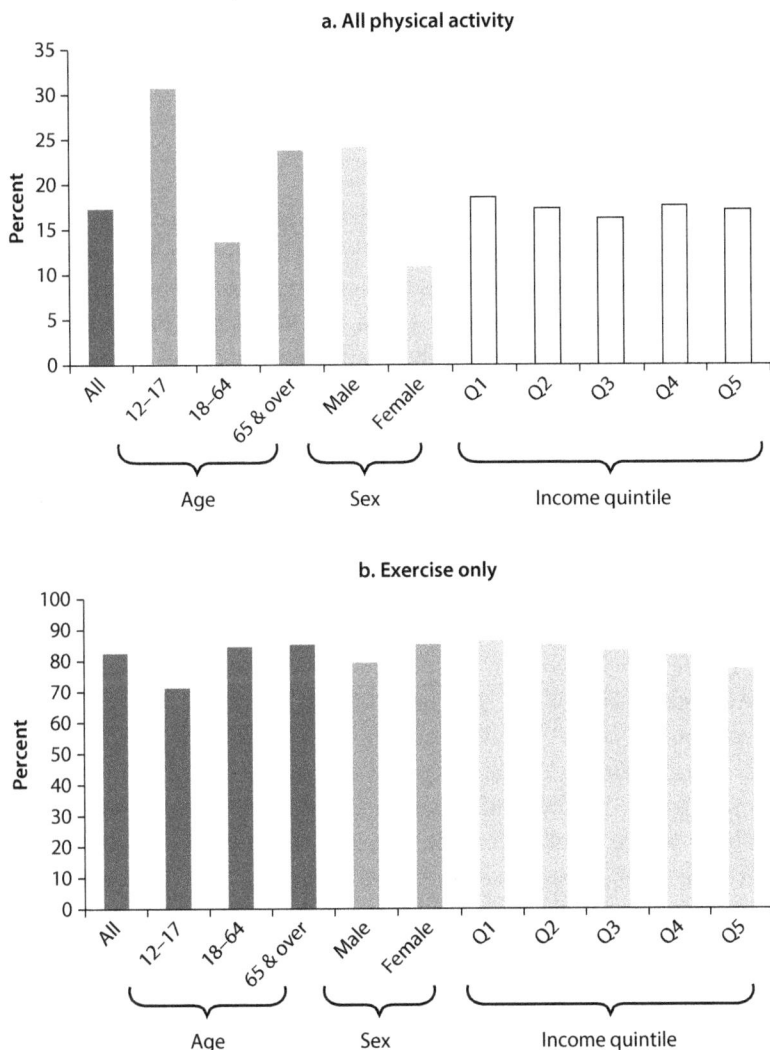

a. All physical activity

b. Exercise only

Source: INEC 2004.

activity from exercise. The all-physical-activity graph, includes not only exercise but also time spent on household chores such as cleaning, cooking, ironing, gardening, and fetching wood. Even when other types of physical activity are included, the pattern holds, although with a smaller gradient.

Younger adults are more physically active than older adults, but young people are still highly inactive physically. In Guatemala, older adults in the lowest income levels tend to be more physically inactive than younger adults and people in the highest income levels (figure 2.4). In Mexico in 2006, 35.2 percent of adolescents were physically inactive (engaging in fewer than four hours of moderate to vigorous physical activity per week), 24.4 percent were moderately active (engaging in at least four hours of physical activity per week), and 35.2 percent were active (engaging in at least seven hours of physical activity per week). This, coupled with the fact that more than half of adolescents spend more than 12 hours a week in front of a TV screen, makes for a highly inactive population (Olaiz-Fernández and others 2006).

Tobacco Use

More than one in four adult men and 14.4 percent of adult women in the region smoked in 2006. Although prevalence of tobacco use is not as high as in parts of Eastern Europe and Asia, in some countries in the region, especially in the Southern Cone and in Bolivia, Cuba, and República Bolivariana de Venezuela, between one-third and two-fifths of adult men and one-quarter and one-third of adult women smoked in 2006.

Although there is a higher prevalence of smoking among men than among women, the region has some of the highest percentages of women smokers among other regions of the world. In 2006, the prevalence of tobacco smoking in adult men was 40 percent worldwide, and that of adult women was nearly 9 percent. Europe and the Americas had the highest smoking prevalence among women, with 22 percent of women smoking in Europe and 17 percent smoking in the Americas (WHO 2010).

Figure 2.6 shows that the prevalence of tobacco smoking among adults in LAC decreased between 2006 and 2009. As the figure shows, the smoking prevalence among adults has decreased in almost every country in the region, with particularly notable reductions in Mexico and Uruguay. The sole exceptions were Brazil, where the percentage of men and women smokers increased slightly; Bolivia, where smoking largely increased among men; and Costa Rica, where smoking among women slightly increased.

Particularly worrisome is the high prevalence of smoking among young people in LAC. Smoking generally starts in early adolescence, and those who begin smoking that early are less likely to quit and more likely to become regular smokers than those who start later (WHO 2010). Figure 2.7 shows the countries in the world with highest levels of tobacco smoking among young people, ranked by female smoking prevalence. Chile had the fourth highest prevalence of tobacco smoking among young women. According to the same data source, Ecuador and Nicaragua are the only LAC countries among the 15 countries worldwide with highest tobacco prevalence among young men, with 31 percent and 30 percent, respectively (not shown in the table). In contrast to the prevalence figures among adults, many countries in the region—Argentina, Brazil, Chile, Haiti, and Uruguay—have higher smoking prevalence among young women than among young men (figure 2.8).

Between 2008 and 2010, tobacco smoking among young people increased in some LAC countries. In that interval, tobacco smoking among youth significantly increased in Brazil and in six Caribbean countries, although it decreased in El Salvador, St. Kitts and Nevis, and República Bolivariana de Venezuela. In Peru,

Figure 2.6 Age-Standardized Rates of Current Smoking of Any Tobacco Product among Adults, by Sex, Selected Latin American and Caribbean Countries, 2006 and 2009

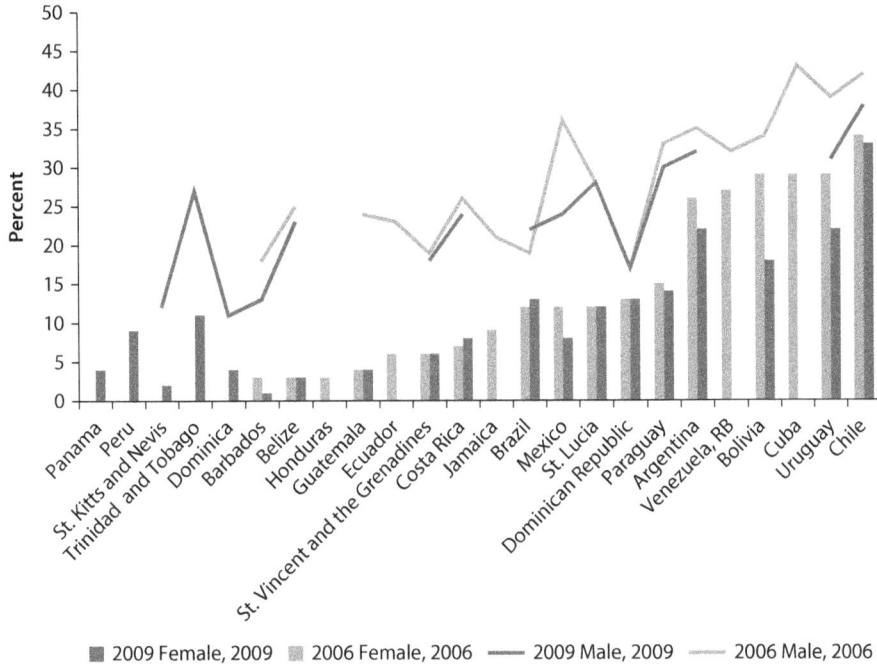

■ 2009 Female, 2009   ■ 2006 Female, 2006   —— 2009 Male, 2009   ---- 2006 Male, 2006

Source: WHO Global Health Observatory Data Repository Tobacco Control.

Figure 2.7 Rates of Current Use of Any Tobacco Product among Youth 13–15 Years Old, by Sex, Selected Countries, 2008

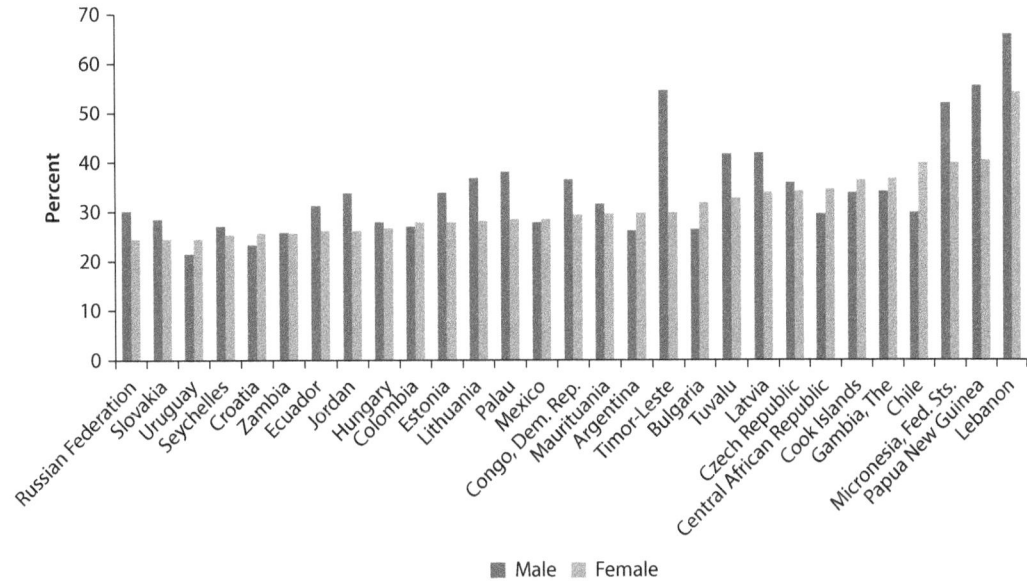

■ Male   ■ Female

Source: WHO database from the Global Youth Tobacco Surveys.

Figure 2.8 Rates of Current Use of Any Tobacco Product among Youth 13–15 Years Old, by Sex, Selected Latin American and Caribbean Countries, 2008 and 2010

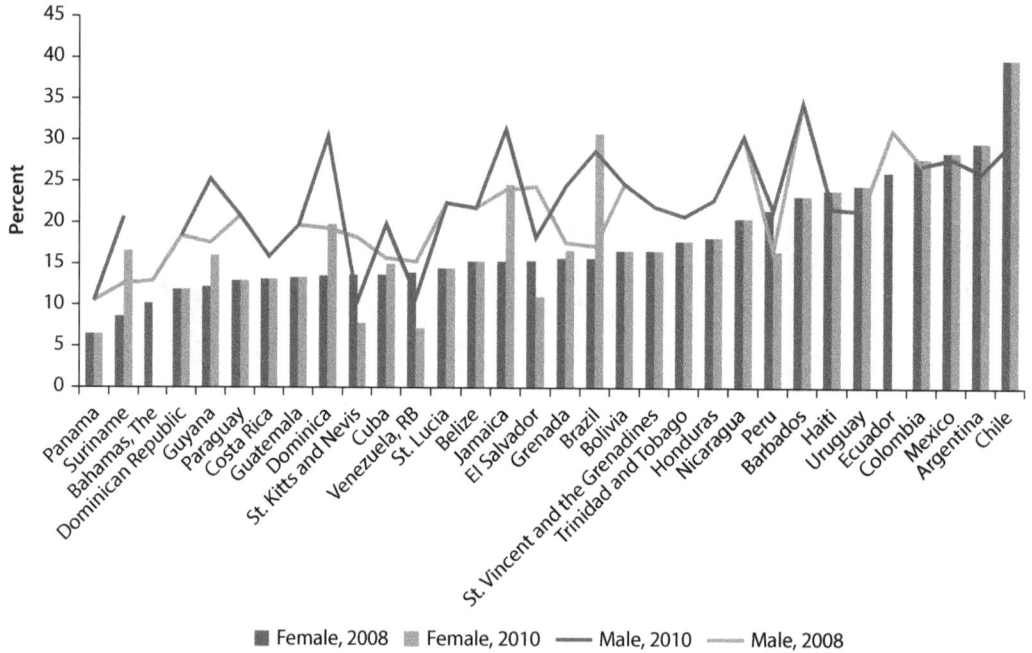

■ Female, 2008   ■ Female, 2010   ── Male, 2010   ── Male, 2008

Source: Global Youth Tobacco Surveys from WHO Global Health Observatory – Tobacco Monitoring.

it increased among boys, but decreased among girls. In all other countries prevalence remained the same (figure 2.8).

In countries with available information, smoking is more prevalent among low-income men, a pattern that reverses among women. According to demographic and health surveys conducted most recently in Bolivia, the Dominican Republic, Guyana, and Peru, smoking among men decreases with household asset level, whereas it increases among women (figure 2.9). The only exception is Guyana, where smoking prevalence among the poorest and the wealthiest asset quintiles was virtually equal (3.5 percent among the poorest quintile versus 3.6 percent among the wealthiest quintile). Similar results were found in Uruguay in the 2009 Global Adult Tobacco Survey (GATS). Using a socioeconomic index that categorizes the population into four groups, results from this survey show that among the poorest quarter of the population, 35 percent of adults smoke, whereas among the wealthiest quarter, only 19.6 percent do (see chapter 5).

Tobacco is one of the leading health risk factors worldwide, and tobacco smoking, including second-hand smoke, is among the first five health risk factors in LAC. Table 2.6 presents part of the results of the Global Burden of Disease Study 2010. The study estimated the disability-adjusted life years lost due to the leading health risk factors worldwide and by region (Lim and others 2012). As the table shows, for all LAC subregions tobacco use is among the first five health risk factors; it is the third risk factor in southern Latin America and in the Caribbean.

Figure 2.9 Percentage of Women Smokers in Bolivia and Guyana, and Percentage of Men Smokers in the Dominican Republic and Guyana, by Asset Quintile, Various Years

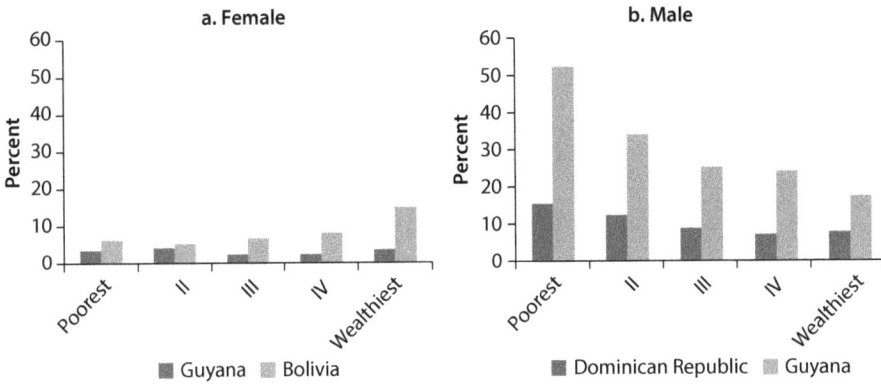

a. Female

b. Male

■ Guyana ■ Bolivia

■ Dominican Republic ■ Guyana

Source: Demographic and health surveys, final report: Bolivia, 2008; the Dominican Republic, 2007; Guyana, 2009; Peru, 2004–08.

Tobacco use increases the risk of cancer of the lung, mouth, pharynx, esophagus, larynx, bladder, pancreas, and other cancers. Its use has also been associated with infertility and delayed conception. Smoking during pregnancy increases the risk of premature birth, stillbirth, and neonatal death (WHO 2009, 2010). Smoking also increases the risk of developing chronic obstructive respiratory disease and coronary heart disease. Both first-hand and second-hand smoke can harm health.

Alcohol Abuse

The highest per capita alcohol consumption in the region is in the Caribbean countries and in some countries in South America; the lowest is in Central America. Figure 2.10 shows that, between 2003 and 2005, the yearly average of adult per capita alcohol consumption in Caribbean countries was as high as 11.9 liters of pure alcohol in St. Lucia, the highest in the hemisphere, and more than 8 liters in Grenada, Guyana, and St. Kitts and Nevis. Not all Caribbean countries have such high levels of adult consumption, however. In Jamaica and Cuba, for example, yearly consumption levels were below 6 liters of alcohol per adult in those same years. Some South American countries, particularly Argentina, Brazil, and Ecuador, also have relatively high per capita consumption. Argentina has the third highest alcohol consumption in the hemisphere, with a yearly per capita consumption of pure alcohol of about 10 liters (WHO 2011b).

WHO (2011b) ranked Belize, Ecuador, Guatemala, Nicaragua, Mexico, and Paraguay as the five countries in the region with the highest risk to health due to their pattern of alcohol consumption. Some of these countries have the highest alcohol consumption among drinkers: Ecuador, with a staggering 29.9 liters of pure alcohol per capita per year consumption among drinkers, followed by Mexico with 27 liters and Nicaragua with 20 liters. Some of these countries are also characterized by high rates of episodic heavy drinking. Table 2.7 shows that

Table 2.6 Health Risk Factors Ranked by Attributable Burden of Disease, by Subregion in the Americas, Western Europe, and Worldwide, 2010

	Global	Western Europe	United States and Canada	Argentina, Chile, and Uruguay	Brazil and Paraguay	Central America, Colombia, Mexico, and Venezuela, RB	Andean subregion	Caribbean
High blood pressure	1	2	4	2	2	4	2	1
Tobacco smoking, including second-hand smoke	2	1	1	3	4	5	5	3
Alcohol use	3	4	3	4	1	1	1	5
Household air pollution from burning solid fuels	4	...	...	23	18	11	7	9
Diet low in fruits	5	7	7	6	6	7	10	8
High BMI	6	3	2	1	3	2	3	2
High fasting plasma glucose	7	6	5	5	5	3	6	4
Physical inactivity and low physical activity	10	5	6	7	8	6	8	7
Diet high in sodium	11	10	11	11	9	13	13	15
Diet low in nuts and seeds	12	9	8	8	10	8	12	10
Iron deficiency	13	32	35	17	14	12	4	6
High total cholesterol	15	8	9	9	11	10	16	16
Diet low in vegetables	17	13	13	10	16	20	14	11
Diet high in processed meat	22	12	12	18	7	9	15	24

Source: Lim and others 2012.
Notes: Shaded cells show the leading five risk factors for each region; BMI = body mass index. Ellipses signify that there were no data because the risk factors were not quantified.

Figure 2.10 Yearly Average of Per Capita Consumption of Pure Alcohol among Adults 15 Years Old and Older, Latin American and Caribbean Countries, 2003–05

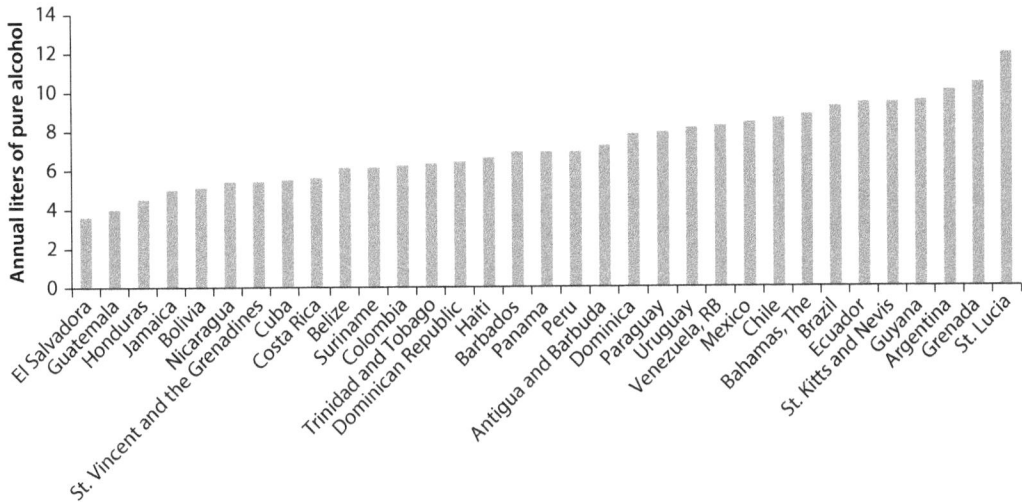

Source: WHO, Global Status Report on Alcohol and Health 2011b.

in Brazil, Nicaragua, and Paraguay, approximately 30 percent or more of adult males reported an episode of heavy drinking per week, indicating a risky consumption pattern. In Argentina, on the other hand, although per capita alcohol consumption is among the highest in the region, the country's consumption pattern is not as risky, since consumption among drinkers is not as high.

Alcohol consumption among men tends to be higher than that among women. In Mexico among 20–29-year-olds, for example, 60 percent of men, compared to 20 percent of women, consumed five or more alcoholic drinks at least once a month. Nationwide, alcohol consumption among both men and women tends to decrease with age (Olaiz-Fernández and others 2006).

Alcohol abuse is the leading health risk factor in most of LAC. As seen in table 2.6, alcohol is the leading health risk factor in most of the region's countries, given the disability-adjusted life years lost attributed to its use. Only in the Caribbean and in the southernmost LAC countries is alcohol use not the main health risk factor, although it ranks among the first five. Alcohol increases the risk for more than 60 types of diseases and injuries (WHO 2011b), such as liver cirrhosis, epilepsy, poisoning, road traffic accidents, violence, and several types of cancers such as mouth, esophagus, liver, colon, and rectum.

Intermediate Risk Factors

High Blood Pressure

More than two in five adult men and one in three adult women in the region have high blood pressure or take medication to treat it (figure 2.11). High blood pressure (systolic blood pressure higher than 140 or diastolic blood pressure higher than 90) is the leading risk for developing heart disease and can lead to

Table 2.7 Pattern of Alcohol Consumption, Selected Latin American and Caribbean Countries, 2003–05

Countries	Total abstainers (%)	Total per capita consumption (in liters of pure alcohol)	Drinkers' per capita consumption (yearly average)	Heavy episodic drinking, males 15–85+ years old males, 2003 (%)
Argentina	17.5	10	12.12	17.5
Barbados	59.0	6.9	16.89	14.2
Belize	64.6	6.1	17.15	28.2
Bolivia	40.1	5.1	8.55	—
Brazil	50.5	9.2	18.51	32.4
Canada	22.4	9.8	12.59	15.5
Chile	32.4	8.6	12.65	—
Colombia	19.4	6.2	7.66	—
Costa Rica	44.3	5.6	9.96	13.8
Cuba	54.4	5.5	11.78	
Dominica	41.0	7.8	13.29	26.2
Dominican Republic	43.3	6.4	11.31	22.0
Ecuador	68.6	9.4	29.87	25.3
Guatemala	77.2	4	17.66	—
Jamaica	57.0	5	11.63	—
Mexico	69.0	8.4	27.16	12.6
Nicaragua	73.8	5.4	20.5	32.7
Paraguay	38.3	7.9	12.77	37.7
Peru	31.0	6.9	10	7.0
United States	34.6	9.4	14.43	13.0
Uruguay	53.0	8.1	17.92	11.5

Source: WHO 2011b.
Note: — = not available.

other chronic diseases such as kidney failure. High blood pressure ranks among the first five health risk factors in most of LAC; it ranks first in the Caribbean and second in most other countries (table 2.6). As mentioned earlier, some risk factors are more prevalent in certain sections of the population or in certain countries. Such is the case for high blood pressure, which appears to be highly prevalent in lower-income countries, compared to higher-income countries in and outside LAC. Adults in Caribbean countries are more likely to have a high prevalence of high blood pressure than do adults elsewhere in the region, which might explain the higher death rates due to heart disease experienced in this group of countries. Outside the Caribbean, a relatively large percentage of adults in countries such as Brazil, Chile, Cuba, and República Bolivariana de Venezuela have high blood pressure, and this prevalence increases with age.[9]

High Cholesterol

High cholesterol levels in the blood are also a major risk factor for heart disease. In contrast to the pattern seen with high blood pressure, however, high

Figure 2.11 Percentage of Adults Older than 20 Years with High Blood Pressure (SBP ≥ 140 or DBP ≥ 90, or Who Are on Medication), Selected Latin American and Caribbean Countries and OECD and Regional Averages, 2008

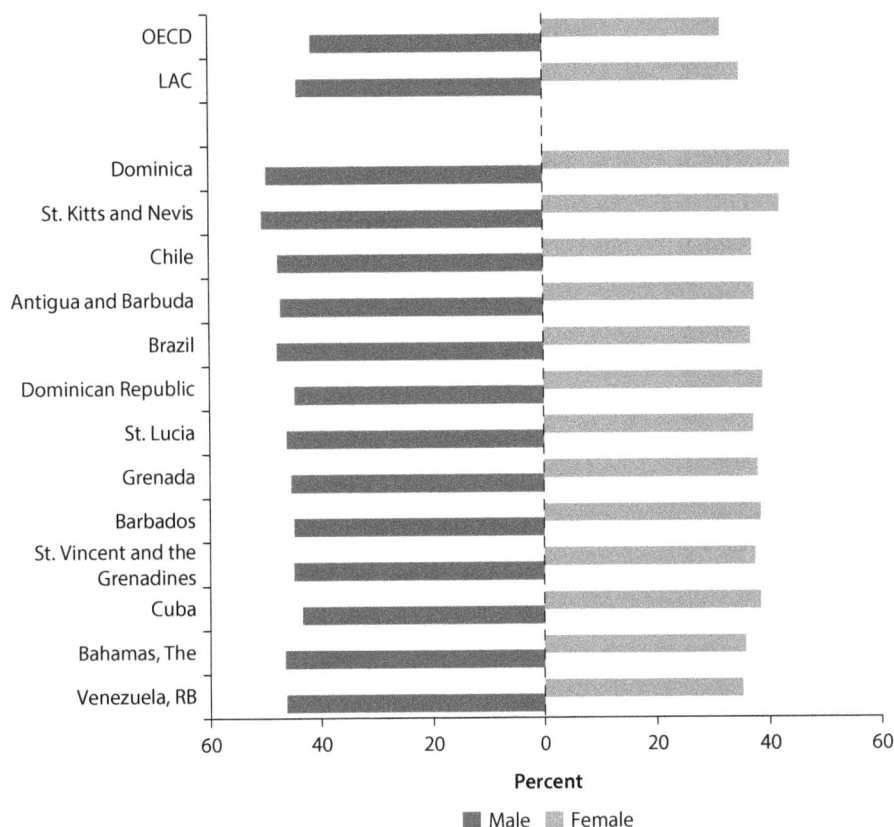

Source: Global Health Observatory Data Repository, Noncommunicable Diseases, Risk Factors. http://apps.who.int/gho/data /node.main.A867?lang=en.
Notes: DBP = diastolic blood pressure; LAC = Latin America and the Caribbean; OECD = Organisation for Economic Co-operation and Development; SBP = systolic blood pressure.

cholesterol is less prevalent in the region than in higher income OECD countries (figure 2.12). Argentina, The Bahamas, Brazil, and Chile have the highest percentage of persons with high blood cholesterol in the region (WHO 2008). Even these high rates in the region are still relatively low compared to those in high-income countries in the OECD.

High Blood Glucose
The percentage of people with high levels of fasting glucose in the blood in LAC is significantly higher than in OECD countries, particularly among women and in Caribbean countries (figure 2.13). In fact, high fasting plasma glucose is among the first five health risk factors in all of LAC, particularly in central Latin America, where it is estimated that it is the third leading health risk factor (table 2.6). In most of the region's countries, women are more likely

Figure 2.12 Age-Standardized Percentage of Adults 20 Years Old or Older with High Blood Cholesterol (≥5.0 mmol/L), by Sex, Selected Latin American and Caribbean Countries and OECD and Regional Averages, 2008

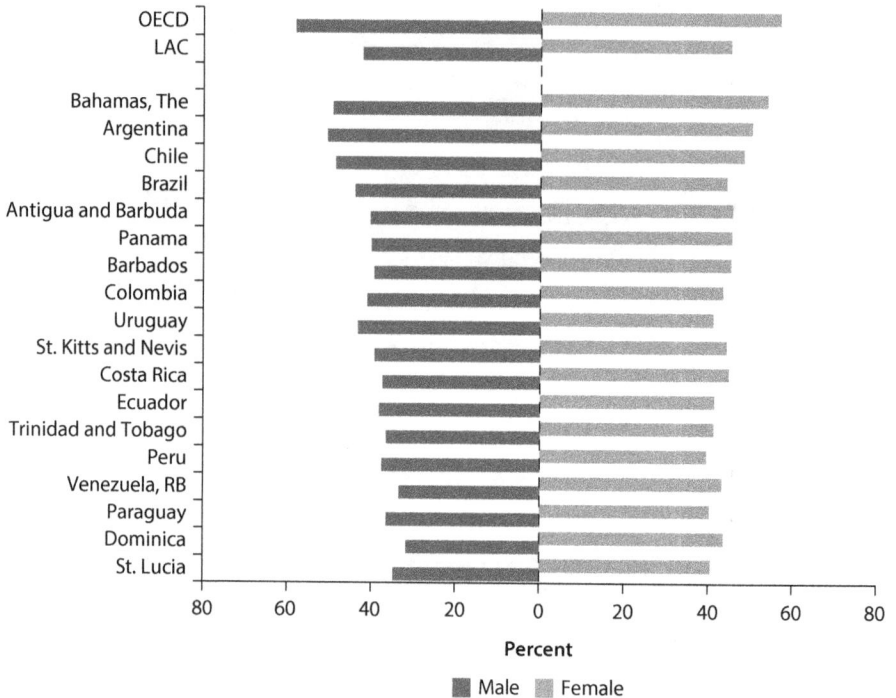

Percent

■ Male ■ Female

Source: WHO 2008. Global Health Observatory Data Repository, Noncommunicable Diseases, Risk Factors. http://apps.who .int/gho/data/node.main.A867?lang=en.
Notes: LAC = Latin America and the Caribbean; OECD = Organisation for Economic Co-operation and Development.

to have high blood-glucose levels than men, except in Argentina, Chile, El Salvador, and República Bolivariana de Venezuela (these countries are not included in figure 2.13, as they have a lower percentage of adults with high blood glucose than the countries shown). Caribbean countries have some of the highest shares of adults with high blood glucose; these countries also have some of the highest diabetes-related death rates in the world, as mentioned previously. High blood-glucose levels are markers for the risk of developing diabetes. Diabetes, in turn,[10] is a risk factor for cardiovascular diseases, blindness, kidney failure, and gangrene.

Overweight and Obesity

The average Latin American and Caribbean adult, particularly the adult woman, is overweight. BMI[11] is the most commonly used measure of overweight and obesity. A person with a BMI equal to or higher than 25 is considered overweight, and someone with a BMI equal to or higher than 30 is considered obese. The mean estimated BMI for adult men and women in the region is 25.4 and 27.0, respectively, and half of adult men and two-thirds of adult women in the

Figure 2.13 Age-Standardized Percentage of Adults with High Blood-Glucose Levels (≥7 mmol or Who Are on Medication), by Sex, Selected Latin American and Caribbean Countries and OECD and Regional Averages, 2008

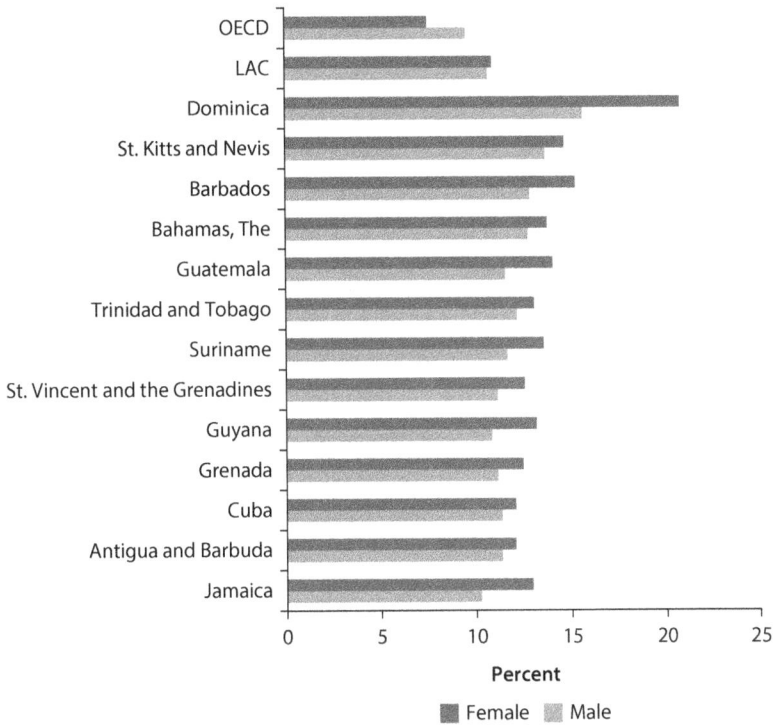

Source: WHO 2008. Global Health Observatory Data Repository, Noncommunicable Diseases, Risk Factors. http://apps.who.int/gho/data/node.main.A867?lang=en.
Notes: LAC = Latin America and the Caribbean; OECD = Organisation for Economic Co-operation and Development.

region are overweight or obese, surpassing rates of overweight and obesity in OECD countries (figure 2.14).

Overweight and obesity rates in parts of the region also appear to be higher than in many OECD countries. Figure 2.15 shows that several Caribbean countries, as well as Mexico and República Bolivariana de Venezuela, have significantly higher estimated rates of overweight and obesity than Canada, the United States, and other OECD countries. In Mexico, overweight and obesity affect 70 percent of the population (71.9 percent of women and 66.7 percent of men) between the ages of 30 and 60.

Moreover, the prevalence of overweight and obesity in the region has increased over time, and yet very few countries in LAC have data on overweight and obesity trends. There are some exceptions, Brazil for instance, has information on these two conditions for men and women for several years; available data indicate an increase in the prevalence of overweight in men and women (BMI ≥ 25). Figure 2.16 shows the increasing percentage of overweight adult women in some of the region's countries. These trends are not linear,

Figure 2.14 Mean Average Body Mass Index (BMI) among Adults 20 Years Old and Older, Selected Latin American and Caribbean Countries and OECD and Regional Averages, 2008

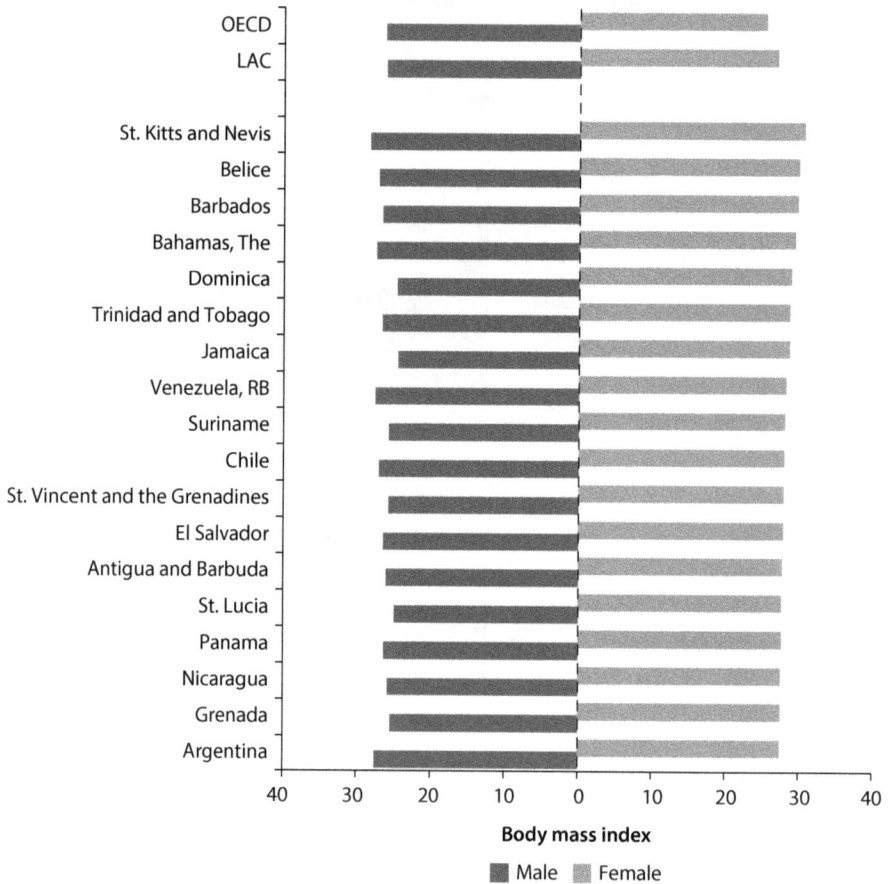

Sources: WHO 2008; Global Health Observatory Data Repository, Noncommunicable Diseases, Risk Factors. http://apps .who.int/gho/data/node.main.A867?lang=en.
Notes: BMI = body mass index; LAC = Latin America and the Caribbean; OECD = Organisation for Economic Co-operation and Development.

however, and some countries, such as Haiti and Peru, which have relatively low percentages of overweight women, have seen little change and even slight decreases during some periods.[12] More recent data from Peru (presented in table 2.8) shows increases in the rate of obesity among women in that country. In addition, according to Argentina's 2009 National Risk Factor Survey more than half of the population (53.4 percent) was overweight or obese that year, with an increase in obesity rates from 14.6 percent in 2005 to 18 percent in 2009 (Ferrante and others 2011). In Mexico, obesity rates have also increased significantly: in 1993, obesity prevalence among adults was 21.5 percent, in 2000 the rate had climbed to 24 percent, and by 2006 the figure topped 30 percent for adults older than 20 years (34.5 percent of women and 24.2 percent of men were obese) (Olaiz-Fernández and others 2006).

Figure 2.15 Age-Standardized Percentage of Overweight Adults Older than 20 Years (BMI ≥ 25), by Sex, Selected Latin American and Caribbean Countries, 2008

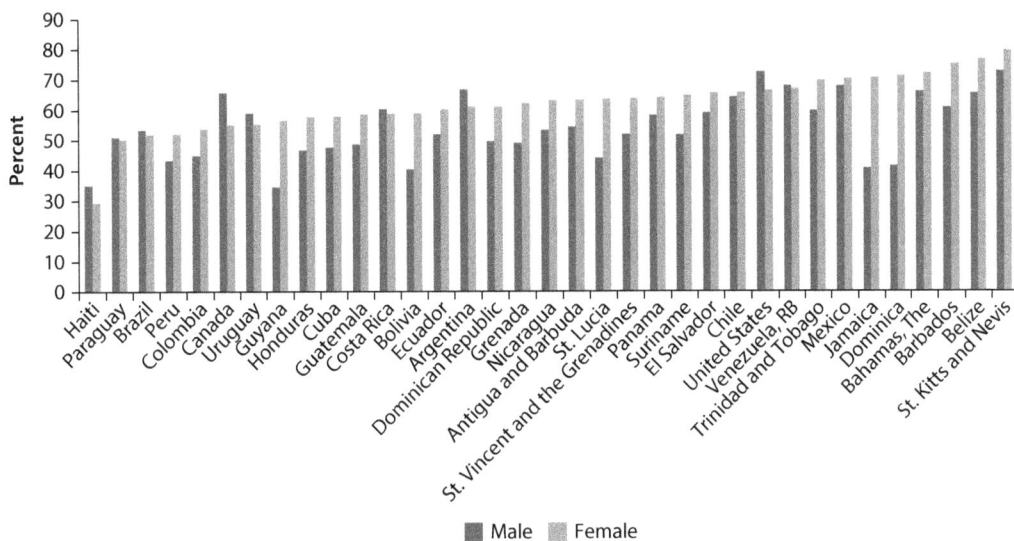

Source: WHO 2008. Global Health Observatory Data Repository, Noncommunicable Diseases, Risk Factors. http://apps.who.int/gho/data/node .main.A867?lang=en.
Note: Figures for some countries are estimates. BMI = body mass index.

Middle-class women are the most likely to be obese. In Bolivia, Colombia, and Peru, the percentage of obese women from middle-class households is higher than the percentage of obese women from the wealthiest or the poorest households (table 2.8). On average, the percentage of obese women has increased over time in all countries. And not only have obesity rates among women increased, but the distribution of obesity across socioeconomic quintiles also has changed. In Peru, women in the wealthiest households were the most likely to be obese in 1996; by the year 2000, however, the share of obese women was highest midway across the socioeconomic distribution. In Colombia in 2005, women in the poorest quintile were the least likely to be obese; by 2010, the percentage of obese women from households in the poorest quintile was higher than that of those in households in the richest quintile, and similar to women in the fourth quintile. In Guyana, the only country where there is information on obesity among men by wealth quintiles, rates increase as the socioeconomic level increases. There, adult women are almost three times as likely to be obese as are men. Among the countries shown in the table, Guyana has the highest percentage of obese women. These percentages are high across all income quintiles; after the second quintile these percentages do not change much.

A large percentage of children also are overweight or obese. Figure 2.17 shows that in at least five LAC countries for which data are available, more than 9 percent of children under five are overweight, with percentages being

Figure 2.16 Trends in the Percentage of Overweight Women (BMI ≥ 25), Selected Latin American and Caribbean Countries, Various Periods

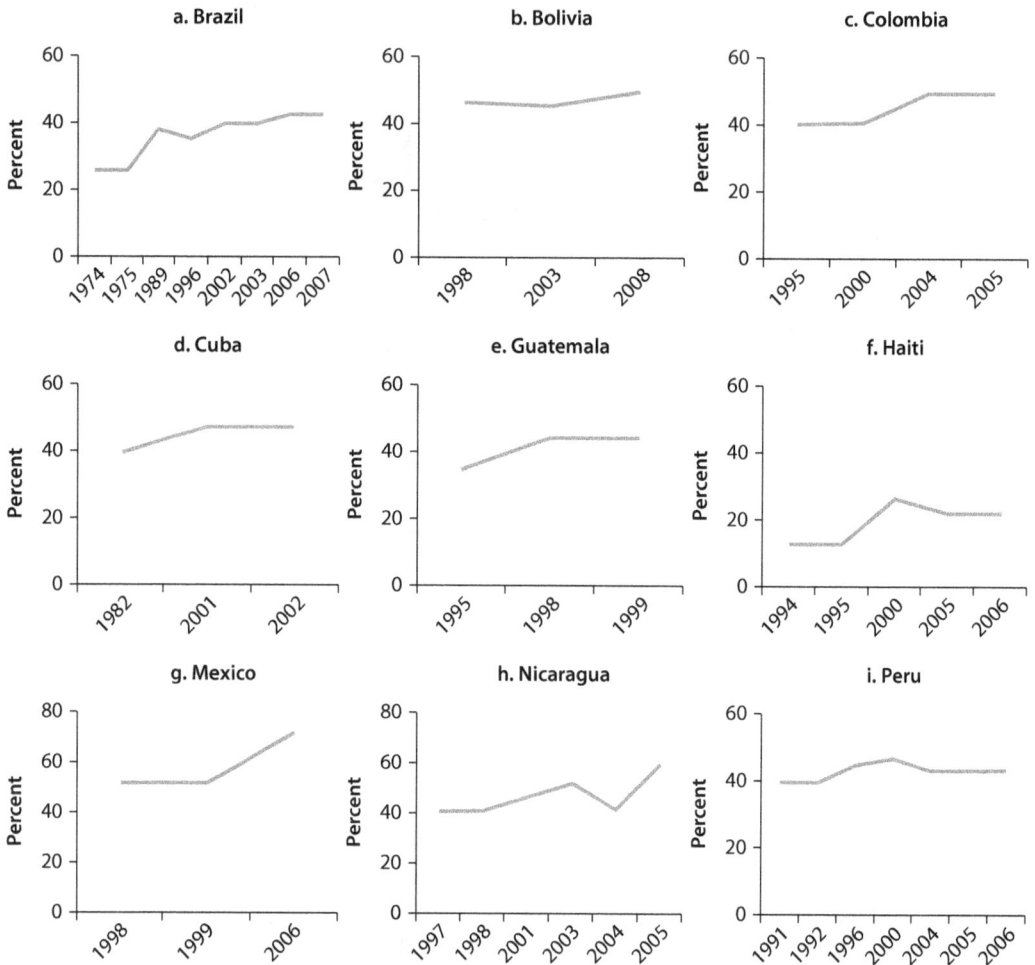

Source: WHO Global Data Base on Body Mass Index.
Note: BMI = body mass index.

significantly higher among older children. According to a 2010 OECD report, in Brazil in 2006, 22 percent of children between the ages of 7 and 10 were overweight; in Mexico, 31 percent of children aged 7–17 years were overweight (Sassi 2010).

In most LAC countries, a high prevalence of overweight and obesity coexists with a high prevalence of chronic malnutrition. As discussed earlier in this chapter, in Guatemala almost 60 percent of adult women, 50 percent of adult men, and approximately 6 percent of children under five years old are overweight or obese. At the same time, the rate of chronic malnutrition among children in that country is approximately 43 percent.[13] These two conditions can even coexist in the same household across the region, and they are often

Table 2.8 Obesity Rates among Nonpregnant Women (15–49 Years Old) in Selected LAC Countries and among Adult Men in Guyana, by Wealth Quintile, Various Years

	Poorest	II	III	IV	Wealthiest	Total
Peru, 1996	2.9	7.2	11.5	13.1	15.7	9.3
Peru, 2000	3.6	9.5	15.8	18.0	14.3	13.0
Peru, 2007–08	4.7	11.4	16.3	16.6	13.2	13.1
Peru, 2011	7.7	16.9	20.8	21.0	15.6	17.0
Bolivia, 2003	5.9	12.2	16.4	19.1	17.5	15.1
Bolivia, 2008	8.3	15.6	20.2	23.1	16.8	17.4
Colombia, 2005	10.8	12.2	13.0	13.2	12.0	12.3
Colombia, 2010	15.0	17.8	15.6	14.9	12.6	15.2
Guyana, 2008						
Among nonpregnant women	17.5	22.7	20.5	23.8	22.8	21.7
Among men	3.8	7.0	7.5	9.6	14.1	8.5

Sources: Demographic and health surveys.
Note: LAC = Latin America and the Caribbean.

Figure 2.17 Percentage of Chronically Malnourished (Stunted) and Overweight Children under 5 Years Old, Selected Latin American and Caribbean Countries, 2010

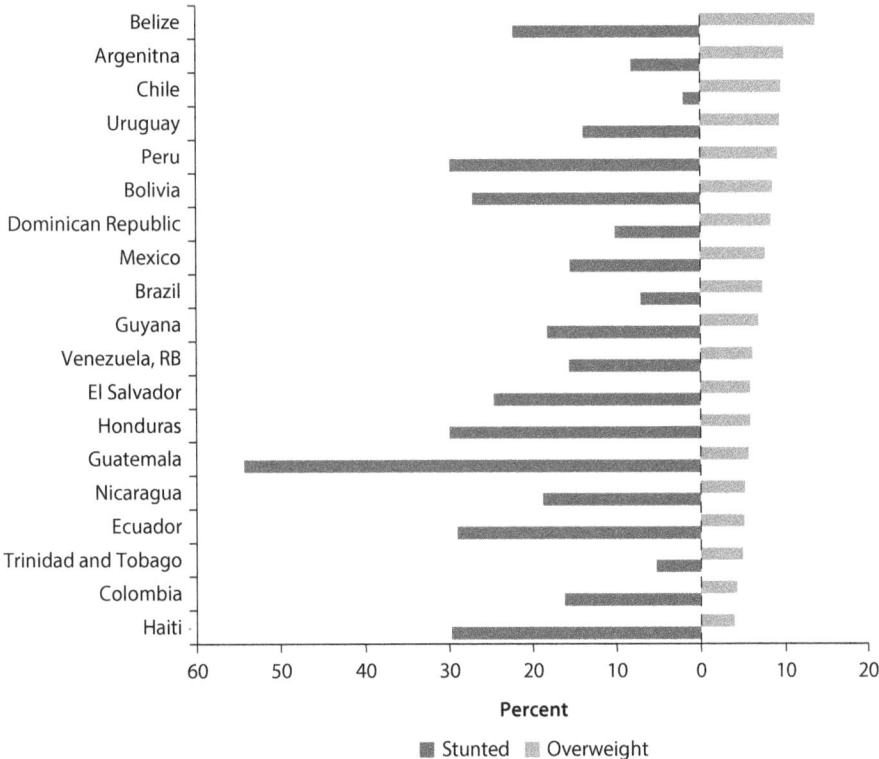

Source: WHO 2011c.

interrelated: low birthweight, for instance, is associated with increased rates of high blood pressure, heart disease, stroke, and diabetes in mothers (WHO 2005). Three of the four countries in the world with the highest percentage of households having both overweight mothers and stunted (chronically malnourished) children are in the region: Bolivia (11 percent of households), Guatemala (13 percent), and Nicaragua (almost 10 percent) (Garret and Ruel 2003). However, in other countries in the region, the rate of childhood obesity is similar to or higher than the rate of chronic malnutrition, as is the case in Argentina, Brazil, Chile, and Trinidad and Tobago (figure 2.17).

Evidence is growing regarding the harmful effects of overweight and obesity on health. Overweight and obesity are precursors for chronic conditions, because they increase the risk of developing high blood pressure, cholesterol, and fasting blood glucose. A high BMI is among the first five health risk factors in LAC, due to the attributable disability-adjusted life years lost associated with it (table 2.6). Being overweight or obese increases the risk of developing cardiovascular diseases (mainly ischemic heart disease and stroke), diabetes, some cancers (such as colon, breast, and endometrial cancers), and musculoskeletal diseases (such as osteoarthritis).

Notes

1. These figures come from 2010 World Bank data, available at http://data.worldbank.org/topic/urban-development.

2. The surveys used for this study are different across countries, and, thus, it is impossible to make fully reliable country comparisons; for instance, average calorie intake in Costa Rica seems to be lower than that of Guatemala and Nicaragua, which are lower income countries. The household survey used to examine dietary patterns in Costa Rica is an income and expenditure survey which has a different design and instruments than those used in the other two countries, which were living conditions surveys. Nevertheless, it is possible to evaluate differences within countries and observe general trends in dietary patterns in the region.

3. For additional information, please visit the Centers for Disease Control and Prevention's posting on this topic: http://www.cdc.gov/heartdisease/index.htm.

4. For additional information, visit http://www.who.int/dietphysicalactivity/pa/en/index.html.

5. For additional information, please visit http://www.who.int/dietphysicalactivity/pa/en/index.html.

6. Estimates are based on Costa Rica's 2004 multipurpose household survey (Encuesta de Hogares de Propósitos Múltiples 2004).

7. Estimates are based on Costa Rica's 2006 national living conditions survey (Encuesta Nacional de Condiciones de Vida [ENCOVI] 2006).

8. Estimates are based on Costa Rica's 2004 multipurpose household survey (Encuesta de Hogares de Propósitos Múltiples 2004 [INEC]).

9. Data come from WHO's Global Health Observatory Data Repository, Noncommunicable Diseases, Risk Factors, which is available at http://apps.who.int/gho/data/node.main.A867?lang=en.

10. Diabetes mellitus is a disease characterized by the body's insufficient production of insulin or improper response to insulin, a hormone produced by the pancreas that absorbs glucose and turns it into energy.

11. Body mass index (BMI) is a reliable indicator of body fatness; it is calculated by dividing a person's weight by his or her height squared.

12. Additional information on the prevalence of overweight and obesity in the region can be found at WHO's Global Health Observatory Data Repository, at http://apps.who .int/gho/data/node.main.A903.

13. The figure of 43 percent of stunted children is based on the old growth reference, not the new WHO standard; the old reference was used to keep the numbers comparable across time. According to the new standards, 54.5 percent of children in Guatemala are stunted.

Bibliography

Brown, I. J., I. Tzoulak, V. Candeias, and P. Elliott. 2009. "Salt Intakes around the World: Implications for Public Health." *International Journal of Epidemiology* 1–23. doi: 10.1093/ije/dyp139.

Bonilla-Chacin, M. E., and L. T. Marcano-Vázquez. 2012. "Promoting Healthy Living in Central America: Multisectoral Approaches to Prevent Noncommunicable Diseases." *HNP Discussion Paper Series* N. 71848. World Bank, Washington, DC.

Bonilla-Chacin, M. E., L. T. Marcano-Vázquez, R. Sierra, and U. Aldana. 2013. Dietary patterns and non-communicable diseases in selected Latin American countries. *Health, Nutrition, and Population (HNP) Discussion Paper.* Washington DC, World Bank. http://documents.worldbank.org/curated/en/2013/03/18132174/dietary-patterns -non-communicable-diseases-selected-latin-american-countries.

Cotlear, D. 2010. *Population Aging. Is Latin America Ready?* Washington, DC: World Bank.

Drewnowski, A., and B. Popkin. 1997. "The Nutrition Transition: New Trends in the Global Diet." *Nutrition Review* 55 (2): 31–43.

Ferrante, D., N. Apro, V. Ferreira, M. Virgolini, V. Aguilar, M. Sosa, P. Perel, and J. Casas. 2011. "Feasibility of Salt Reduction in Processed Foods in Argentina." *Revista Panamericana de Salud Pública* 29 (2): 69–75.

Ferrante, D., B. Linetzky, J. Konfino, A. King, M. Virgolini, and S. Laspiur. 2011. "2009 National Risk Factors Survey: Evolution of the Epidemic of Chronic Noncommunicable Diseases in Argentina. Cross Sectional Study." *Revista Argentina de Salud Pública* 2 (6): 34–41.

Garret, J., and M. Ruel. 2003. "Stunted Child-Overweight Mother Pairs: An Emerging Policy Concern." *FCND Discussion Paper* 148, International Food Policy Research Institute, Washington, DC.

Hawkes, C. 2007. WHO Commission on Social Determinants of Health. *Globalization, Food and Nutrition Transitions.* Globalization and Health Knowledge Network, Research Papers. Ottawa: Institute of Population Health.

Hu, F. B., and W. C. Willett. 2002. "Optimal Diets for Prevention of Coronary Heart Disease." *The Journal of the American Medical Association* 288 (20): 2569–78.

Instituto Nacional de Estadística. 2006. Encuesta Nacional de Condiciones de Vida 2006. Guatemala, Guatemala.

Instituto Nacional de Estadística e Informática. 2001. *Encuesta Demográfica y de Salud Familiar 2000*. Report prepared by J. Reyes and L. Ochoa. Lima, Peru.

Instituto Nacional de Estadística e Informática. 2009. *Perú: Encuesta Demográfica y de Salud Familiar 2007–08*. Lima, Peru.

Instituto Nacional de Estadística e Informática. 2012. *Perú: Encuesta Demográfica y de Salud Familiar 2011*. Lima, Peru.

Instituto Nacional de Estadísticas y Censos de Costa Rica (INEC), *Encuesta de Hogares de Propósitos Múltiples, 2004*.

Kearney, J. 2010. "Review: Food Consumption Trends and Drivers." *Philosophical Transactions of the Royal Society B* 365: 2793–807.

Lim, S. S., A. D. Lopez, C. J. L. Murray, M. Ezzati, T. Vos, A. D. Flaxman, G. Danaei, K. Shibuya, H. Adair-Rohani, M. Amann, H. Ross Anderson, K. G. Andrews, M. Aryee, C. Atkinson, L. J. Bacchus, A. Bahalim, et al. 2012. "A Comparative Risk Assessment of Burden of Disease and Injury Attributable to 67 Risk Factors and Risk Factor Clusters in 21 Regions, 1990–2010: A Systematic Analysis for the Global Burden of Disease Study 2010." *Lancet* 380: 2224–60.

Ministerio de Salud de la Nación. 2006. *Primera Encuesta Nacional de Factores de Riesgo 2005*. http://www.msal.gov.ar/ent/images/stories/vigilancia/pdf/encuesta_factores _riesgo_2005_completa.pdf.

Ministerio de Salud de la Nación. 2011. *Segunda Encuesta Nacional de Factores de Riesgo para Enfermedades no Transmisibles 2009*. http://msal.gov.ar/ENT/VIG/Areas _Tematicas/Factores_de_Riesgo/PDF/Segunda_Encuesta_Nacional_De_Factores _De_Riesgo_2011.pdf.

Ministerio de Salud Pública, Dirección General de Salud, División Epidemiología. 2009. *1era Encuesta Nacional de Factores de Riesgo de Enfermedades Crónicas No Transmisibles*. Montevideo, Uruguay.

Ministerio de Salud y Deportes and Instituto Nacional de Estadísticas. 2009. *Bolivia: Encuesta Nacional de Demografía y Salud 2008*. Report elaborated by R. Coa and L. Ochoa. La Paz, Bolivia.

Ministry of Health (MOH), Bureau of Statistics (BOS), and ICF Macro. 2010. *Guyana Demographic and Health Survey 2009*. Georgetown, Guyana: MOH, BOS, and ICF Macro.

Olaiz-Fernández, G., J. Rivera-Dommarco, T. Shamah-Levy, R. Rojas, S. Villalpando-Hernández, M. Hernández-Avila, and J. Sepúlveda-Amor. 2006. *Encuesta Nacional de Salud y Nutrición 2006*. Cuernavaca, MX: Instituto Nacional de Salud Pública.

Popkin, B. 2006. "Global Nutrition Dynamics: The World Is Shifting Rapidly Toward a Diet Linked with Noncommunicable Diseases." *American Journal of Clinical Nutrition* 84 (2): 289–98.

Saad, P. 2010. "Demographic Trends in Latin America and the Caribbean." In *Population Aging: Is Latin America Ready?* edited by D. Cotlear. Directions in Development, Human Development Series. Washington, DC: World Bank.

Sassi, F. 2010. *Obesity and the Economics of Prevention: Fit or Fat*. Paris: OECD.

Serra-Majem, L., D. MacLean, L. Ribas, D. Brulé, W. Sekula, R. Prattala, R. Garcia-Closas, A. Yngve, M. Lalonde, and A. Petrasovits. 2003. "Comparative Analysis of Nutrition Data from National, Household, and Individual Levels: Results from a WHO-CINDI Collaborative Project in Canada, Finland, Poland, and Spain." *Journal of Epidemiological Community Health* 57: 74–80.

Thow, A. M., and C. Hawkes. 2009. "The Implication of Trade Liberalization for Diets and Health: A Case Study from Central America." *Globalization and Health* 5 (5).

USDA (United States, Department of Agriculture) and HSS (Department of Health and Human Services). 2010. *Dietary Guidelines for Americans, 2010.* 7th ed. Washington, DC: Government Printing Office.

WHO (World Health Organization). 2003. *Diet, Nutrition and the Prevention of Chronic Diseases: Report of a Joint FAO/WHO Expert Consultation.* WHO Technical Report Series 19. Geneva: WHO.

———. 2004. *Global Strategy on Diet, Physical Activity and Health.* Geneva: WHO.

———. 2005. *Preventing Chronic Diseases. A Vital Investment.* Geneva: WHO.

———. 2008. *The Global Burden of Disease: 2004 Update.* Geneva: WHO.

———. 2009. *Report on the Global Tobacco Epidemic 2009.* Geneva: WHO.

———. 2010. *Gender, Women and the Tobacco Epidemic.* Geneva: WHO.

———. 2011a. *Global Status Report on Noncommunicable Diseases 2010.* Geneva: WHO.

———. 2011b. *Global Status Report on Alcohol and Health.* Geneva: WHO.

———. 2011c. *World Health Statistics 2010.* Geneva: WHO.

Wright, J., and C. Y. Wang. 2010. "Trends in Intake of Energy and Macronutrients in Adults from 1999–2000 through 2007–2008". *NCHS Data Brief* 49, National Center for Health Statistics, Atlanta, GA, November 2010.

CHAPTER 3

Economic Impact of NCDs in Latin America and the Caribbean

Edmundo Murrugarra and María Eugenia Bonilla-Chacín

Noncommunicable diseases (NCDs) not only represent an important health burden in Latin America and the Caribbean (LAC), they also pose an increasing economic and development threat to households, health systems, and economies throughout the region. These conditions require continuous contact with the health system for long periods of time and, if not controlled, can result in costly hospitalizations. NCDs also are responsible for great productivity losses due to worker absenteeism, disability, and premature death. In addition, out-of-pocket expenditures for services and medicines can impoverish households with members that suffer from these conditions (Nikolic, Stanciole, and Zaydman 2011). Much of this economic burden to households, health systems, and economies is avoidable, however, as many NCDs can be prevented or controlled.

This chapter analyzes the economic burden of NCDs in the region. Using existing household surveys, the chapter shows the impact of NCDs on household out-of-pocket expenditures and on the labor market in selected countries in the region. To put this discussion in perspective, the chapter ends with a brief overview of the existing literature on the economic impact of NCDs in the region's health systems.

Household Out-of-Pocket and Catastrophic Health Expenditures Associated with NCDs

This section reviews household out-of-pocket and catastrophic health expenditures in households that have members who have an NCD, using household surveys from selected countries in the region. Data from Colombia, Jamaica, Nicaragua, and Peru show that out-of-pocket expenditures in households that include someone with a chronic condition more than double those of households that do not, with the greatest difference seen in expenditures on drugs. In Colombia and Nicaragua, households with a chronic-disease patient are also more likely to incur catastrophic health expenditures.

Data from a few of the region's countries show that the use of health care services is higher among persons who report that they have a chronic condition, regardless of gender, age, education level, socioeconomic status, or urban/rural residence. These results were found in all countries with available data: Brazil, Chile, Colombia, Nicaragua, and Peru (figure 3.1). NCDs in general require continuous contact with the health system over long periods of time. If a household lacks insurance against such expenditures, these diseases can greatly damage its economic welfare, possibly impoverishing it.[1]

Households that include a member with an NCD have higher out-of-pocket expenditures than households that do not. In Colombia, Nicaragua, and Peru, for example, households with a member with an NCD pay (as a percentage of total household expenditure) about twice as much as households that do not have a member who suffers from a chronic condition. The pattern across income levels differs from country to country, however. While in Colombia the poorest households with a member who has an NCD pay more (as percentage of total household expenditure), in Peru the poorest households pay as much as wealthier ones, and in Nicaragua, the wealthiest pay more (see table 3.1).

In Colombia and Nicaragua, households with a member who suffers from a chronic condition are also more likely to incur catastrophic health expenditures, particularly poor households. The percentage of households with a member with an NCD that incur catastrophic health expenditures (defined as households that spend more than 20 percent of total expenditures in health care) is twice as high or higher than that in households without a member with an NCD. In Colombia,

Figure 3.1 Utilization of Health Services by Persons with a Chronic Condition and by Those without, by Age Group, Urban or Rural Residence, Educational Level, and Economic Status

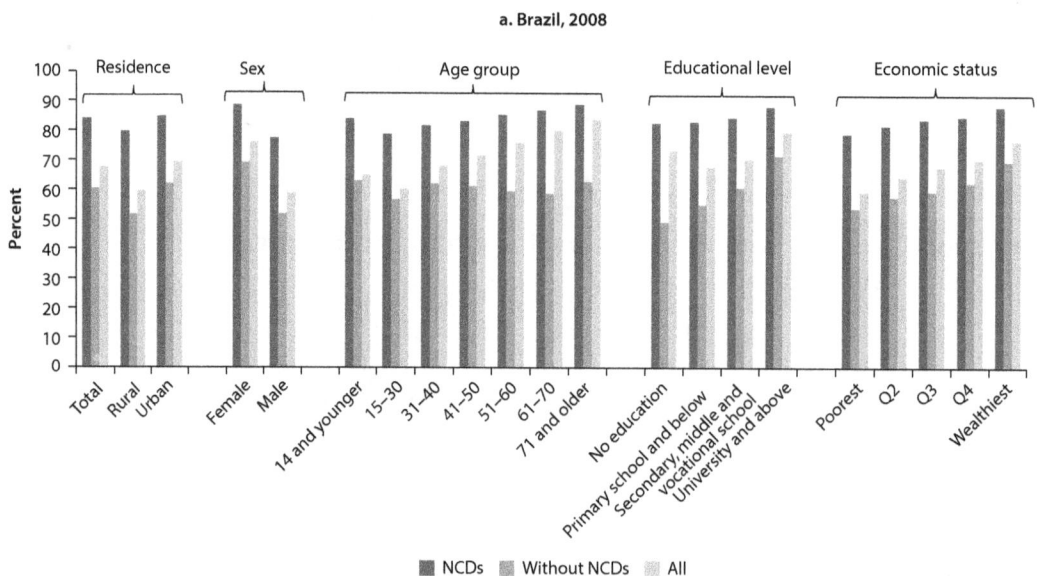

a. Brazil, 2008

NCDs   Without NCDs   All

figure continues next page

Figure 3.1 Utilization of Health Services by Persons with a Chronic Condition and by Those without, by Age Group, Urban or Rural Residence, Educational Level, and Economic Status *(continued)*

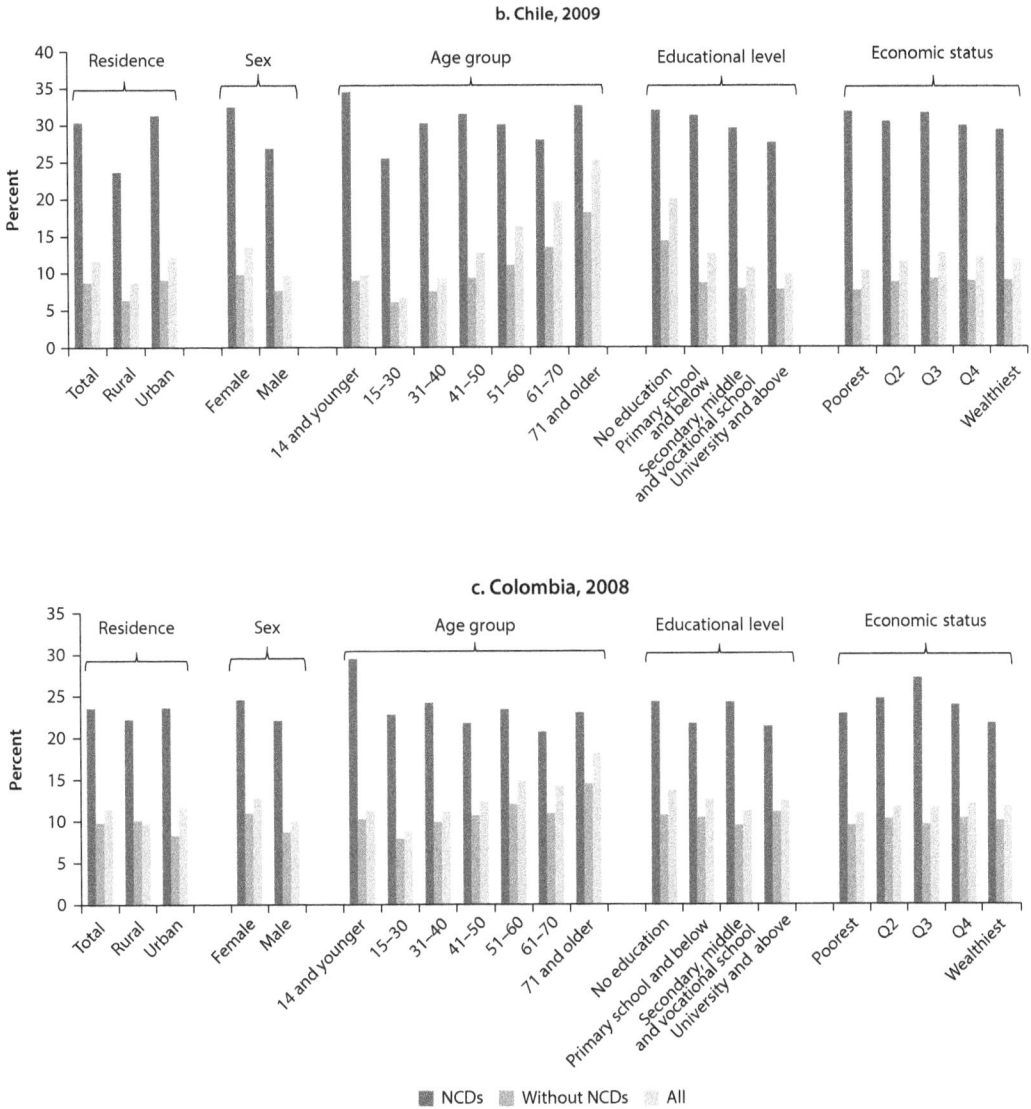

b. Chile, 2009

c. Colombia, 2008

■ NCDs ▨ Without NCDs ░ All

figure continues next page

Figure 3.1 Utilization of Health Services by Persons with a Chronic Condition and by Those without, by Age Group, Urban or Rural Residence, Educational Level, and Economic Status *(continued)*

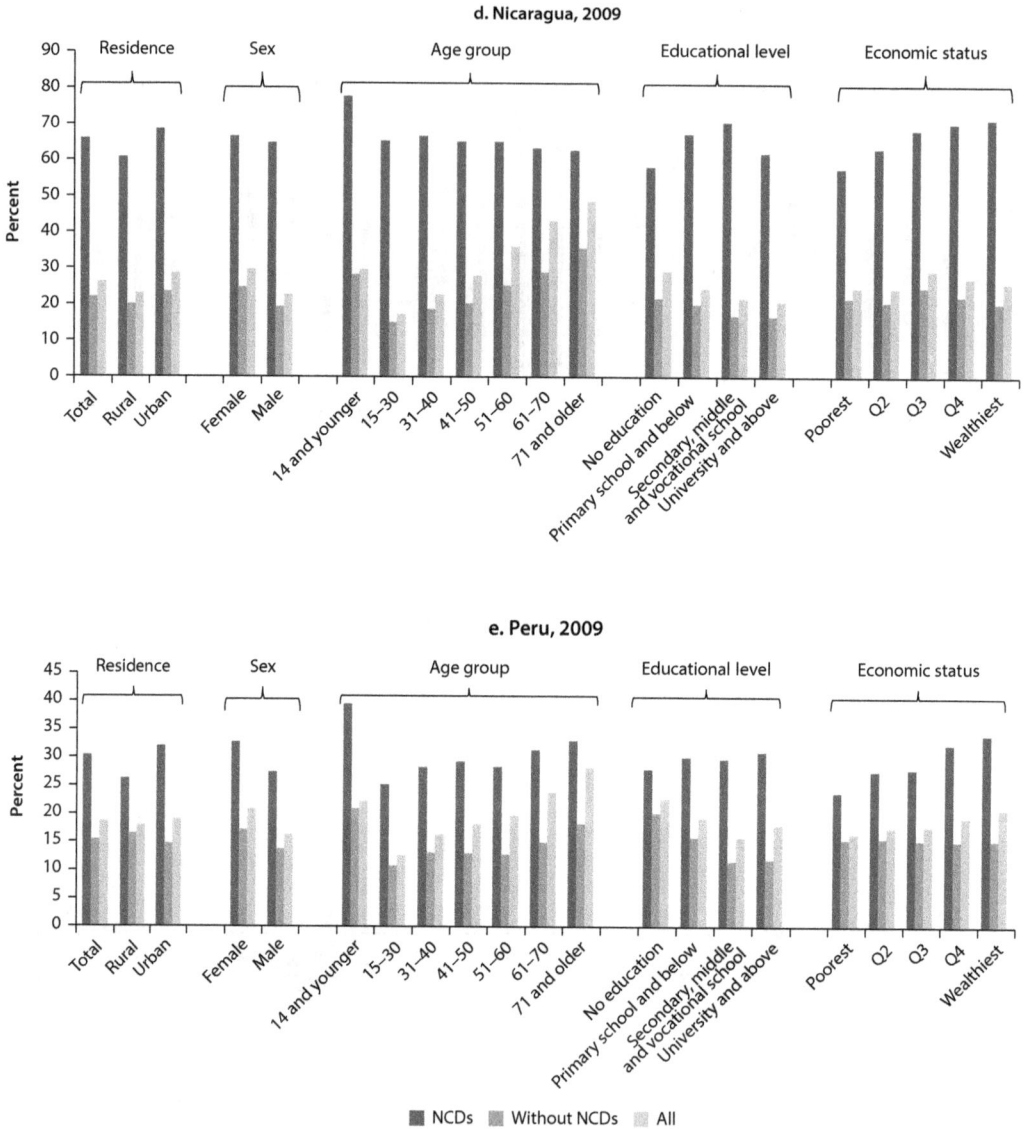

d. Nicaragua, 2009

e. Peru, 2009

■ NCDs   ■ Without NCDs   ▨ All

Source: Estimates from Brazil, Pesquisa Nacional Por Amostra de Domicilios (PNAD 2008); Chile, Encuesta de Caracterizacion Socioeconómica Nacional (CASEN 2009); Colombia, Encuesta de Calidad de Vida, 2008; Nicaragua, Encuesta de Hogares sobre Medición de Nivel de Vida, (EMNV) 2009; and Peru, Encuesta Nacional de Hogares, 2008.
Note: NCDs = noncommunicable diseases.

Table 3.1 Out-of-Pocket Health Expenditures and Catastrophic Expenditure on Health by Households with a Member with an NCD and by Households without, by Income Level

Colombia, 2008

All persons, payers and nonpayers (in Col$)	Household health expenditure (normalized by total household expenditure)			Percentage of households with catastrophic health spending (more than 20 percent of total household expenditures)			Percentage of households with catastrophic health spending (more than 30 percent of total household expenditures)		
	Without NCDs	With NCDs	Total	Without NCDs	With NCDs	Total	Without NCDs	With NCDs	Total
All	3.7	7.1	4.8	5.1	10.5	6.9	2.7	5.7	3.7
Poorest	4.6	9.2	6.2	7.1	16.5	10.3	4.3	10.9	6.5
Q2	4.6	8.5	5.9	6.6	12.9	8.8	5.1	8.5	6.3
Q3	3.7	6.5	4.7	4.1	7.4	5.3	1.9	4.1	2.7
Q4	3.3	6.6	4.5	3.8	8.7	5.5	1.5	4.4	2.6
Wealthiest	3.1	6.1	4.1	4.2	8.5	5.6	2.0	3.3	2.4

Nicaragua, 2009

Average monthly expenditure (hospitalization fee not included) sample, all households	Household health expenditure (normalized by total household expenditure)			Percentage of households with catastrophic health spending (more than 20 percent of total household expenditures)			Percentage of households with catastrophic spending (health spending more than 30 percent of total household expenditures)		
	Without NCDs	With NCDs	Total	Without NCDs	With NCDs	Total	Without NCDs	With NCDs	Total
All	3.55	6.49	4.61	2.26	5.69	3.50	0.76	2.00	1.21
Poorest	4.13	6.37	4.90	2.50	5.40	3.50	1.35	1.69	1.47
Q2	3.33	6.17	4.37	2.25	5.05	3.27	0.36	1.48	0.77
Q3	3.64	6.41	4.77	2.34	7.10	4.28	0.13	3.16	1.36
Q4	3.43	6.29	4.45	2.50	3.31	2.79	1.00	1.36	1.13
Wealthiest	2.90	7.44	4.42	1.59	7.64	3.62	0.68	2.33	1.24

Peru, 2009

Average monthly expenditure	Household health expenditure (normalized by total household expenditure)			Percentage of households with catastrophic health spending (more than 20 percent of total household expenditures)			Percentage of households with catastrophic spending (health spending more than 30 percent of total household expenditures)		
	Without NCDs	With NCDs	Total	Without NCDs	With NCDs	Total	Without NCDs	With NCDs	Total
All	2.6	4.1	3.7	29.6	19.6	23.3	29.2	18.2	22.3
Poorest	2.5	4.2	3.5	45.1	38.2	41.3	44.5	36.6	40.2

table continues next page

Table 3.1 Out-of-Pocket Health Expenditures and Catastrophic Expenditure on Health by Households with a Member with an NCD and by Households without, by Income Level *(continued)*

Peru, 2009

Average monthly expenditure	Household health expenditure (normalized by total household expenditure)			Percentage of households with catastrophic health spending (more than 20 percent of total household expenditures)			Percentage of households with catastrophic spending (health spending more than 30 percent of total household expenditures)		
	Without NCDs	With NCDs	Total	Without NCDs	With NCDs	Total	Without NCDs	With NCDs	Total
Q2	2.5	3.8	3.3	32.0	25.1	27.9	31.5	24.0	27.1
Q3	2.4	3.9	3.4	27.4	19.0	22.1	27.2	18.1	21.5
Q4	2.6	4.4	3.9	22.9	14.8	17.6	22.4	13.2	16.4
Wealthiest	2.9	4.3	3.9	24.1	13.6	17.1	23.8	12.1	16.0

Sources: Colombia, estimates from the 2008 quality of life survey (Encuesta de Calidad de Vida, 2008); Nicaragua, calculation using the 2009 household survey on quality of life measurement (Encuesta de Hogares sobre Medición de Nivel de Vida, [EMNV 2009]); and Peru, national household survey (Encuesta Nacional de Hogares).
Note: Col$ = Colombian pesos; NCDs = noncommunicable diseases; Q2 = second quintile; Q3 = third quintile; Q4 = fourth quintile.

about 10 percent of households with a member with an NCD incur catastrophic health expenditures; in Nicaragua about 6 percent of households with a member with a chronic disease do. Poor households in Colombia are more affected, with more than 16 percent of poor households with a member with an NCD reporting catastrophic health expenditures (table 3.1); in Nicaragua, wealthier households that include a member with an NCD are more likely to incur catastrophic health expenditures. In Peru, the pattern reverses—households without a member with a chronic condition are more likely to incur catastrophic health expenditures; the socioeconomic distribution is more regressive among households were a member has a chronic condition, however.

On average, people with NCDs make far greater out-of-pocket payments for health services than people without an NCD, with expenditures for drugs accounting for most of this difference. As seen in table 3.2 this pattern holds in the three countries for which data are available. In Colombia, Nicaragua, and Peru persons with a chronic condition spend more than twice as much on drugs as do persons without such a condition. Hospitalization expenditures are also higher for people with a chronic condition, particularly in Peru.

Noncommunicable Diseases and Labor-Market Outcomes: Evidence from Selected Latin American Countries

The onset and progression of NCDs may impact labor market outcomes.[2] Since NCDs lead to impairments that limit workers' functional capabilities, they can lower the maximum effort that a person can undertake or that person's responsiveness. NCDs can affect labor-market status in three critical areas: labor-force participation and type of employment; labor supply or hours worked; and labor

Table 3.2 Individual Health Expenditures by Persons with an NCD and by Those without, by Income Level

Colombia, 2008

Individuals who made a payment (in Col$)	Copay		Consultation[a]		Medication		Transportation		Hospitalization		Total		
	Without NCDs	With NCDs	Without NCDs	With NCDs	Without NCDs	NCDs	Without NCDs	With NCDs	Without NCDs	With NCDs	Without NCDs	With NCDs	Total
All	2,836	3,259	18,602	19,910	13,724	23,030	5,699	8,743	2,065	2,564	42,926	57,506	46,511
Poorest	1,050	1,758	14,525	16,078	13,359	22,914	1,050	1,758	2,163	4,740	35,719	54,310	40,142
Q2	1,707	1,450	13,571	7,578	12,728	16,569	1,707	1,450	1,525	1,504	36,153	35,090	35,911
Q3	915	1,787	11,368	7,820	10,452	14,751	915	1,787	2,129	3,307	29,269	35,534	30,812
Q4	1,670	2,909	14,075	10,573	10,962	21,284	1,670	2,909	1,799	1,569	35,154	44,652	37,667
Wealthiest	6,671	6,278	30,688	43,036	16,868	33,531	6,671	6,278	2,493	2,507	62,873	94,808	71,152

Peru, 2009

Individuals who made a payment in the month prior to the survey (in S/.)	Consultation[a]		Medication		Hospitalization		Other[b]		Total		
	Without NCDs	With NCDs	Without NCDs	With NCDs	Without NCDs	With NCDs	Without NCDs	With NCDs	Without NCDs	With NCDs	Total
All	26.4	44.0	18.7	47.7	55.7	62.3	13.9	19.7	25.9	58.8	36.8
Poorest	18.0	42.4	13.4	39.4	61.3	34.1	3.6	6.5	15.5	40.6	21.8
Q2	16.6	28.9	13.5	30.1	33.3	42.1	4.7	8.5	15.4	35.1	20.7
Q3	17.3	27.6	14.8	33.4	38.5	51.7	8.3	10.6	18.6	39.6	25.0
Q4	23.6	34.9	18.9	46.2	47.1	65.6	11.2	18.4	24.6	56.2	35.5
Wealthiest	39.4	60.0	27.6	64.1	85.6	79.8	23.9	28.0	42.0	80.9	57.1

table continues next page

Table 3.2 Individual Health Expenditures by Persons with an NCD and by Those without, by Income Level *(continued)*

Nicaragua, 2009

Individuals who made a payment in the month prior to the survey (in C$)	Consultation[a]		Medication		Hospitalization		Transportation		Other[b]		Total	
	Without NCDs	*With NCDs*	*Without NCDs*	*With NCDs*	*Without NCDs*	*With NCDs*	*Without NCDs*	*With NCDs*	*Without NCDs*	*With NCDs*	*Without NCDs*	*With NCDs*
All	282.3	431.4	174.2	412.6	6,468.4	7,101.6	51.6	48.2	176.5	351.1	211.1	482.6
Poorest	149.7	361.2	121.1	288.7	..	..	66.8	60.7	136.4	217.6	145.2	301.9
Q2	206.0	257.9	130.5	259.0	5,000.0	750.0	44.8	56.5	134.1	306.9	152.4	315.3
Q3	294.4	374.6	158.8	377.1	..	10,000.0	46.1	40.8	173.9	286.6	187.7	440.3
Q4	273.7	307.8	180.5	386.7	2,484.2	4,201.8	42.2	45.3	201.4	186.4	211.1	385.3
Wealthiest	404.2	632.9	352.7	703.8	11,165.5	6,521.9	58.0	42.3	248.4	711.5	430.0	912.1

Sources: Colombia, estimates from the 2008 quality of life survey (Encuesta de Calidad de Vida 2008) and national household survey (Encuesta Nacional de Hogares); Nicaragua, calculation using the 2009 household survey on quality of life measurement (Encuesta de Hogares sobre Medición de Nivel de Vida [EMNV 2009]); Peru, estimates from the 2008 national household survey (Encuesta Nacional de Hogares 2008).

Note: .. = negligible.

a. Includes medical consultation, lab tests, x-rays, and other exams.
b. Includes eyeglasses, contact lenses, and other medical products.

earnings, which may partially affect productivity (Kahn 1998; Gordo 2011; Lechner and Vazquez-Alvarez 2011; Schultz 2008, 85–118; Mete and others, 2008, 67–84). This section shows evidence from Brazil, Chile, Colombia, El Salvador, and Honduras that suggests that NCDs have a greater negative impact (5 percent or higher) on labor market participation in more formal economies such as Chile's or Brazil's. The combination of NCDs' effect on labor participation, hours worked, and productivity suggests that these diseases could have a negative impact of about 0.25 percent of gross domestic product (GDP), which could increase to 0.40 percent once the effect of related disability is included.

NCDs and Disability: Data and Analytical Challenges

This section relies on a range of indicators for NCDs and disability that are available in existing household surveys in LAC. Household survey information about NCDs and disability can vary significantly from country to country due to the nature of the questions, conditions specified, recall period, and source, all of which can affect the prevalence figures and the analysis. Information about NCD prevalence also could have a substantial bias, depending on the type of question asked. The data used in this study are described in appendix A, detailing specific information on the country, survey used, and type of information on self–reported health status, NCD, and disability.

Labor-Force Participation

Evidence from selected countries suggests that the impact on labor-force participation differs significantly across countries. This section provides a preliminary assessment of the impact of NCD and disability on labor market outcomes. Figure 3.2 shows the rates of labor-market participation for Brazil, Chile, Colombia, El Salvador, and Honduras, separating out the total population participation and the participation of the population with NCDs. In countries that have greater social insurance coverage (disability insurance and pension mechanisms) and that are at a more advanced aging stage (such as Brazil, Chile, and Colombia), persons affected by NCDs have significantly lower participation rates, compared to the average population. These differences in participation show differences across age groups, underscoring the need for age-specific assessments, especially for older workers.

Participation patterns may reflect differences in aging and in social-insurance coverage or differences in knowledge or awareness of NCDs across countries. On average, individuals with NCDs in Brazil and Chile have about 5 percentage points lower participation, compared to almost 20 percentage points lower participation in Colombia. In El Salvador and Honduras, however, labor market participation among individuals with NCDs is not distinguishable from that of the average population. This may suggest that in countries that lack social insurance coverage or where coverage is very low (such as in those two countries) individuals need to keep working regardless of their health status.

Differences across age groups in formal and more informal economies merit specific assessments by age and type of employment. These aggregate differences

Figure 3.2 Labor-Force Participation for the Population with NCDs and for the Overall Population, by Age

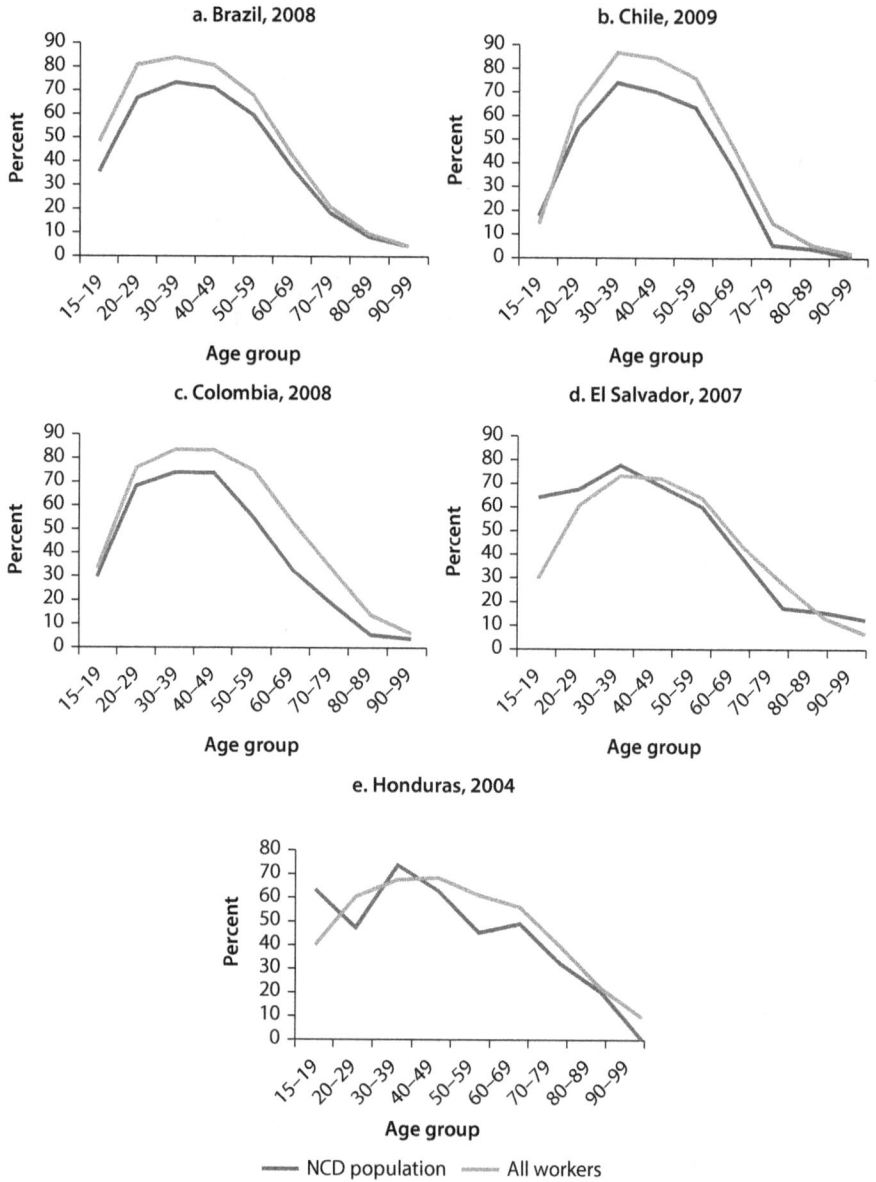

a. Brazil, 2008

b. Chile, 2009

c. Colombia, 2008

d. El Salvador, 2007

e. Honduras, 2004

—— NCD population   ——— All workers

Source: Author estimates based on national household surveys described in appendix A.
Note: NCD = noncommunicable disease.

in participation may also hide differences by sex, education, and type of employment, among other socioeconomic dimensions. In Chile, for example, where
women are significantly more likely to report an NCD (17 percent of females
reporting, compared to 11 percent of males), labor participation rates differ
widely between men and women. In males, these rates are almost identical

(78 percent for non-NCD groups and 77 percent for NCD groups), whereas among females, the NCD group shows a participation rate more than 15 percent lower compared to the non-NCD group (42 percent and 50 percent, respectively) (Contreras and others 2012). The differences in participation rates across age groups may also hide differences in the impact across types of employment. Young workers tend to work in the informal sector, and older workers tend to be self-employed. As these groups have different social insurance coverage and face different opportunity costs (e.g., pensions) the impact of NCD-associated disability can vary significantly from age group to age group. This is especially relevant in LAC economies, where workers continue to work until their late 60s or 70s.

Intensity of Labor Supply

Individuals with NCD-related disabilities who can still work may have to adjust their labor supply intensity. The severity of the NCD or the degree of difficulty a person has in performing activities of daily living (ADLs) may determine whether a person can continue to work, or, if symptoms are severe enough, whether that person must withdraw from the labor market. Still, while these individuals may decide to continue working, they may have to cut back on their hours if the required effort is too much, thereby adjusting their labor supply intensity.

Workers with NCDs show more pronounced differences in hours worked across the life cycle, with fewer hours worked early and late in life and more hours worked in their 30s and 40s. Figure 3.3 shows the average number of weekly hours worked by average workers and by those with NCDs for the selected countries. Consistently, workers with NCDs report significantly fewer hours worked than do average workers, and they also have more pronounced life cycle variations (fewer hours worked early and late in life, and more hours worked in their 30s and 40s). This pattern is observed in Colombia and Brazil, but less so in Chile. A possible explanation may be the differential effect that NCDs have on type of employment. Since formal-sector workers are eligible for some type of health or disability insurance, they may be better able to quit the labor market than informal workers, and a disproportionate number of NCD-affected workers work in the informal sector.

The relatively high intensity of labor supply among NCD workers, compared to that of the rest of the population may be associated with a lack of insurance, as discussed earlier, and by the need to compensate for lower productivity. NCD-affected individuals work between 3 percent and 6 percent fewer hours per week than do average workers. The reduction is relatively similar across countries, with Colombia leading the reduction in hours with 6.3 percent lower hours, followed by Brazil (5.3), El Salvador (4.3), Chile (2.3), and Honduras (with negligible differences). These findings, together with the differences observed in younger and older workers, suggest that these differences need to be assessed further.

A detailed review of specific NCDs shows that some of these diseases are more likely to trigger reductions in work intensity than do others. The relationship

Figure 3.3 Intensity of Labor Supply (Average Number of Weekly Working Hours) for the NCD-Affected Population and for All Workers, by Age

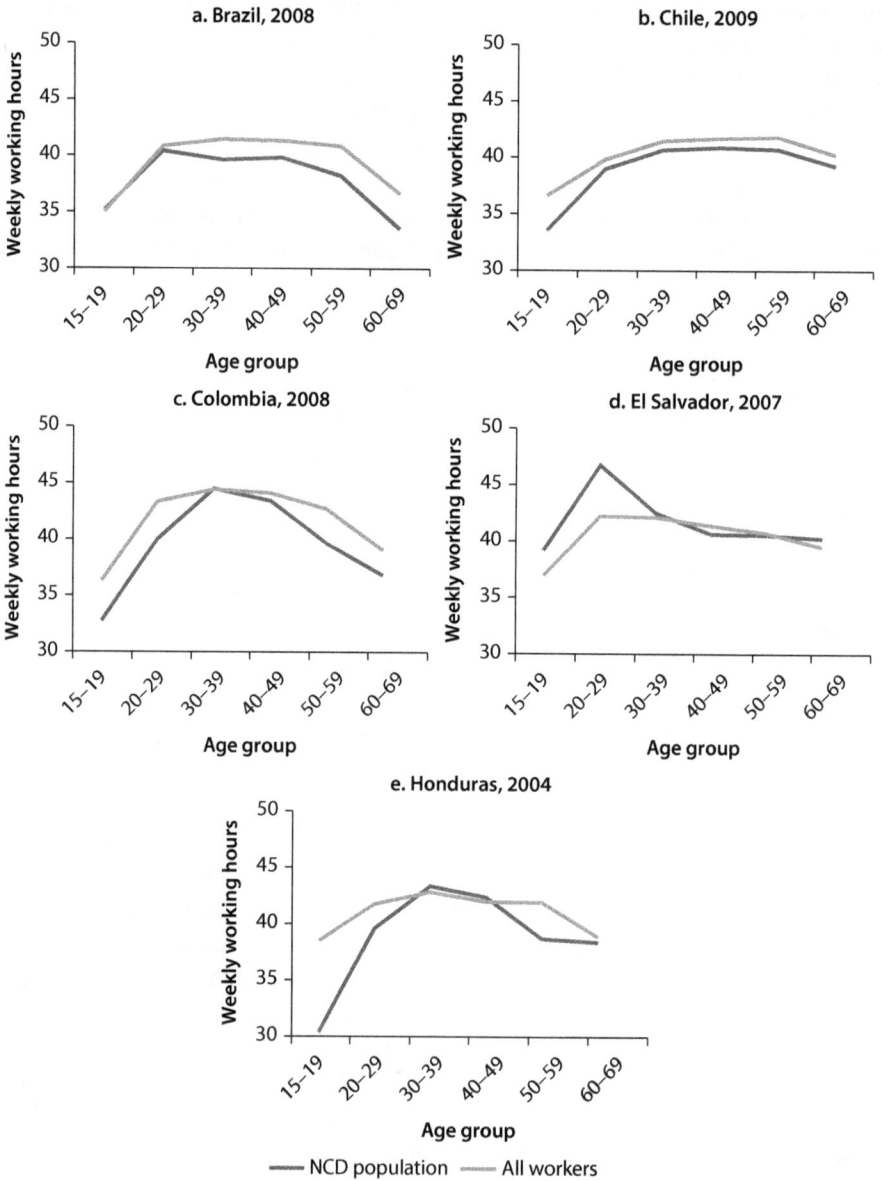

a. Brazil, 2008

b. Chile, 2009

c. Colombia, 2008

d. El Salvador, 2007

e. Honduras, 2004

—— NCD population —— All workers

Source: Author estimates based on national household surveys described in appendix A.
Note: NCD = noncommunicable disease.

between NCDs and work intensity can be examined in more detail using Brazil's National Household Sampling Survey (PNAD) data, where information on health status is more precise—the survey asks for a medical diagnosis of specific diseases, not just self-reported status. However, some individuals may experience symptoms of certain NCDs but have yet to be diagnosed due to a lack of medical consultation, for example. Among Brazil's older workers (older than 50 years), illnesses such as arthritis and, to a lesser extent, cardiovascular diseases, have a greater effect in lowering hours worked than does kidney disease (figure 3.4). This means that while workers with any NCDs work longer hours, those with certain NCDs work fewer, suggesting that different NCDs have a varying impact on labor outcomes. The development of data sources and methods for examining the differential effect across ages and by type of illness is a pending agenda.

NCD and Labor Earnings

The effect that NCDs have on workers' productivity may be reflected in labor earnings. There has been little discussion about the impact of NCDs

Figure 3.4 Average Number of Weekly Hours Worked by Persons with an NCD and by All Workers, by Age and Specific Disease, Brazil, 2008

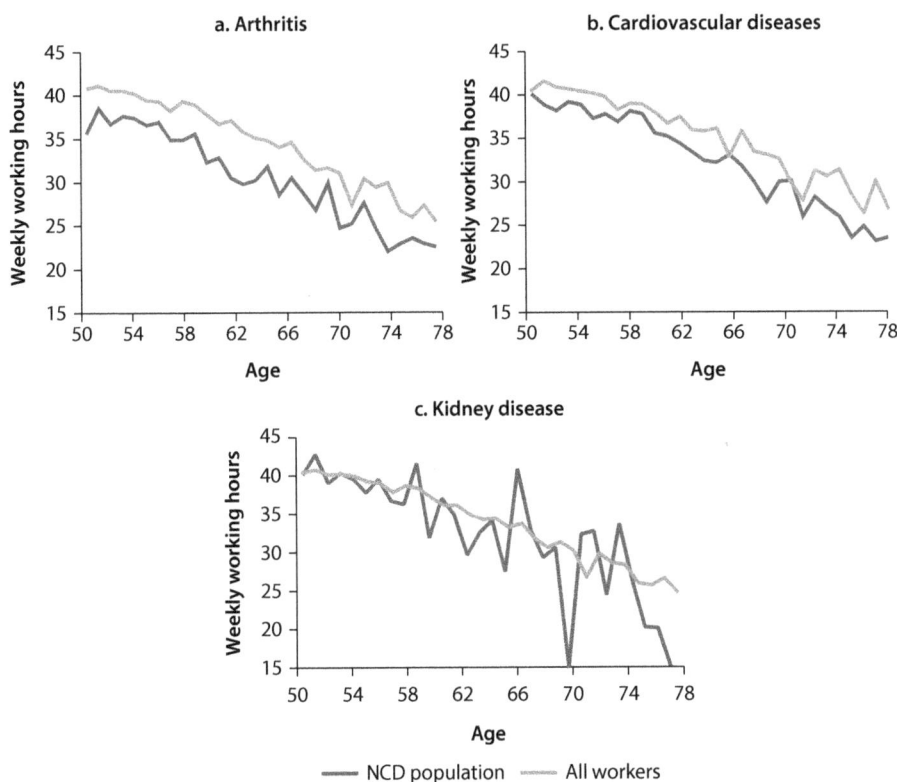

Source: Author estimates based on national household surveys, as described in appendix A.
Note: NCD = noncommunicable disease.

on productivity, because measuring labor productivity is problematic. Labor earnings, or hourly earnings, are the result of technological factors, workers' skill, and productivity, and institutions such as labor market regulations define the margin for wage adjustments. An examination of the association between NCDs and labor earnings needs to account for these differences. An important distinction to be made is NCDs' differential effect by type of employment. As discussed earlier, while workers with NCDs may have some income protection in the formal sector (through health insurance), workers in the informal sector have no such safeguards, and the self-employed may adjust their level of effort and performance. In rural areas, for instance, self-employed agricultural workers may simply work similar hours but at a much lower productivity. Assessing the correlation of NCDs and labor earnings would require a more detailed analysis by type employment and, in principle, controlling for changes across types of employment and occupation.

NCDs reduce hourly earnings, but at significantly different degrees across age groups. As discussed earlier, NCDs trigger changes in hours worked, so productivity measures must account for these changes. Hourly earnings are estimated for all workers, except unpaid ones that are excluded from the sample. Figure 3.5 shows average hourly earnings (measured in local currency) across the life cycle for workers with NCDs and for workers without NCDs in Brazil, Chile, Colombia, El Salvador, and Honduras. In Brazil and Chile, workers with NCDs have lower incomes than those without NCDs, mainly during their adult working life. These differences can represent 30–40 percent of non-NCD earnings in their 40s, but tend to decline later in life. In Brazil, the average NCD worker earns 11 percent less than a non-NCD worker, but for workers in their 40s the difference could represent 40 percent less. In Chile, Contreras and others (2012) found that workers with NCDs earn 6 percent less than average workers, controlling for other characteristics. In Colombia, El Salvador, and Honduras, these differences are less clear, and also vary substantially across the life cycle. If measured around age 40, workers with NCDs earn between 15 percent less in Colombia and 40 percent less in El Salvador, but aggregate differences are offset and result in similar earnings.

An assessment of hourly earnings will require more detailed data in order to separate out the impact of NCDs, especially at older ages. Unfortunately, despite the fact that it is known that aging individuals have higher incidences of NCDs, the data are insufficient to conduct a critical analysis. The onset of NCDs is closely connected to labor participation, type of employment (physically demanding or not), education level, and employment sector (informal, self-employed, salaried), as these factors affect insurance coverage. Such factors become especially relevant during aging years, as older persons' ability to carry out physical tasks, mobility, and other needs begin to deteriorate. High quality longitudinal data would allow for an accurate assessment of these changes during the later working years, which in fact requires good collection of labor market outcomes, objective assessments of health conditions, and a complete collection of household characteristics.[3]

Figure 3.5 Average Hourly Earnings (in Local Currency) for Workers with an NCD and for All Workers, by Age

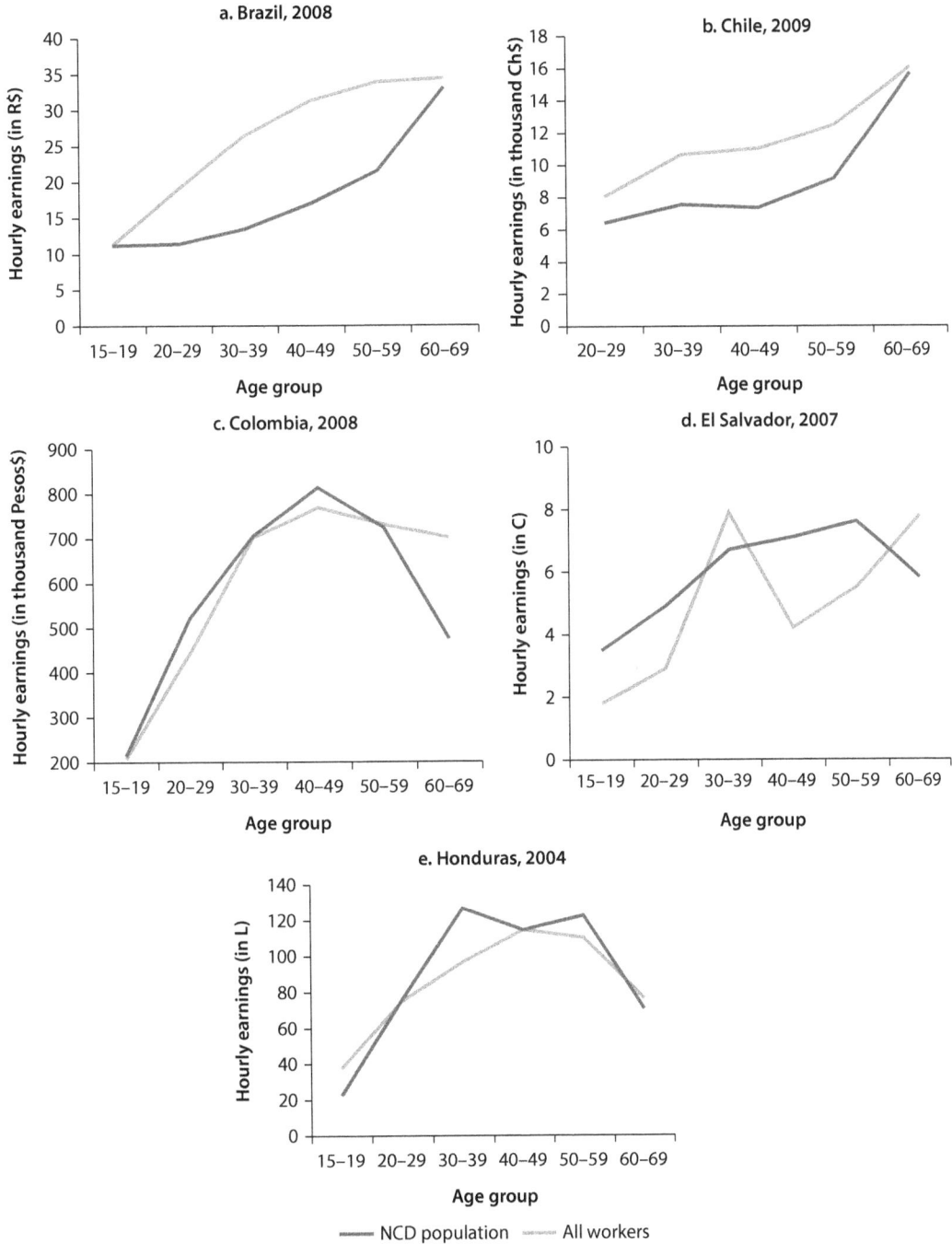

a. Brazil, 2008

b. Chile, 2009

c. Colombia, 2008

d. El Salvador, 2007

e. Honduras, 2004

— NCD population   — — All workers

Source: Author estimates based on national household surveys, as described in appendix A.
Note: NCD = noncommunicable disease.

The Economic Cost of NCDs to Health Systems in the Region

According to a report issued by the World Economic Forum (Bloom and others 2011), the region of the Americas ranks second worldwide, after Europe, in experiencing the highest economic consequences from cardiovascular disease, with total costs reaching US$ 175.6 billion in 2010. The global cost of cardiovascular diseases will increase from US$ 863 billion in 2010 to US$ 1,044 billion in 2030. About US$ 474 billion (55 percent) of the current cost are due to direct health care costs, and the remaining 45 percent are due to productivity losses from disability or premature death, or from time lost from work because of illness or the need to seek care (Bloom and others 2011). Table 3.3 shows the costs attributable to cardiovascular diseases in the Americas, including screening, primary-prevention, secondary-prevention, acute-hospital-care, and productivity-loss costs.

Diabetes costs the global economy nearly US$ 500 billion in 2010, and the figure is estimated to increase to US$ 745 billion by 2030, with developing countries accounting for the largest share (Bloom and others 2011). The World Economic Forum report foresees that the burden of cost from diabetes will increasingly shift from high-income countries to lower- and upper-middle-income countries (Bloom and others 2011). Among low- and middle-income countries worldwide, total diabetes-related costs were highest in Latin American and Caribbean (Adeyi and others 2007).

A recent Pan American Health Organization (PAHO) study estimated the annual cost of diabetes in the Americas at US$ 201 billion. Of the total amount, US$ 95 billion was attributed to direct costs and approximately $106 billion, to indirect costs. This study found that in the Americas, the per capita cost of diabetes care was highest in the United States (US$ 12,243) and lowest in Colombia (US$ 442). The average per capita expenditure on health was highest in the United States (US$ 4,432) and lowest in Haiti (US$ 24).[4] Table 3.4 shows the estimated total indirect and direct cost (in millions of US$) attributed

Table 3.3 Costs Attributable to Cardiovascular Diseases, Region of the Americas, 2010

Region of the Americas	Total costs (without productivity costs)	Productivity costs	Total costs (including productivity costs)	Per-capita total costs	Per-capita total costs (adults only)
AMR-A (United States, Canada, and Cuba)	165.9	108.2	274.0	736	1,206
AMR-B (all other countries in the region)	8.8	17.2	26.0	52	108
AMR-D (Bolivia, Ecuador, Guatemala, Haiti, Nicaragua, and Peru)	0.9	2.1	3.1	36	91

Source: Bloom and others 2011.
Note: Costs are shown in billions of US$, except for per-capita values.

Table 3.4 Estimated Direct and Indirect Costs Due to Diabetes, Region of the Americas, 2004

Area	Total	Indirect	Direct	Per-capita direct	Per-capita health expenditures
North America	151,546.3	54,221.1	97,252.2	15,516	6,839.1
Caribbean (Spanish-speaking)	2,050.4	1,054.5	995.9	2,711	275
Caribbean (English-speaking)	1,030.3	812.3	218	3,388	1,511
Central America	2,616.7	1,788.3	828.4	4,120	994
South America	44,346.8	37,696.2	6,704.6	6,838	3,211

Sources: Data from the Symposium on Diabetes Economics, sponsored by the Declaration of the Americas on Diabetes (DOTA), the International Diabetes Federation (IDF), and the Pan American Health Organization (PAHO), in coordination with the Latin American Diabetes Association (ALAD), and held in São Paolo, Brazil, on 27 September 2004. http://www1.paho.org/common/Display.asp?Lang=E&RecID=7746.

to diabetes. The data was the result of the combination of this and a previous study (Barceló and others 2003, 19–27).

The total economic cost of cancer globally was estimated at US$ 895 billion in 2008, representing 1.5 percent of the world's GDP. According to a study from the American Cancer Society, the most costly types of cancers are those caused by tobacco use: cancers of the lung, bronchus, and trachea. Together, these cancers account for almost US$ 180 billion globally. An estimated 2.8 million new cases of cancer were detected in the Americas in 2009. According to the World Economic Forum report, the cost of the new cases of cancer in the Americas was $153 billion, which included medical costs, nonmedical costs, and loss of productivity, but not costs related to cancer screening and prevention and lost income due to cancer mortality. The report cited lung cancer as the most expensive cancer, followed by prostate and breast cancers.

Notes

1. A multivariate analysis of health care utilization in Colombia and Peru (not shown) shows that persons reporting a chronic condition, those that have health-insurance coverage, and women are more likely to utilize health services. While a household's socioeconomic level does not significantly affect the probability of using a health service in Colombia, it does so in Peru, where people in wealthier households are more likely to use health services. Finally, while in Colombia people in urban areas are more likely to use health services, in Peru the pattern reverses.

2. Others have pointed out the potential effects of NCDs and disability on workers not affected by NCDs (Schultz 2008). Such is the case in firms and sectors where team activities are prevalent or where one worker's performance affects the performance of others.

3. Surveys that can shed light on these transitions include the Mexican Health and Aging Study (MHAS), a prospective panel study of health and aging in Mexico that included a nationally representative sample of Mexicans aged 50 and over in 2001 and their spouses or partners regardless of their age; and the Mexican Family Life Survey (MxFLS), a multi-thematic and longitudinal database which collects, in a single instrument, a wide range of information on socioeconomic indicators, demographics, and

health indicators on the Mexican population. See MxFLS (http://www.ennvih-mxfls
.org/) and MHAS (http://www.mhas.pop.upenn.edu/).

4. Data from the Symposium on Diabetes Economics, sponsored by the Declaration
of the Americas on Diabetes, the International Diabetes Federation, and the
PAHO, in coordination with the Latin American Diabetes Association, and held
in São Paolo, Brazil, on September 27, 2004. http://www1.paho.org/common
/Display.asp?Lang=E&RecID=7746.

Bibliography

Adeyi, O., O. Smith, and S. Robles. 2007. *Public Policy and the Challenge of Chronic
Noncommunicable Diseases*. Directions in Development Series. Human Development.
Washington, DC: World Bank.

Barcelo, A., C. Aedo, S. Rajpathak, and S. Robles. 2003. "The Cost of Diabetes in Latin
America and the Caribbean." *Bulletin of the World Health Organization* 81 (1).

Bloom, D. E., E. T. Cafiero, E. Jané-Llopis, S. Abrahams-Gessel, L. R. Bloom, S. Fathima,
A. B. Feigl, T. Gaziano, M. Mowafi, A. Pandya, K. Prettner, L. Rosenberg, B. Seligman,
A. Z. Stein, and C. Weinstein. 2011. *The Global Economic Burden of Noncommunicable
Diseases*. Geneva: World Economic Forum.

Contreras, D., J. Ruiz-Tagle, and P. Guzmán. 2012. "Socio-Economic Impact of
Noncommunicable Diseases and Disabilities in Chile." Unpublished paper, Regional
Study on Noncommunicable Diseases, March 25, 2012.

Departamento Administrativo Nacional de Estadística, Dirección de Metodología y
Producción Estadística y Dirección de Metodología y Producción Estadística. 2008.
Encuesta Nacional de Calidad de Vida. Bogota, Colombia.

Gordo, L. 2011. "Compression of Morbidity and the Labour Supply of Older People"
Applied Economics 43 (4): 503–13.

Instituto Brasileiro de Geografia e Estatística. 2008. *Pesquisa Nacional Por Amostra de
Domicilios (PNAD 2008)*.

Instituto Nacional de Estadística e Informática. 2008. *Encuesta Nacional de Hogares sobre
Condiciones de Vida en el Perú*. Lima, Peru.

Instituto Nacional de Información de Desarrollo. 2009. *Encuesta de Medición del Nivel de
Vida 2009*. Managua, Nicaragua.

Kahn, M. 1998. "Health and Labor Market Performance: The Case of Diabetes." *Journal of
Labor Economics* 16 (4): 878–99.

Lechner, M., and R. Vazquez-Alvarez. 2011. "The Effect of Disability on Labour Market
Outcomes in Germany." *Applied Economics* 43 (4–6): 389–412.

Mete, C., H. Ni, and K. Scott. 2008. "The Impact of Health Shocks on Employment,
Earnings, and Household Consumption in Bosnia and Herzegovina." In *Economic
Implications of Chronic Illness and Disability in Eastern Europe and the Former Soviet
Union*, edited by C. Mete. Washington, DC: World Bank.

Ministerio de Desarrollo Social. 2009. *Encuesta de Caracterización Socioeconómica
Nacional*. Santiago, Chile.

Nikolic, I. A., A. E. Stanciole, and M. Zaydman. 2011. *Chronic Emergency: Why NCDs
Matter*. Health, Nutrition, and Population Discussion Paper Series. Washington, DC:
World Bank.

Rijo, M. and J. Hana Ross. 2010. *The Global Economic Cost of Cancer.* Atlanta, GA: The American Cancer Society.

Schultz, T. 2008. "Health Disabilities and Labor Productivity in Russia in 2004." In *Economic Implications of Chronic Illness and Disability in Eastern Europe and the Former Soviet Union,* edited by C. Mete, 85–118. Washington, DC: World Bank.

CHAPTER 4

Governance of Multisectoral Interventions to Promote Healthy Living: International Examples

Claudia Trezza and María Eugenia Bonilla-Chacín

Many of the premature deaths and much of the disability caused by noncommunicable diseases (NCDs) can be prevented or controlled through targeted clinical preventive and control services and population-wide preventive interventions. This chapter examines the multisectoral policies and programs that governments in several countries, particularly in the Organisation for Economic Co-operation and Development (OECD) and Latin America and the Caribbean (LAC), have implemented to prevent NCDs at the population level, focusing on the governance challenges in their design and implementation.

This chapter reviews several experiences involving the implementation of multisectoral interventions to promote healthy living. Most interventions reviewed here reflect the characteristics of those that World Health Organization (WHO) considers as "best buys," because they are "cost-effective, of low cost, and can be implemented in low resource settings." Most aim at controlling tobacco use and alcohol abuse, and include such efforts as fiscal policies, banning smoking in public spaces, raising awareness and increasing knowledge about the dangers of tobacco, banning tobacco advertising, restricting the availability and access to alcohol, limiting the hours of alcohol sales, and restricting alcohol purchases and sales among some age groups. Some of these best buys also aim at improving diet, particularly by decreasing sodium and trans-fat consumption (WHO 2011a). WHO considers interventions to be highly cost-effective ("best buys") if they provide an additional year of healthy life, measured in disability-adjusted life years (DALYs), for under the per capita income in a given country or region.

Other cost-effective interventions not considered "best buys" that were reviewed here included efforts related to restrictions on marketing of foods and beverages high in salt, fat, and sugar, especially to children; using taxes and subsidies to promote healthy diets; and enforcing drunk driving laws. Other effective interventions for which cost-effectiveness evidence is still limited also were reviewed, such as modifications to the built environment as a way to increase physical activity, and community-based interventions to promote a healthy diet and increased physical activity. The chapter also reviews international experiences with policies aimed at raising awareness about healthy diets and physical activity. While the experiences reviewed here are not all-inclusive, they were selected because there was available detailed information on their design and implementation and, thus, could shed light on the governance of these processes.

Concerns often have been raised about whether government interventions designed to change diet, increase physical activity, and reduce the consumption of tobacco and alcohol abuse are justified, as these changes are viewed as individual choices taken within well-functioning market structures. However, there are several market and rationality failures associated with lifestyle-related goods (e.g., choices regarding food, physical activity, tobacco use, and alcohol abuse) that can justify a government's intervention in these markets (Sassi and Hurst 2008). For instance, the consumption of lifestyle related goods can generate negative externalities, or can harm third parties in ways that are not fully reflected in the cost to the individual consumer. The harmful effects of second-hand smoke and the violence and traffic accidents caused by alcohol abuse, for instance, are examples of direct negative externalities associated with risk factors for NCDs and injuries. And there is additional spillover on the economy from these choices, since the consumption of "lifestyle" related goods can generate high costs to the health system, the household, and the overall economy, as was discussed in the previous chapter; these costs are not taken into account by those who consume these goods. There is also evidence of spillover effects within households and social networks, such as the effect on children's diets as a result of the dietary choices of adult household members.

A government intervention targeting the market for "lifestyle" goods can also be justified if it can reverse information and rationality failures that are often present in these markets (Sassi and Hurst 2008). Often, consumers do not have all the information on the negative or positive impacts of these goods, and so the government must step in to provide such information (e.g., information on the harmful effects of tobacco use and alcohol abuse or on the benefit to health from physical activity). Recent literature also points to different "rationality failures" related to the consumption of "lifestyle"-related goods such as food, alcohol, and tobacco. These rationality failures are related to the addictive or habitual nature of some of these goods, time preferences that heavily discount future costs or benefits, and lack of self-control, among others.

A government intervention might also be justified if it corrects unintended health consequences derived from existing government policies. For example, the government may wish to offset urban planning and transport policies that discourage physical activity, or agricultural policies that increase the relative price of fruits and vegetables while lowering the price of fats and sugars and others (Sassi and Hurst 2008).

Finally, a government intervention might be undertaken to narrow inequalities in the exposure to health risk factors. As has been seen earlier in this publication, some health risk factors are more prevalent among the poor.

The Health Sector's Role

Although the policies reviewed in this chapter are multisectoral, the health sector has a key role to play in ensuring that interventions to prevent and control NCDs actually occur. The health sector is the one that can initiate dialogue among relevant actors and that can ensure that actions to prevent risk factors are designed and implemented. It is also the health sector that must assess the extent of the NCD problem and the factors driving it (Meiro-Lorenzo and others 2011). Indeed, one of the most important national and health sector responses to NCDs is surveillance. To prevent and control chronic conditions, it is vital to have information on their prevalence, as well as on the direct and intermediate risk factors that can trigger these diseases. In addition, the health sector needs to launch secondary prevention measures aimed at the most at-risk populations and control measures for those already with these conditions (these are not, however, the focus of this document).

Multisectoral Interventions to Prevent Risk Factors

In an effort to learn from the best and most promising practices, this chapter describes these programs' main characteristics and the governance challenges in their design and implementation. It aims at understanding the processes whereby successful or promising public policies and programs to prevent health risk factors have been developed and implemented. In so doing, the chapter will examine: the major stakeholders who influenced and shaped policy decisions; their positions, incentives, and strategies; the institutional arrangements that framed the decision-making process; the public's perception of the policies; the interaction among various stakeholders during the decision-making and implementation processes; and the lessons learned from these experiences. Since this chapter is based on a literature review, the assessment of the governance challenges in the design and implementation of the policies is limited by the information available.

Every intervention can be classified according to the policy lever used to induce a behavioral change (Gostin 2000), be it economic incentives or disincentives, the informational environment, direct regulation, indirect regulation, or deregulation. Taxes on and subsidies for certain foods, and taxes on tobacco and alcohol generate an economic incentive to reduce consumption, in the case of taxes, or to increase consumption, in the case of subsidies. Media campaigns aimed at promoting healthy eating and physical activity are an example of policies that seek to change the existing informational environment. And policies aimed at reducing the intake of sodium and trans fats are often statutory regulations. Most of the policies and programs use a combination of these policy levers. Most community-based programs, for example, are comprehensive programs that often create incentives, change the informational environment, and develop regulations. The tobacco- and alcohol-abuse control programs reviewed in this publication are also comprehensive, often using various policy levers aimed at changing behavior. In the case of tobacco, these programs create economic incentives by levying taxes on tobacco products, change the informational environment by informing the public about the harmful effects of tobacco consumption, and issue direct regulations by banning smoke in public spaces. In terms of alcohol abuse, these programs have created regulations to limit the availability of alcohol products, have created indirect regulations by controlling the permissible blood-alcohol level among drivers, and have created economic incentives to reduce consumption by levying taxes on alcohol, among other measures. Whenever possible, the discussion indicates the type of policy lever used to induce behavioral change in the interventions reviewed.

A wide variety of communities, cities, countries, and regions have carried out the population-based preventive policies and programs. These policies are multisectoral, often involving several government agencies, the private sector, and civil society organizations. These different stakeholders often do not face the same incentives, which might make their positions difficult to reconcile. Within the government, different agencies outside the health sector often participate in the decision-making process, including transportation, planning, agriculture and commerce, education, and finance agencies, as well as members of the legislative branch.

Interventions to Promote Healthy Diets

This section reviews the decision-making process involved in the design and implementation of some successful or promising experiences aimed at promoting a healthy diet. It first reviews several experiences designing and implementing interventions such as salt reduction strategies, regulations on the amount of allowed trans fats in processed foods, and policies aimed at raising awareness about healthy diets through nutrition labeling and social media campaigns. The section also reviews policies aimed at restricting the marketing of foods high in salt, fat, and sugar, and taxes and subsidies to promote healthy diets.

Salt-Reduction Strategies

In low- and middle-income countries, estimates indicate that a 15 percent reduction in the mean salt intake in the population could avert 8.5 million cardiovascular deaths in a span of more than 10 years, and that reducing salt consumption amounts to US$ 0.40 per person per year (Asaria and others 2007). High sodium (a major salt component) intake is associated with high blood pressure, which increases the risk for heart disease, stroke, and renal disease, underlying the importance of putting in place strategies to reduce it.

Recently there has been some controversy surrounding the recommendation to decrease sodium intake (for example, in Cohen and Townsend 2012; Taubes 1998). However, the conclusions and recommendations of WHO, the Centers for Disease Control and Prevention (CDC), and many other experts on the subject remain the same—reducing sodium or salt intake reduces the risk for high blood pressure. As mentioned earlier, WHO recommends keeping the level of salt intake among adults to under 5 g per day (WHO 2006).

Although salt may pose a danger to health, it is also a relatively inexpensive way for the food industry to preserve some foods and improve the taste of its products (Institute of Medicine 2010). Consequently, public health advocates and the food industry often are at odds when it comes to policies aiming at reducing salt intake.

In the 1980s, as a way to respond to the high prevalence of cardiovascular diseases and high cholesterol among its residents, the government of North Karelia, Finland, launched a community-based program to change the population's overall lifestyle, especially in terms of smoking and dietary habits. The dietary strategy focused on reducing salt intake and fat and increasing the consumption of fruits and vegetables (Puska and others 2009).

In what is considered to be one of the most successful examples of a multisectoral approach, the North Karelia government enlisted the participation of the health services, schools, social services, nongovernmental organizations (NGOs), supermarkets, the food industry, community leaders, and the media in the intervention. Particularly effective was the pressure brought to bear on the food industry to lower sodium content in food. This was done through a massive informational and awareness campaign, which guaranteed consumer demand for less salty products, and through labeling regulations, which required listing sodium levels on prepackaged foods. As part of the campaign, project coordinators and advertising firms contracted by the city, developed leaflets, books, and posters to raise awareness about the intervention. Magazines and videotapes providing information on smoking prevention and nutrition counseling, financed through advertising, were released. Radio and TV campaigns were created with the intent of promoting healthy lifestyles. Newspaper stories, most probably pitched by the government's public affairs officers, covered the issue as a news event during the project period. Clear and persuasive messages through these channels changed North Karelian's consumption and purchasing habits (Puska and others 2009). In response to the growing consumer awareness, supermarkets and restaurants began decreasing salt content in their foods and producing healthier products.

The North Karelia program turned out to be extremely effective in reducing sodium intake. And because of its positive results, the program was extended nationwide, but results in this broader project were not as successful as those in the North Karelia pilot (Puska and others 2009). To further reduce sodium consumption, in the late 1980s the Ministry of Trade imposed labeling regulations. The industry was required to place nutrition information on product packages, including sodium and salt content, and products were classified and labeled in three categories according to the level of salt in butter, margarine, sausages, bread, and breakfast cereals. A 1992 law imposed additional restrictions, listing the maximum salt concentration of soups, sauces, and salted mushrooms (Puska and others 2002). A 20 percent decrease in salt intake among the population occurred in the 30 years since the program was put in place nationwide. In 2007 salt intake was 7–8 g in women and 9–10 g in men (Puska and others 2009).

In an effort to avoid government regulations and to continue to please consumers' palates while reducing salt in their products, food companies, particularly in the United States, have invested resources in numerous creative initiatives. One strategy involved changing consumers' taste. Food companies have engaged in so-called "silent reductions," designed to lower sodium so gradually that regular consumers will not notice the change in the product and can slowly ratchet down their taste preferences for salt. Food manufacturers, such as Unilever and PepsiCo, have invested in research for sodium substitutes and enhancers, as well as for other innovations designed to lower the level of sodium in foods, thus enabling advertised and silent reductions in the sodium content of their products (Institute of Medicine 2010). Although these actions did not lead to reductions in salt intake and were not consistently carried out throughout the food industry, they exemplify how industry can contribute toward the fight against NCDs.

One of the most important examples of salt-reduction efforts in LAC, the case of Argentina, is documented in the next chapter.

Replacing Trans Fats—Regulation

Regulations to reduce trans-fat intake are considered by the WHO as a "best buy"[1] intervention to prevent NCDs at the population level. It is estimated that replacing trans fats with polyunsaturated fats through regulation would yield a cost-effectiveness ratio between US\$ 25 and US\$ 73 per DALY averted (Willett and others 2006).

In 2006, New York City's Board of Health imposed a two-stage phase out of trans fats in all of the city's food-service establishments, enforceable through fines of up to US\$ 2,000. The goal was for restaurants to reduce trans-fat levels to 0.5 g per serving. Restaurants opposed the ban, and the city government, in an effort to address the concerns expressed by the restaurants, gave them extensions to reach the trans-fat level goal. But before the ban went into effect, New York City had attempted to push the restaurants to voluntarily phase out their trans-fat levels. The city sent letters to New York restaurants and food suppliers asking them to stop using trans fats and offering technical assistance. The city also trained more than 7,000 persons on how to switch from trans fats to polyunsaturated fats. Despite these efforts, data showed that no reduction in the use of trans fats had been accomplished after a year. The city government concluded that a regulatory mandate was needed (Mello 2009).

The New York City regulation was also successful because of the solid research base that the city government made available to the public to gain its support for the ban. During the passage of the regulation, messages to the public were highly persuasive in making the link between trans fats and coronary heart disease. Particularly important in making the case to the public that regulation was necessary, was an Institute of Medicine recommendation that trans-fat consumption be minimized (Mello 2009).

In Denmark, a 1993 scientific article suggesting a positive association between the intake of trans fatty acids and the risk of coronary disease led that country's governmental institutions and the food industry to reduce trans-fat content in food production. Subsequent scientific studies reinforcing such a link led to the passage of government legislation regulating the industrially produced partially hydrogenated fat (IP-TFA) content of all food products to a maximum of 2 percent of the total fat content (Stender and others 2006).

In LAC, both Argentina (see the case study in the next chapter) and Puerto Rico have regulated trans fats. Other Latin American countries, including Chile, Costa Rica, the Dominican Republic, and the Common Market of the South (MERCOSUR) countries (Argentina, Brazil, Paraguay, and Uruguay), are in the process of discussing trans-fat reductions and including them in nutrition labels (PAHO 2008).

Nutrition Labeling—The Informational Environment

Nutrition labels have been effective in changing behavior among certain groups (mainly younger people, women, people with higher levels of education, and those who already have an interest in diet and health) (Guthrie and others 1995). There is, however, some evidence on unintended negative consequences of food labeling. For instance, Mathios (1998) found evidence that after the introduction of the US Nutrition Labelling and Education Act (NLEA) consumers shifted purchases of cooking oils toward those higher in saturated fats and lower in mono-saturated fats; however, in another research the same author found that NLEA improved dietary choices in the salad dressing market (Mathios 2000). All this said; nutrition labels have played a crucial role in promoting health, especially if their underlying goal is to achieve long-term dietary improvements across populations and if they can encourage food companies to develop more foods with lower quantities of less healthy nutrients (Hawkes 2004). Available studies suggest that nutrition labels on food products help consumers make healthier food choices and encourage healthier diets among people who read the labels (Hawkes 2004).

Although food labeling in the United Kingdom is not mandatory, the labeling format used by U.K. companies is considered among the most effective, mainly because the labels are clear and easily understood. In March 2006, food companies in the United Kingdom were encouraged to use the so-called Traffic Light System (TLS), which highlights total fat, saturated fat, sugar, and salt content on the front panel of packages through a colored scheme. The United Kingdom Food Standard Agency encouraged companies selling products especially high in calories, such as pizza, sausages, burgers, pies, sandwiches, and breakfast cereals, to use such a labeling system. Thanks to a widespread consumer education campaign about the harmful effects of unhealthy nutrients, many persons read the labels, and food companies began competing to provide healthier products that could appeal to consumers who were concerned about health. The labeling scheme has proven effective, with 80 percent of U.K. food products being labeled (Van Camp and others 2010).

In the United States, the 1994 Nutrition and Education Bill mandated that all packaged foods include nutrition labels. The system has proven effective in increasing the use of labels. More shoppers reported using nutrition labels after the legislation was implemented, and meal planners increasingly used them to select foods. According to surveys conducted after the law went into effect, consumers made healthier choices because of the nutrition labels, an increasing amount of food companies improved the quality of their products, and overall diet improved in the United States (Hawkes 2004). Other countries are switching from a voluntary to a mandatory system of nutrition labeling. In Europe, for example, nutrition labeling was voluntary until recently.

In most countries, regulation on nutrition labeling only covers processed foods, not food served in restaurants. But with more and more people across the globe eating foods prepared outside the home (Lin and others 1999), however, some cities, states, and countries have begun contemplating, and sometimes enforcing, regulations on restaurants, in addition to food manufacturers. Faced with high levels of obesity, coronary heart disease, and diabetes in New York City,[2] a regulation was adopted in 2006 making it mandatory for restaurants that had chosen to make calorie information publicly available (about 10 percent of the city's restaurants) to post such information on menus and menu boards.[3] Although some restaurant chains were providing nutrition information to consumers before the legislation went into effect, the information was found to have an insignificant impact on consumer knowledge and information about the products. A survey conducted by the city found that only 8 percent of customers reported seeing the calorie information. Survey results showed that the information was not displayed where and when the consumers made their purchases, making it difficult for them to make healthy choices. The New York City regulation requires calorie content values of all menu items to be available at the point of decision.[4] The regulation was meant to "enable New Yorkers to make more informed, healthier choices … to reduce obesity."

Before the regulation went into effect, however, Mayor Michael Bloomberg had already put forth two laws to combat these health risks—a ban on trans fatty acids and a law requiring laboratories to report cases of diabetes to a citywide registry. By then, consensus was high among New Yorkers regarding a law that regulated the information that restaurants provided to consumers. Before the legislative process, the city conducted and studied polls to gauge the public's acceptance of menu labeling. A 2005 national poll showed that 83 percent of adults wanted information about nutrition to be available in restaurants. A telephone poll, conducted shortly after the law came into effect, showed that 80 percent of New Yorkers supported the expansion of the law to cover the entire state (Mello 2009).

The city faced some obstacles along the way, however. The New York State Restaurant Association (NYSRA) sued the Board of Health for its initial proposal, arguing that the city's regulation clashed with federal regulations (federal preemption claim), which give restaurants some flexibility in how they provide information to customers and prohibit states from regulating claims made by restaurants, unless they are associated to health risks. NYSRA's suit also argued that the regulation violated free speech, in that it restricted how restaurants communicated nutrition information to their consumers. The federal preemption claim was dismissed by the district court, which rejected the argument on the basis that the regulation reduced consumer confusion and promoted information that could help reduce obesity. The law came into effect seven months later, this time with revised rules that applied not just to restaurants that voluntarily made disclosures regarding calories, but to any New York City restaurant that is part of a chain with 15 or more outlets nationwide and that serves standardized portions. NYSRA again tried to block the regulation's implementation. This time, the U.S. Food and Drug Administration (FDA) intervened, stating its support for the Board of Health's stance. Since July 2008, the city has been issuing fines to noncompliant restaurants (Mello 2009).

Imposing standards on restaurants that differ from or are not specifically spelled out in federal regulations has not been easy (Mello 2009), but this situation is likely to change. The 2010 U.S. Health Care Act (the Affordable Care Act) made nutritional labeling on menus mandatory for chain restaurants with 20 or more outlets. While results of the New York City regulation have yet to be evaluated, a 2008 study found widespread support for the new legislation (Armstrong 2008).

Argentina, Paraguay, and Uruguay only required nutrition labels when a health claim was made, but since 2003, MERCOSUR-level regulations have imposed mandatory labeling. As of 2006, nutrition labels must include information on the energy value and the protein, carbohydrate, total-fat, dietary-fiber, saturated-fat, trans-fat, and sodium content of foods.[5] República Bolivariana de Venezuela requires nutrition labels only on foods with special dietary uses, and Chile only requires nutrition labeling when a health claim is made. The rest of the countries had no regulations in place as of 2004 (Hawkes 2004). In 2001, the Brazilian Ministry of Health approved a resolution for the mandatory nutrition labelling of all processed foods including the Brazilian serving sizes (Coitniho and others 2002).

Social Media Campaigns—Changing the Informational Environment

Studies suggest that media campaigns can be effective (at least in generating awareness) if they are developed on the basis of research on the beliefs and attitudes of target audiences, if the messages are tailored to those specific audiences, and if multiple communication channels are used to deliver the message (Henly and Raffin 2010). The "1% or Less" social-marketing campaign conducted in Wheeling, West Virginia, is a good example. The campaign's goal was to reduce the consumption of foods high in saturated fat as a way to decrease the risk of heart disease among Wheeling residents. Because whole milk is one of the six main foods with a high saturated-fat content consumed by Americans, the social media campaign focused on encouraging residents to switch from whole or 2-percent milk to 1-percent or fat-free milk. The campaign relied on paid advertisements and public relations instruments to disseminate the message. Paid advertisements were outsourced to a professional ad agency; the messages encouraging viewers and listeners to switch to low-fat milk as a way to reduce their risk of heart disease were broadcast on television and radio and run on newspapers. As part of the public relations campaign, a campaign advisory group made up of community leaders and local health professions was established. This group helped to develop the campaign messages and gave credibility to the campaign. In addition, a series of media events—including press conferences with prominent local physicians and tasting events—were launched to pitch the story to news directors and the media. The campaign was effective in changing people's behavior. After just six weeks, 36 percent of milk drinkers indicated that they had changed to low-fat milk, compared with 3.6 percent in the control community, and low-fat milk sales had increased from 29 percent to 46 percent in the intervention group (Reger and others 2002). Six months after the campaign, the changes in consumption and sales of low-fat milk remained.

Social marketing campaigns intended to improve diets are usually pursued as part of a larger intervention to improve diet. The Together Let's Prevent Childhood Obesity (EPODE) project, which will be examined later (see the section on community-based programs), is an example of a community-based program in France that used social marketing campaigns to improve diet and increase physical activity.

Regulating Advertising—The Informational Environment

Advertising has an effect on preferences, purchasing behaviors, and food consumption among children (Hastings and others 2003). In 2007, businesses worldwide spent more than US$ 9.6 billion marketing foods and beverages, US$ 1.7 billion of which was directed to children and adolescents (FTC 2008).

To avoid regulation, food companies often negotiate with governments and develop self-regulation. Companies prefer this, as it generally doesn't involve strict monitoring practices. Moreover, by developing their own guidelines, companies can promote an image of corporate social responsibility in the face of an increasingly well-informed consumer body. Some companies adhere to the International Chamber of Commerce code, which is more protective of children. Other multinational companies have developed their own codes of conduct and standards for their advertising. In 2006, the Clinton Foundation and the American Heart Association developed school beverage guidelines in collaboration with industry. Three companies in particular (Coca Cola, PepsiCo—both of which represent 75 percent of the world's beverage market—and Cadbury Schweppes) helped develop the guidelines, which included restrictions on caloric and nutrient content and on advertising their products in elementary schools (Hawkes 2004).

The 2007 Children's Food and Beverage Advertising Initiative, which involves 15 major food companies, also developed advertising restrictions that applied to children under the age of 12.[6] This initiative bans ads in elementary schools and calls on companies to devote no less than 50 percent of their child-directed advertising to promoting a healthy diet (Sharma and others 2010). These codes are not mandatory, however, and there is no mechanism in place to monitor or sanction companies that violate them. Relatively few companies have committed themselves to standards and guidelines, and the standards have not been applied consistently across industry. Studies show that the advertising of unhealthy dietary practices is intensifying, despite the increase in self-regulatory restrictions (Kunkel and others 2009). This general failure to effectively change the advertising behavior of the food industry led WHO to call on governments to impose mandatory regulations on the advertising of food companies (Oommen and Anderson 2008).

In the United Kingdom, self-regulating measures undertaken by the food industry were not successful in decreasing consumption of high-energy foods among children. Obesity rates were among the highest in Europe, and children in the United Kingdom were found to consume high levels of fat, sugar, and salt. As awareness about the risks of an unhealthful diet began to increase in the country, a study by Hastings and Carins (2010) showed an association between advertising and food preferences among children.[7] In January 2008, the government opted for statutory regulation and imposed scheduling restrictions to stop unhealthy foods from being advertised during programs mostly watched by children age 16 and younger. As a way to establish which products fell into the category of "unhealthy" foods, the government developed a nutrient profiling system, which scored each food based on its levels of fat, salt, and sugar (Ofcom 2007).

To determine which programs would fall under the restriction, Ofcom, the government-approved regulatory authority for the broadcasting and telecommunications industries in the United Kingdom, developed an index which identified television programs whose viewers included 20 percent or more of children 16 and younger. The programs that crossed over that threshold were subject to the regulation. The regulation proved somewhat successful: There was a 41 percent decrease in television advertising for unhealthy foods; however, there was an increase in advertising in other types of media (Hastings and Carins 2010). Other OECD countries have put in place some regulations reducing the intensity of marketing for energy-dense, nutrient-poor foods targeted at children.

In LAC, food marketing to children is widespread and promotes foods high in fat, sugar, and salt, often through giveaways and contests to increase consumption among children. Marketing in Latin America is mostly done on TV, but school-based advertising is also common, especially for soft drinks (PAHO 2011). Some countries have either passed or are in the process of enacting legislation on advertising, however.

The Government of Chile is developing self-regulatory measures on food advertising to children (Hawkes 2007). And in Mexico, the food industry has developed a self-regulatory code on advertising food and nonalcoholic beverages to children (Código de Autoregulación de Publicidad de Alimentos y Bebidas No Alcohólicas dirigida al Público Infantil), which includes detailed guidelines on what kinds of messages are appropriate for children (PAHO 2011), a recently approved amendment to Mexico's General Health Law states that the content of advertisements for junk food should not encourage unhealthy eating habits (PAHO 2011).

In Brazil, the Ministry of Health (MOH) has proposed several bills to restrict advertising to children, and the Ministry's National Health Surveillance agency put together a working group that drafted a proposal which included several recommendations to restrict advertising of foods high in fat, sugar, and salt and low in nutrient value. The proposal was considered unconstitutional on the grounds that the agency is not charged with regulating on this matter. In parallel, the State of São Paulo proposed a law to combat overweight and obesity, which would require the government to adopt measures regulating food marketing to children, in partnership with the advertising sector, media companies, civil society, and industry (Hawkes 2007).

On the basis of WHO's 2004 Global Strategy on Diet, Physical Activity and Health, the Pan American Health Organization (PAHO) issued a series of recommendations to countries on the regulation of advertising. These recommendations were discussed with Member Countries in July 2011 (PAHO 2011).

Fiscal Measures—Economic Incentives and Disincentives

In contrast with the regulatory strategies on unhealthy products directed at industry that were just discussed, taxes on products deemed "unhealthy" directly affect the consumer, influencing or restricting his or her choices and raising arguments about the right of governments to interfere in personal choices. And countries react differently to government taxes. As discussed earlier, the food industry generally opposes taxation, as this can decrease its profits. Consumer attitude toward imposed taxes at the point of purchase varies, however.

In the United States, for example, imposing a tax at the point of purchase has been greatly debated. The country's proponents of levying taxes on unhealthy foods say that leaving industry to self-regulate has been ineffective in improving diet, and that imposing taxes on unhealthy foods is a cost-effective way to get people to eat healthier foods. They argue further that the money raised through taxes can be invested in subsidies for healthier foods such as fruits and vegetables, and could end up saving the government health dollars.[8] Opponents argue that imposing such taxes on what someone eats is an infringement on personal freedom, and that public health goals should be attained using other types of mechanisms that don't infringe on personal choices and liberties.[9] Moreover, because low-income consumers are more sensitive to price changes, excise taxes have been criticized for being regressive and for imposing a greater burden on lower income populations (Robertson and others 2007).

Evidence demonstrates that taxing soda drinks, as is the current practice in the United States, leads to a moderate reduction in soft drink consumption in children and adolescents, but the reduction of soda consumption is offset by increases in consumption of other high-calorie drinks (Fletcher and others 2010). Evidence also has shown that although, overall, the current low tax level on sodas has had little impact, some groups of children—children already overweight, children from low-income households, and African-American children—are more sensitive to these taxes, particularly when the sodas are available at school (Sturm and others 2010).

Jacobson and Brownell (2000) concluded that acceptance of taxes on sodas across the United States would be greater if the revenues they generate were invested in nutrition programs or used to subsidize the purchase of healthy foods. A poll conducted among New Yorkers in conjunction with a proposition to increase taxes on soft drinks, found that 52 percent supported a "soda tax," but the number rose to 72 percent when respondents were told that the revenue would be used for obesity prevention (Brownell and Frieden 2009). Similarly, Sturm and others (2010) have suggested that taxes on sodas would have a greater impact if the revenues were invested in obesity prevention efforts rather than through their direct impact on children's consumption of soda. Yet, no state had used the tax revenue to subsidize the healthy foods or nutrition programs. Rather, these tax revenues had gone to support other services such as schools and transportation. In all these states, taxes had been levied simply to generate revenue.

Poland's experience in eliminating large subsidies for butter and lard is another international example of how fiscal measures can be effective in changing dietary habits. In the early 1990s, the Government of Poland lifted those subsidies and, as a result, the consumption of nonhydrogenated vegetable oils increased rapidly, partially substituting the consumption of butter and lard. This dietary change brought about a decrease in coronary heart disease of about 28 percent between 1990 and 1999 (Willett and others 2006).

Finally, Denmark levied a tax on foods high in saturated fats at the end of 2011, only to eliminate it a year later after extensive criticism from the food industry for raising prices and increasing its administrative burden; the food industry also produced statistics showing that the consumption of fatty foods did not change during the time the tax was effective. A study conducted by the University of Copenhagen, however, showed that consumption did decrease in the first three months after the tax was levied, although it was not clear whether this drop was due to hoarding in days before the levy was enacted.[10]

Interventions to Promote Physical Activity

Social Media Campaigns—The Informational Environment

This section documents examples of social media campaigns to promote physical activity. These policies were included in this section since WHO considers them "best buys" (WHO 2011a). However, other reviews indicate that there is not enough evidence on the effectiveness of some types of social media campaigns. For instance, the US independent Task Force on Community Preventive Services implemented a review of these interventions at community level and concluded that there was insufficient evidence to determine the effectiveness of stand-alone mass media campaigns or classroom-based health education focused on providing information to promote physical activity.[11]

One of the best known social media campaign to promote physical activity was waged in the United States by the CDC. The campaign, dubbed VERB, focused on changing the sedentary lifestyle and increasing physical activity in "tweens," (children 9–13 years old) among several ethnic groups; the tweens' parents were the campaign's secondary target. Launched in 2002, the campaign was based on extensive research conducted among tweens and parents designed to understand their behaviors and attitudes toward physical activity. The research involved focus groups, interviews, and surveys among different minorities and ethnic groups. Based on the findings, the campaign was planned using commercial marketing techniques and applying them toward the public health goal of increasing physical activity (Wong 2004). In order for the campaign to be effective, the messages promoted physical activity as a desirable occupation, stressing those elements of physical activity that tweens value, such as playing, having fun, and being with friends. The reasoning was that tweens would more easily give up sedentary behaviors, such as watching TV and playing video games, if the physical activities were portrayed as opportunities to have fun.

VERB messages encouraged tweens to come up with physical activities they liked, rather than telling them how much and how often to exercise. Television ads showed people from different races and ethnic backgrounds having fun while doing physical activities. To build the VERB brand, campaign planners involved popular athletes and celebrities who were linked to the public health campaign. Paid television ads were timed to ensure that, when they aired, a greater audience of tweens and their parents would see them. Separate advertisements and commercials were directed to the parents, encouraging them to discuss physical activity with their children. VERB was also present in cultural festivals and street fairs to enhance the program's popularity in the community. Partnerships with community organizations, corporations, and websites were formed to promote the VERB brand and to raise awareness (Wong 2004). Thanks to partnerships built with park organizations, schools, churches, and businesses, accessible and safe outdoor environments were created for tweens. After one year, 75 percent of children surveyed were aware of the campaign and levels of reported time spent engaged in physical activities had increased (Huhman and others 2005).

In LAC, an important social media campaign called "Agita São Paulo" (Get Moving, São Paulo) has been particularly successful in raising awareness about physical activity. Growing concerns about the increasing rates of chronic diseases in São Paulo, led the city to develop a massive and sophisticated mass media campaign aimed at encouraging physical activity among residents. In 1990, data indicated that the prevalence of a sedentary lifestyle among males and females aged 18–70 in the city was 69.3 percent (Matsudo and others 2003). After two years of broad consultations with health advisors across the globe, and thanks to consultations with the government, nongovernmental institutions, and private companies, "Agita São Paulo" was launched in 1996. It was designed to increase knowledge about the health benefits of physical activity and to raise people's physical activity levels. Simple messages were used to encourage children, working age adults, and seniors to engage in at least 30 minutes of moderate physical activity a day on most days of the week.

To raise awareness and encourage physical activity, program planners organized "mega-events," which brought together large sections of the population and were usually linked to popular events such as carnivals and festivals that attracted mass media coverage. "Agita Melhor Idade" (Get Moving for Better Aging), specifically designed to encourage the elderly to become more physically active, consisted of a walk on the national and international days of older adults. A key element in determining the results of the intervention was the development of partnerships across different sectors. To raise awareness about mega events and to encourage physical activity, the planners partnered with numerous institutions that helped to develop and distribute flyers, posters, and videos, and to spread the "accumulate minutes of physical activity every day" program message. Messages centered on becoming physically active while engaging in everyday activities, such as walking the dog, gardening, and doing home chores. Messages about walking and climbing stairs were posted along the transportation system, and dancing, the country's favorite leisure activity, was used in messages directed at all sectors of the population (Matsudo and others 2003).

Funds from the state Secretariat of Health allowed program planners to create areas where residents could engage in physical activity. Parks were redesigned and gyms were made more accessible. An educational component was also added, with exercise included in student curricula (Anderson and others 2009). The intervention proved successful in increasing physical activity among residents. According to United States Agency for International Development (USAID), the cost of the intervention was US$ 0.01 per person, and its cost-effectiveness was US$ 248 per DALY averted (Anderson and others 2009). Awareness of the program increased significantly, and those who knew of the program reported being more likely to be physically active (Matsudo and others 2002). Frequency of moderate physical activities increased from 3.5 days to 5.0 days per week, and the duration of exercise increased from 40 minutes to 120 minutes per day. Among school-age children, those doing 150 minutes of exercise per week increased from 20 percent to 40 percent of boys and from 4 percent to 42 percent of girls (Anderson and others 2009).

WHO acknowledged the program's success and deemed it a useful model for other developing countries. As a result, the model was applied throughout Brazil; the MOH launched the nationwide program, "Agita Brazil" (Get Moving, Brazil) in 2000. In addition, Argentina, Colombia, Costa Rica, Ecuador, Guatemala, Mexico, Panama, Paraguay, Peru, Uruguay, and República Bolivariana de Venezuela also replicated the program. In 2000, the Physical Activity Network of the Americas, which all of these countries joined, was created with the CDC and PAHO support.

Modifying the Built Environment to Increase Physical Activity

A number of interventions aimed at promoting physical activity have involved modifying the built environment to reduce motor-vehicle use and make these spaces more appealing and safer for pedestrians and bicyclists. For instance, high levels of hypertension and diabetes in Chicago's low-income Logan Circle area led community members to implement outdoor physical activities modeled after Colombia's Ciclovía program (see chapter 5) and to raise awareness among neighbors to improve safety in their community (Bennett and others 2007; Gomez-Feliciano and others 2009).

Governments sometimes turn to transportation policies, specifically on walking and biking, to encourage physical activity. Known as traffic calming strategies, these policies have helped cities reduce traffic-related injuries (Van Schagen 2003). Cities are increasingly using traffic calming techniques as part of a wider plan to tackle a broad array of modern challenges. New York City, for example, has put in place various programs to promote environmental sustainability, attract businesses and tourists, and increase physical activity and improve public health among residents. Recently, the city doubled its miles of bike lanes to almost 500 in only three years. The strategy is intended to attract greater numbers of cyclists and to make streets safer for drivers, pedestrians, transit riders, and cyclists. On average, bike lanes reduce injury resulting from crashes for all road users by at least 40 percent. The commissioner is also developing policies to open up the city to pedestrians through pedestrian plazas to eliminate gridlock, as in Times Square, and adding express bus service lines to the outer boroughs, to reduce the number of cars on the expressways and roads.[12]

Although most New York City voters support bike lanes because they are greener and healthier, the plan has come under attack by some residents and businesses. Two community organizations, "Neighbors for Better Bike Lanes" and "Seniors for Safety," sued the Department of Transportation (DOT) for allegedly providing skewed data and flawed information about the benefits to be derived from the original bike lines. More specifically, DOT was accused of inflating the number of bicyclists who used the lanes and understating the number of accidents that had occurred since the bike lanes expanded. The organizations demanded that the new bike lanes be removed (Shaer 2011). Businesses also opposed the expansion, stating that because the added bike lanes inconvenienced city drivers and curtailed parking for deliveries, the bike lanes hindered sales, harming the city's economy (Goodman 2010). This is not the first time bike lanes have created such acrimonious debates in the city: in 1980, then-Mayor Edward Koch added bike lanes in Manhattan, but they were quickly removed following protests, mainly from business associations.

The city defeated the DOT lawsuit (Chaban 2011), and a recent poll conducted by the mayor's office shows that support for bike lanes exceeded 60 percent. In response to the criticism in the suit, the city cited the latest data, showing that only four pedestrians had been killed in bike-pedestrian accidents between 2001 and 2005. From 2006 through 2010, as cycling doubled, only three pedestrians were killed in bike-pedestrian accidents.[13] Along with the expansion of the bike lanes, the Mayor has partnered with third-party contractors to establish a bike-share program that would allow riders to rent bikes at kiosks for a small fee.

Built environments that promote health in cities and communities are an important component of WHO's Healthy Cities Project, an initiative that began in high-income OECD countries. This effort recognizes the multisectoral nature of health promotion and aims at placing health high on the social, economic, and political agendas of local governments. About 90 cities are members of the WHO European Healthy Cities Network, and 30 national Healthy Cities networks across WHO's European Region have more than 1,400 cities and towns as members.[14]

In LAC, the Healthy Municipalities and Communities movement follows the European Healthy Cities approach of promoting health at the local level. Many LAC countries have healthy municipalities or healthy communities' initiatives, including Argentina, Brazil, Costa Rica, Cuba, El Salvador, Guatemala, Honduras, Nicaragua, Mexico (about 1,000), Panama, Paraguay, Peru (130), Trinidad and Tobago, and Uruguay.[15]

In LAC, a CDC-funded project called Guide for Useful Interventions for Physical Activity (GUIA) is being implemented to develop evidence-based strategies to promote physical activity in the region. Among the initial findings of GUIA's review are the promising results of community-wide policies and planning, combined with locally funded physical activity classes, to increase physical activity in communities (Hoehner and others 2008). The literature on the evaluations of such interventions in Latin America is scant, although there are a few cases of community-wide interventions in the region that show some evidence of success. Among them is the case of Bogotá, a city with a built environment that promotes physical activity (documented in the next chapter).

Community-Based Interventions to Promote Healthy Diets and Increase Physical Activity

Workplace Programs

Among the most successful work-based programs to improve diet and increase physical activity is the Treatwell 5-a-Day Program in the United States, which used a combination of environmental and behavioral approaches to improve diet among employees. The study sought to assess the effectiveness of a work-based nutrition intervention involving families and designed to promote greater consumption of fruits and vegetables. When the study was conducted, only 20–30 percent of Americans met the recommendation to consume five or more servings of fruits and vegetables each day (Sorensen and others 1999).

The program encompassed 22 community health centers located in underserved areas. Its behavioral and educational component involved the subjects' periodic exposure to the program's media campaign, promotion of the cancer information service hotline, and a nutrition presentation on how to purchase and prepare healthy foods. Through an Employee Advisory Board, workers were able to participate in the planning and coordination of program activities and events. This proved particularly helpful in organizing festivities, discussion series, and educational campaigns carried out throughout the program to raise awareness among employees. Employee families also participated in the intervention. Newsletters and letters sent to families, as well as family picnics and parties, were used to raise awareness about the importance of eating healthy foods. To change the environment, healthy foods were offered in workplace vending machines, at special occasion meals, and in break rooms. Catering policies for meetings and functions were modified to include fruits and vegetables and other low-fat options. Point-of-choice labeling of fruits and vegetables, posters, videos, and brochures in employee eating areas also were used to increase awareness and change behavior.

The program's results were that: participating workers increased their consumption of fruits and vegetables by 19 percent. The involvement of employee families made it easier to bring about the changes, as individual behaviors are more easily changed within a social context, in this case the workplace and the family (Sorensen and others 1999).

School-Based Interventions

The Child and Adolescent Trial Cardiovascular Health (CATCH) program used a health-promoting school approach. The largest school-based health study in the United States, CATCH incorporated educational, behavioral, and school-environment components. The goal was to decrease cardiovascular disease risk factors in children by reducing fat consumption and increasing physical activity. This was a case-control study involving a total of 96 schools, 28 schools from third grade through fifth that included school-food-service changes, enhanced physical education, and classroom health curricula; 28 additional schools received these components plus family education. Meals offered in intervention school cafeterias were lower in total fat, saturated fat, and sodium content. Training sessions and monthly visits conducted by intervention staff were intended to influence menu planning, food preparation methods, and advertising in school cafeterias. Cafeteria staff members were provided with guidelines and educational materials on ways to prepare healthy foods, using more vegetables, fruits, and beans in entrees and salads. Students also were encouraged—through the educational component—to increase their fruit and vegetable consumption. Through the physical education component, standardized physical education interventions were put in place, including curriculum and staff development, and follow-up in randomly assigned schools. Families were involved in activities in and outside of school to raise awareness about the campaign (see French and Stables 2003; McKenzie and others 1996; and Nader and others 1999).

Results show that an intervention in a food-service cafeteria successfully reduced total fat, saturated fat, sodium, and calories in foods served there, as well as increasing fiber, vitamin A, and Vitamin C (French and Stables 2003). The intervention also succeeded in increasing the children's moderate-to-vigorous physical activity, with intervention children reporting 12 more minutes of daily vigorous physical activity and running 18.6 yards more than control children (McKenzie and others 1996). Ultimately, children in the intervention schools consumed less fat and saturated fat and self-reported greater physical activity, compared to the control schools (Nader and others 1999).

Pathways, a randomized control study conducted among Native American schoolchildren also used a multicomponent approach to evaluate the effectiveness of reducing body weight. Among its four components was the involvement of family members in program activities, which was meant to assist the children in creating supportive environments toward building healthy behaviors. A physical education component included 30-minute sessions per week of moderate-to-vigorous physical activity, as well as 2–10-minute exercise breaks. Children were handed out low-fat snack packs and were given tips to bring home so their families could prepare healthful snacks. The program included school activities, such as physical activities for a healthy lifestyle, family fun nights, and workshops. Results from the study showed significant positive changes in fat intake and in food- and health-related knowledge and behavior (Caballero and others 2003).

Other Community-Based Programs

One of the most successful community-based, multisectoral approach programs was the North Karelia, Finland, intervention previously described. Apart from the sodium intake reduction component, this intervention successfully engaged a multitude of stakeholders, including supermarkets, health care professionals, and schools.

Critical to the intervention was the collaboration between the government and the food industry. The government placed considerable pressure on the food industry to produce healthier foods and reduce certain elements from the production process, such as salt and fat. But the project was not all stick; it also used carrots, with the government offering incentives to help industry switch to producing healthier foods. For example, one of the program's main focuses was to reduce dairy consumption, because dairy products high in sodium and saturated fat were one of the most consumed foods in the city until the intervention began. But the campaign negatively affected the dairy industry. To offset industry's excessive losses, the government launched a program to help dairy farmers switch to growing berries, a promising new product, especially since the campaign promoted consumption of fruits and vegetables. To help make the switch from dairy to berry farming, in 1985 the Ministry of Agriculture and the Ministry of Commerce financed a collaborative project involving berry farmers, the berry industry, and commercial and health authorities. The partnership sought to find innovative ways, including through information and education campaigns and new product development, to promote berry consumption. Berry consumption rose gradually, and many dairy farmers switched to berry production (Puska and others 2002). Collaboration between the project and the food industry also played an important role in the intervention. As part of the goal of substituting butter with vegetable oil for cooking, the project coordinated with the food industry to promote and market spreads high in vegetable oil and low in total fat (Puska and others 2009).

Another effective example is EPODE, a community-based program designed to reduce the prevalence of childhood obesity. The program began in 1991 with a pilot project in two northern communities in France (Fleurbaix and Laventie) under the name Fleurbaix Laventie Ville Santé. Given the pilot's success and faced with high obesity rates among children across the country, in 2004 the Government of France expanded the model to 10 additional cities, under the name EPODE. EPODE's successful methodology has now been replicated in 331 European cities and towns, as well as in sites outside Europe.

The pilot study set out to investigate the impact of a school-based nutrition program on BMI levels and rates of overweight and obesity in children 5–12 years old. The interventions were found to successfully decrease the rates of overweight and obesity in the two communities—the rate of overweight and obese children in Fleurbaix and Laventie was 8.8 percent, while that in control towns was 17.8 percent (Adamo 2007). Interventions then were extended to the entire population of the two pilot cities through community-based educational activities that focused on physical activity and nutrition.

EPODE is a preventive program that involves all city stakeholders, including mayors, shop owners, schoolteachers, doctors, pharmacists, caterers, restaurant owners, sports associations, the media, scientists, and various branches of town government. It aims to raise awareness, change nutrition behaviors, and encourage a healthy lifestyle among children ages 5–12 and their families (Katan 2009). The program encourages children and their families to eat healthier foods and to balance food intake with physical activity. At its core, the program relies on sophisticated social marketing techniques to change individual behavior. The EPODE messages are simple, easily understood, and encourage children to try fruit compotes or add fruits to their vegetables, rather than telling them what to eat. Moreover, the messages try to avoid stigmatizing children that do not participate in the program. Messages portray healthy behavior as an opportunity for children to have fun and play, rather than as health activities ("Playing is already moving!") (Henley and Raffin 2010).

Community-based activities provide families with hands-on experience on how to promote healthy behavior. The nutrition-based education component involves cooking classes, food tasting experiences, agricultural discovery sessions, and meals provided to families in schools. The physical activity component consists in organizing walk-to-school days and outdoor games on weekends, as well as developing sporting facilities and playgrounds, mapping out walking itineraries, and hiring sports instructors (Katan 2009).

Community-Based Programs in Latin America

Initial findings from the GUIA project's review of interventions in Latin America designed to encourage physical activity, found some promising results.

Brazil's population has a low degree of participation in moderate-to-high levels of physical activity, ranging from 10.5 percent in São Paolo, to 14.7 percent in Recife, and to 21.5 percent in Brasilia (Simoes and others 2009). In 2003, Brazil's MOH launched a nationwide program to promote healthy living. One of the program's components involves the promotion of leisure-time physical activity and better nutrition. Within this framework, the government initiated the "Academia das Cidades" (ACP) program, which set up gyms in several cities across Brazil. Quantitative and qualitative evaluations in the cities of Curitiba and Recife were conducted and published as part of the GUIA, indicating some evidence of success.

In Recife, the evaluation was conducted through a cross-sectional study that examined the effect that ACP had had on increasing leisure-time physical activity among adults. Through the program, the government contracted physical-education teachers to supervise leisure-time physical activity, provide nutrition education, and take health measurements such as blood pressure and BMI in the city's public spaces. Leisure activities include aerobics classes, walking groups, and dance. Supervised leisure is part of the public health care system and is open to community members between 10 a.m. and 5 p.m.; about 10,000 persons have enrolled in the program since 2002.

Telephone interviews were conducted with over 2,000 Recife residents, who were asked about their level of physical activity and their participation in and exposure to ACP activities. Results from the survey indicate that there has been a 25-percent increase in physical activity since the ACP sites were launched, suggesting that the program has been successful (Simoes and others 2009).

A similar evaluation was conducted in Curitiba. Curitiba is Brazil's seventh largest city, and it has a tradition of carrying out innovative and integrated urban planning efforts aimed at a healthier lifestyle. Since the 1970s, the city's green spaces have increased from under 1 m^2 per person to 52 m^2 per person. The city promotes physical activity throughout many public facilities and public recreation areas through various programs run by the municipal Sports and Leisure Secretariat and the municipal government. Probably because of Curitiba's long-standing tradition in promoting a healthier lifestyle, results from the telephone surveys here found greater participation levels in ACP than did the Recife survey. While current and former participation in the Recife ACP ranged between 1.9 percent and 3.9 percent, in Curitiba participation ranged between 5.6 percent and 11 percent. Awareness about the program also was higher in Curitiba, with 9 out of 10 people reporting knowing about the program, compared to only 61.7 percent reporting so in Recife. This intervention adds to the evidence suggesting that community-based physical activity interventions can increase physical activity levels (Reis and others 2010).

The city of Curitiba also hosted another important intervention designed to increase physical activity in the community. The city's municipal Sports and Leisure Secretariat put in place the program, called CuritibAtiva, in 1998. The program involves multiple stakeholders and sectors in the city. It comprises a multitude of activities: some short-term, such as marathons and dances, others long-term, such as physical-activity classes. Some activities are tailored to specific audiences, such as school games for young people, and others target the community at large, such as a walking campaign and various civic activities. Activities to raise awareness about the program and to increase knowledge about its health benefits were also introduced (Ribeiro and others 2010). The program is being evaluated as part of the GUIA project through complex logic models that gather information from the multiple stakeholders responsible for the program. The evaluation will provide information to program coordinators on the intervention's gaps and overlaps, and will allow other cities in the region to adapt the CuritibAtiva model to their own needs (Ribeiro and others 2010).

Tobacco-Control Policies

Thanks to existing tobacco-control policies, tobacco prevalence in OECD countries has decreased significantly over the last decades. Most of this drop has resulted from tax increases, regulations setting up smoke-free environments, and public awareness campaigns. Since the 1960s, tobacco prevalence in OECD countries dropped from about 40 percent to 20 percent; in Canada and the United States, prevalence decreased from 42 percent in 1965 to 16 percent in 2009 (OECD 2011).

The most cost-effective interventions to control tobacco use are now part of the WHO Framework Convention on Tobacco Control (FCTC). A total of 174 countries have adopted the FCTC since 2003. The treaty establishes minimum standards for member countries to enact tobacco control, but countries are encouraged to develop more stringent national policies. Policies range from pricing and tax regulations (Article 6); to packaging and labeling of tobacco products (Article 11); education, communication, training, and public awareness campaigns (Article 12); sales to minors (Article 16); and measures to tackle the illicit trade of tobacco (Article 15) (WHO 2011b). Countries across the globe have undertaken many of the FCTC's strategies to reduce tobacco use. The Convention provides an international context that facilitates the adoption of tobacco-control policies globally.

Increasing the Price of Tobacco Products—Economic Incentives and Disincentives

Raising taxes increases the overall price of tobacco products and reduces tobacco demand, cigarette smoking, and other tobacco use (Harris 1987; Keeler and others 1996). Smoking reduction due to taxes is seen both in the frequency of use and in the prevalence of use. Raising taxes on cigarettes induces cessation, prevents relapse, reduces initiation, and lowers the numbers of cigarettes consumed by smokers.

The greatest reductions occur among youth and young adults. Adolescents and young adults are twice to threefold more sensitive to tobacco price changes than adults (Task Force on Community Preventive Services 2001). Racial and ethnic minorities, less educated groups, and lower income populations are also significantly susceptible to price hikes (Chaloupka 1998). It is estimated that the price elasticity of demand ranges between −0.20 and −0.50 in high-income countries and between −0.50 and −1.00 in low- and middle-income countries

(Chaloupka and others 1999). This means that a tax increase of 10 percent will reduce cigarette demand by 3–5 percent. And the elasticity is greater among young people. The effects are also stronger in low- and middle-income countries, where a 10 percent increase in tobacco tax is estimated to lead to an 8 percent reduction in tobacco use.

In its effort to avert the adoption of tobacco-control measures, the tobacco industry has engaged in a multitude of efforts, including lobbying, public relations campaigns, and research. To thwart regulations and influence political decisions, they often rely on political donations, lobbying, and threats of legal action (Saloojee and Dagli 2000). And to counter tobacco tax increases, companies either oppose the regulation or develop lower priced brands to ensure that their products are accessible to consumers. Industry sometimes develops a variety of price related marketing efforts, such as multi-pack discounts and the distribution of coupons (Chaloupka and others 2002). These strategies can undermine the government's intentions. For example, if tobacco companies react to an increased tax by lowering their price in an amount greater than the tax increase, then the government's revenues will be lower than expected (Harris 1987). Such was the case in Hungary, where tobacco companies responded to tax increases with various tactics, including the development of a lower priced cigarette that could compete with the existing brands, and decreases in the prices of their products which ran counter to the ultimate goal of the government's taxes (Szilagyi and Chapman 2003).

Increasing taxes on tobacco could also provide incentives to smuggling and illegal trade in cigarettes. Tobacco smuggling has been a problem in various countries and states, such as in New York state, following a hike in tobacco taxes (Davis and others 2006), as well as in some Latin American countries such as Brazil, where in 2005, falsification, illegal manufacturing, and cigarette smuggling represented 30 percent of the total number of cigarettes consumed by the population (Müller and Wehbe 2008).[16] In general, however, the extent of cigarette smuggling has less to do with cigarette tax rates than with government policies regarding smuggling, enforcement efforts, and the acceptance of smuggling and black-market sales (Joossens and Raw 2000). Various countries have designed tobacco-control policies that include measures aimed specifically to monitor the tobacco market and deter smuggling. In Scandinavian countries, monitoring systems were imposed on all production and distribution of cigarettes, and unique serial numbers were posted on every cigarette pack as a way to avoid smuggling (WHO 2004a).

As part of their strategy to persuade governments not to pass tobacco-control policies, tobacco companies often point to the economic losses that the country would sustain if such policies were to go through. While raising tobacco prices and reducing its consumption could lower government revenues, studies show that the health benefits gained from the decreased smoke inhaled among smokers and their families compensate for the losses and ultimately translate into greater monetary gains. There is, however, a distinction to be made. Economic losses caused by tobacco-control policies are more or less easily offset, depending on a country's economic dependence on tobacco production. In other words, the economic benefit of tobacco-control policies hinges on whether a country produces tobacco and how much it produces. Increased taxes on tobacco products would, indeed, negatively affect farmers in countries where tobacco production is high. However, even in most countries where tobacco production is high, the land devoted to growing tobacco represents only 0.25 percent–1.5 percent of all cultivated land (World Bank 2003). Moreover, there are examples of successful tobacco-control policies in tobacco producing countries, as is the case of Brazil that will be discussed later on.

Banning Smoking in Public Places—Regulation

In 1986, the U.S. Surgeon General published a report declaring that second-hand smoke caused lung cancer in healthy nonsmokers (HSS 2006). The report also raised a new moral question in the anti-smoking debate, arguing against the notion that smoking constituted a basic civil liberty that should not be restricted by governments. The harmful effect to nonsmokers allowed governments to justify measures to limit smoking (Callinan and others 2010).

In 2002, New York City launched an aggressive and comprehensive tobacco-control program. The program included various components, but it is most widely known for its focus on banning smoking in the city's workplaces, including restaurants and bars. Thanks to strong advocacy from the New York City Health Department, the Smoke-Free Air Act was passed in 2002 and implemented in March 2003. The legislation's 97 percent compliance led to its expansion in 2011, making public parks, beaches, and pedestrian plazas smoke-free.[17] Although New York City had banned smoking in most restaurants in 1995, it continued to allow smoking in bars and bar areas of restaurants (Cooper 2002). Article 1399-n clearly defines areas considered "workplaces" under the act.[18] To comply with the law, New York City officials encouraged workplace owners to discuss the law with customers and employees, to post "no smoking" signs and to remove ashtrays throughout the premises. Under the act, violations are subject to fines ranging from US$ 200 to more than US$ 2,000. Suspension of licenses is also foreseen under the ban.[19] In addition to the smoke-free ban, the program's other components helped make it a success in decreasing smoking consumption. Tax increases, for one, raised the legal retail price of cigarettes by 32 percent, to nearly US$ 7 per pack. In addition, to counter the tobacco industry's marketing messages through traditional advertising, point-of-sale materials, indirect marketing (such as sponsorship of public sporting events), and lobbying, the City engaged in a major print and broadcast anti-tobacco advertising campaign (Frieden and Bloomberg 2007). Smokers also were provided with free courses of nicotine-replacement treatment to help them quit.

Contrary to the tobacco industry and the bar and restaurant associations, New Yorkers widely welcomed the law. A year after the ban was imposed, a Quinnipiac University poll found a 59 percent approval rate of the ban among New York City residents.[20] As for the public health impact of the legislation, the city used three separate surveys to evaluate the effects of the ban on smoking prevalence.[21]

Smoking decreased by 11 percent (from 21.6 percent to 19.2 percent) between 2002 and 2003, following the intervention. The decrease occurred in all five boroughs; across all age groups, races and ethnicities, and education levels; and in both men and women. Almost half of all respondents attributed the air-free act and the decreased exposure to smoke as the primary reason for the decrease in smoking (Frieden and others 2005).

As with most smoking bans, New York City's came with opposition (Frieden and others 2005). Supported by funds from the tobacco industry, the New York Nightlife Association and the Empire State Restaurant and Tavern Association, two lobbying groups for New York City's restaurants and bars, warned against the ban, claiming that it would negatively affect the economy by decreasing profits in the city's bars and restaurants.[22] A study prepared for the two associations to examine the economic impact of the ban, reported that an earlier study had found bars and restaurants in the city negatively affected by the ban. The report stated that following the ban, staffing had been reduced by 16 percent in bars, hotels, and nightclubs, and that three-fourths of bars and restaurants had experienced a 30 percent decline in patronage (Ridgewood Economic Associates 2004).

However, an evaluation conducted by the city contradicted these findings. The city's assessment found that, despite the smoking ban, New York City had experienced increases in jobs, liquor licenses, and business tax payments since the law had taken effect. Moreover, data from the city's Department of Finance found that from April 2003 to January 2004, revenues of city restaurants had increased by about US$ 1.4 million, compared to the same period the year earlier (Elliott 2004).

Increasing Awareness and Knowledge about Tobacco—The Informational Environment

Poland's long anti-smoking battle can be traced by the warning labels placed on cigarette packages. Thanks to the foresight of a few steadfast scientific researchers and a full-fledged media campaign, in 1998 the Polish Parliament passed a law requiring that 30 percent of the two larger sides of cigarette packs include health warnings (Zatonski 2003). This, together with other policies such as tax increases, led to the country's dramatic decrease in total mortality rate (approximately 10 percent between 1991 and 2000).

In The United Kingdom, a 2003 regulation outlawed any published material that purposefully promoted tobacco. A comparative study between countries' varying degrees of stringency of advertising bans found the United Kingdom's comprehensive bans to be the most successful in creating awareness around tobacco and in reducing exposure within the population (Harris and others 2006).

Tobacco-Control Policies in LAC

Most Latin American and Caribbean countries have legislation in place restricting smoking in some public spaces. But these laws are not always clear in delimiting smoke-free areas, and compliance not always assured. The result is that airborne nicotine concentrations in public places continue to be high in some of the region's countries. In Mexico in 2005, for example, airborne nicotine was detected in almost 80 percent of the areas within hospitals, 93 percent of government offices, and 100 percent of spaces in the airport, restaurants, and bars (Navas-Ancien and Valdes-Salgado 2005). Since then, Mexico has taken measures to improve this situation.

The best example of smoke-free policies and one of the best examples of overall tobacco control in LAC is the effort in Uruguay, which in 2006 became the world's first middle-income country to enact smoke-free legislation (Chapter 5). Following Uruguay's implementation of anti-smoking policies, other countries and cities in the region have enacted smoke-free legislation. Mexico City, for example, passed a smoke-free law in February 2008, prohibiting smoking in indoor workplaces and enclosed public places, including public transport, restaurants, and bars. Smoking is allowed in designated areas (Griffith and others 2008). Close collaboration between the city's government, health advocates, and civil society made it possible to enact smoke-free laws, launch a comprehensive media campaign, and raise financial resources to promote the interventions, conduct research, and raise awareness of the smoke-free agenda. People reported decreased exposure to second-hand smoke after the measures were implemented, and support for the intervention among Mexico, DF, residents increased significantly, with 98 percent of them agreeing that second-hand tobacco smoke is dangerous and 97 percent believing that the law benefits their health (WHO 2009).

There are other very promising cases in the region, where sub-national governments have enacted smoke-free legislations. In Argentina (see chapter 5) and República Bolivariana de Venezuela, local governments have passed laws to achieve smoke-free environments. In República Bolivariana de Venezuela, the state of Monagas passed a 100 percent smoke-free law in 2003 to prohibit smoking in enclosed public places, public transportation, and workplaces (Sebrié and others 2008).

A successful example of a tobacco-control policy in a producer country is that of Brazil. Brazil is one of the largest tobacco producers in the world, and yet, the country was able to impose comprehensive tobacco-control policies in the 1980s and 1990s, which significantly decreased demand and tobacco consumption. Brazil is the fourth greatest raw-tobacco producing country in the world after China, India, and the United States. The country produces more raw tobacco than it consumes, 576.6 metric tons a year, or about 7 percent of the world's total tobacco production (Jha and Chaloupka 1999). Da Costa and Goldfarb (2003) detail the unraveling of tobacco control polices in Brazil at the time. As it has in many other countries, Brazil's tobacco industry established strong ties with the government, so much so that the government financed some of the country's tobacco production. Other significant agricultural products did not receive such assistance. Until the late 1970s tobacco companies effectively suppressed any attempt by health advocates or health care professionals to discuss tobacco harm.

The situation changed, however, when international research on the hazard of tobacco began circulating in the country. In 1979, reports about Brazil's mortality rates caused by tobacco began to be disseminated. Concern in the medical community led the National Cancer Association and others to organize meetings and conferences meant to train health professionals about the consequences of tobacco use. Awareness began growing in the country, and in 1987, the MOH commissioned a plan for tobacco control and established the National Tobacco Control Program, which was to play a significant role in tobacco control for the next decades.

The country's progress in tobacco control since the mid-1980s has involved the participation of a number of leaders who were key in determining successful policies in tobacco control. The first was Marcos Moraes, director of the National Institute of Cancer (INCA), who was deeply committed to the cause and was responsible for the increase in information and awareness about tobacco in the 1980s. A vast body of research was conducted and disseminated, and important partnerships and associations were forged toward tobacco control. Another key player was Jose Serra, appointed Minister of Health under the presidency of Fernando Cardoso (1994 and 2002). It is thanks to Serra's commitment that all form of tobacco advertising was banned and cigarette packages were forced to carry pictures of diseases caused by smoking.

The strength and success of these two prominent health leaders, supported by strong health advocacy associations, had to do with their refusal to be swayed by a well organized tobacco industry that used sophisticated and expensive means to block the anti-tobacco movement and anti-tobacco legislation. Industry lobbyists used principles such as the freedom of commercial expression, the right to information, and consumers' freedom of choice, to persuade Brazilians not to support anti-tobacco policies. The companies tapped all communication channels to deliver their messages, sending letters to radio and TV. They created slick smoking lounges to promote tobacco use and to link smoking with sophisticated and comfortable lifestyles. When tobacco advertising was gradually restricted, tobacco companies used point-of-sale advertising; when that was restricted, too, they sponsored sports and environmental events, intending to associate smoking with healthy activities.

The advocacy groups and key players found a window of opportunity in Brazil and used all the instruments available to them, including the media, educational campaigns, and research, to quickly advance the anti-tobacco agenda; they enacted legislation upon legislation, and issued restriction upon restriction, until a comprehensive tobacco-control system was in place.

Countries in the region also impose taxes on tobacco; these taxes have, in general, increased in the last years. Tax rates vary widely, however, ranging from only 12 percent of the price of a 20-cigarette package of the most frequently sold brand in Antigua and Barbuda to more than 70 percent in Argentina, Chile, Uruguay, and República Bolivariana de Venezuela. Most of the rates in the region could be substantially increased (table 4.1).

Table 4.1 National Retail Price of a 20-Cigarette Pack, Countries of the Americas, 2008 and 2010

	2008			2010						
	Price of a 20-cigarette pack of the most sold brand		Taxes (as a % of price of the most sold brand)	Price of a 20-cigarette pack of most sold brand		Taxes (as % of price of the most sold brand)				
Country	International dollars at purchasing power parity	In US$ at official exchange rates	Total tax[a]	Int. dollars at purchasing power parity	In US$ at official exchange rates	Specific excise	Ad valorem excise	Import duties	Total tax[a]
Antigua and Barbuda	3.20	2.41	10	3.12	2.41	0	0	0	12
Argentina[b]	2.11	1.11	69	2.29	1.37	0	69	0	76
Bahamas, The	3.35	2.69	31	3.18	2.69	0	31	0	31
Barbados	8.89	5.50	48	8.57	5.50	34	0	0	48
Belize	4.69	2.50	19	4.63	2.50	10	0	0	21
Bolivia	1.99	0.78	41	2.15	0.85	0	29	0	42
Brazil[b]	1.59	1.03	60	1.96	1.84	26	0	0	60
Canada[b]	6.14	6.17	67	6.61	7.84	58	0	0	67
Chile	3.56	2.07	76	3.91	3.06	0	60	0	76
Colombia[b]	1.48	0.80	34	1.53	1.02	30	10	0	50
Costa Rica	2.33	1.35	56	2.22	1.55	0	44	0	56
Cuba	...	0.30	87	...	...	...	...	...	...
Dominica	2.63	1.30	26	2.63	1.30	13	0	0	26
Dominican Republic[b]	4.87	2.82	57	5.44	3.24	26	17	0	57
Ecuador	3.39	1.70	64	...	1.70	0	54	0	64
El Salvador[b]	2.79	1.40	41	3.51	1.75	26	18	0	55
Grenada[b]	3.87	2.22	41	4.92	2.83	0	34	0	49

table continues next page

Table 4.1 National Retail Price of a 20-Cigarette Pack, Countries of the Americas, 2008 and 2010 (continued)

	2008			2010					
	Price of a 20-cigarette pack of the most sold brand		Taxes (as a % of price of the most sold brand)	Price of a 20-cigarette pack of most sold brand		Taxes (as % of price of the most sold brand)			
Country	International dollars at purchasing power parity	In US$ at official exchange rates	Total tax[a]	Int. dollars at purchasing power parity	In US$ at official exchange rates	Specific excise	Ad valorem excise	Import duties	Total tax[a]
Guyana	3.02	1.17	27	3.55	1.47	0	16	0	21
Honduras[b]	2.23	0.95	45	3.11	1.43	26	0	0	39
Jamaica[b]	9.74	5.05	44	11.57	6.75	36	0	0	51
Mexico[b]	3.58	2.07	61	3.61	2.37	3	46	0	63
Nicaragua[b]	2.90	1.06	20	3.55	1.30	16	0	0	29
Panama[b]	3.32	1.96	32	5.23	3.25	0	42	0	47
Paraguay	0.40	0.20	19	0.51	0.27	0	7	0	18
Peru[b]	2.65	1.27	43	2.87	1.59	31	0	3	50
St. Kitts and Nevis	2.45	1.85	18	3.06	2.41	0	5	0	14
St. Lucia	4.40	2.41	30	4.28	2.41	0	0	0	31
St. Vincent and the Grenadines	3.78	2.00	16	3.78	2.00	2	0	0	16
Suriname[b]	2.59	1.82	58	3.05	2.19	41	0	0	50
Trinidad and Tobago	2.17	2.22	37	3.13	2.51	21	0	0	34
United States[b]	4.58	4.58	37	5.72	5.72	40	0	0	45
Uruguay[b]	2.92	1.85	66	4.09	3.32	54	0	0	72
Venezuela, RB	4.55	3.96	71	5.64	6.17	0	68	0	71

Source: WHO 2011b, Appendix 4.

Note: US$ = U.S. dollars. ... = data not available/ not reported.

a. Total tax includes excise taxes, import duties if applicable, VAT, and other taxes not elsewhere specified, reported as of July 31, 2010, and not reflecting tax increases/changes that might have occurred after that date.

b. The country has increased overall tobacco excises since 2008, but due to price variability the effect is not necessarily apparent in the tax indicators.

Alcohol-Control Policies

Fiscal Policies—Economic Incentives and Disincentives

One of the best-known alcohol-control policies is the anti-alcohol legislation enacted in the Soviet Union during Mikhail Gorbachev's time. The 1985 anti-alcohol legislation was a comprehensive regulation intended to curb the increasing alcohol-abuse problem in the then-USSR. The legislation not only included measures to increase the price of alcoholic beverages, but it also relied on other mechanisms such as reductions of state production and sale of alcoholic beverages, restriction in the hours of sale and number of outlets and serving places, and the shutting down of breweries (Reitan 2001).The policy was very effective in reducing alcohol consumption and, through it, lowering adult mortality rates. Between 1985 and 1987, years when the anti-alcohol policy was in effect, male life expectancy in Russia increased from 61.7 years to 64.9, and female life expectancy increased from 73 years to 74.3. From 1988 to 1994, after the legislation was eliminated, male life expectancy again decreased to 57.6 years and female life expectancy, to 71 years (Leon and others 1997). Despite the large positive impact of the policy, it was greatly opposed. Most of the opposition came from within the Soviet government agencies, particularly the ministries of Finance and of Trade and the Central State Planning Commission, because the policy drastically reduced revenues from alcohol sales from government owned distilleries and from excise taxes (Tarschys 1993).

There also are examples in LAC of effective local initiatives to impose taxes or increase the price of alcohol as means to reduce alcohol consumption. In the city of Paulina, Brazil, city officials increased alcohol prices to curb alcohol consumption. During carnival, the city experienced a high prevalence of emergency room visits and instances of public disorder, mostly related to alcohol consumption. Paulina stepped up efforts to enforce laws regarding the sale of alcoholic beverages to minors and intoxicated persons, and increased regulation of bar permits and infractions against those who drink and drive. During 2003 and 2004, selling spirits to minors around the carnival was prohibited, and the cost of beer was doubled. Evaluations of the initiative found a reduction in medical and police incidents related to alcohol of 70 percent (Monteiro 2007).

Taxes that are too high may have unintended consequences, however, possibly increasing the cross-border production, smuggling, and trade of alcohol, which, in turn, leads to higher alcohol consumption (WHO 2004b). High alcohol taxes can also increase the noncommercial production of alcohol, and this product is not regulated or monitored and can, therefore, be particularly harmful. For example, Brazil's *cachaca*, an alcoholic beverage produced in the region of Minas Gerais region, is cheap, easy to produce, and has a high alcohol content. This makes the drink ripe for illicit production and piracy around the country. Only 10 percent of alcohol distilleries in Minas Gerais are registered (Haworth and Simpson 2004).

Restricting Availability of and Access to Alcohol

Total bans of alcohol sales have only been imposed in Muslim countries and in small indigenous communities. A few governments have imposed total monopolies over the production and sale of alcoholic beverages. In Sweden, the government's chain, Systembolaget, is strongly opposed by the country's grocery store associations for monopolizing the sale of alcoholic beverages containing more than 2.25 percent of alcohol by volume (Holder 2008).

Other countries rely on other strategies to limit the availability of alcohol, such as establishing licensing systems that impose partial control over the sale of alcoholic beverages. Under a licensing system, retailers apply and pay for a license to sell alcohol from the municipality, local government, or the state. Licenses can be suspended if certain rules are broken, say, if owners are caught selling alcohol to underage persons. Most Latin American and Caribbean countries and some United States' states operate through licensing systems (WHO 2004b). Licensing systems have proven effective in reducing alcohol consumption. By providing licenses to alcohol outlets and controlling outlet density, governments can determine the minimum distances between stores or limit the number of licenses granted in certain neighborhood, especially if that neighborhood already has outlets clustered together (Campbell and others 2009; Stewart 2005). Providing licenses to outlets and privatizing the sale of alcohol can be effective in decreasing alcohol consumption because private owners, who have a stake in keeping the business going, will be more likely to respect the rules that come with their licenses (Anderson and others 2009).

Limiting Alcohol-Sale Hours—Regulation

Governments can also regulate the availability of alcohol by determining when alcohol can be sold. In 1992, in the Aboriginal town of Halls Creek, Australia, the government, responding to high rates of alcohol-related violence, restricted the hours for alcohol purchase. In just two years, the regulation, along with educational programs launched in schools and community-wide and the establishment of a treatment program in the town, led to decreased rates of alcohol consumption, crime, and domestic violence (Douglas 1998).

As of 2008, most countries in LAC, except for Bolivia, the Dominican Republic, Jamaica, Nicaragua, Panama, Paraguay, and Peru, have legislation in place that limits the hours during which alcohol can be sold (Ramirez and Ruge 2008). But, as seen with other alcohol legislation, these laws are not always enforced. There are, however, some local-level experiences where alcohol-sale restrictions were imposed and effectively enforced, leading to a significant decrease in alcohol consumption and alcohol-related violence.

The alcohol restrictions in Diadema, Brazil, are a good example. The city is located 20 km from the center of São Paulo. Homicide rates there were high, and most (65 percent) were alcohol-related. Based on research showing that most assaults on and homicides of women occurred in or near bars between 11 p.m. and 6 a.m., in July 2002 the Mayor of Diadema adopted a new municipal code requiring that all alcohol retailers in the city stop selling alcohol at 11 p.m. (for details see Pacific Institute for Research and Evaluation 2004).

To gain political support for the law, Diadema political leaders developed an information and education strategy targeted to residents. A brochure describing the need for the law and its content was distributed to Diadema households. The public education campaign included use of local news and radio announcements, as well as meetings with community leaders. Six months prior to the scheduled adoption of the new alcohol policy the municipal civil guard visited most alcohol retailers and discussed the proposed new law with owners. Three months later, they visited the owners again, asking them to sign a declaration stating that they were aware of the law and the legal consequences of violating it. In addition, an education campaign was conducted among retailers.

Before the legislation went into effect, public opinion polls confirmed the community's approval (83 percent) of the proposed alcohol policy. More recent surveys show that 98 percent of Diadema residents know about the law and 93 percent support the alcohol policy (see Pacific Institute for Research and Evaluation 2004).

Municipal civil-guard officers patrol in the evenings to enforce the law; there also are regular meetings with and reports to the officers. Penalties for violations of the law are adjudicated administratively, not criminally, and the penalties are clearly established in the law; they foresee an initial warning, followed by a fine for a second violation, a temporary license suspension for a third, and a license revocation for a fourth.

Although the data collected on the results of the Diadema experience have limitations, some evidence suggests that the law has been effective in decreasing homicides. It is estimated that Diadema's alcohol policy prevents approximately 11 murders a month in a city of 350,000 persons (Pacific Institute for Research and Evaluation 2004). The Diadema program was used as a model for 120 municipalities, and the state of Pernambuco has recently passed a law to achieve the same effect.

Most countries have some alcohol restrictions in public places such as parks or streets. Policies may range from a prohibition of possessing open alcohol containers in public places to setting and enforcing standards to keep intoxicated persons from public spaces. For example, in response to reported high rates of alcohol consumption and alcohol-related crime, the government of New Zealand imposed various liquor bans throughout the country, progressively restricting alcohol possession district-by-district and limiting alcohol use at certain hours and during specific seasons (Webb and others 2004).

Setting Age Limits for the Purchase and Consumption of Alcohol—Regulation

The minimum legal drinking age (MLDA) in the United States has changed over time. After alcohol prohibition was repealed in 1933, most states set the minimum drinking age at 21, since that was the age of majority in the United States at the time. But beginning with the Vietnam War, many states lowered their MLDAs to 18. By the mid 1970s, however, research showed a significant increase in alcohol-related traffic crashes after the minimum drinking age was lowered, and 25 states increased their age limits between 1976 and 1983; 11 others imposed license revocations (Grant 2011; Komro and others 2011).

The most significant alcohol policy changes occurred between 1984 and 1986, however, when many of states began imposing restrictions. This was due to several forces working together. First, a social media campaign was launched, focusing on the hazards of drinking. Advocacy groups, too, began flourish around this time, mostly focused on drinking and driving. One of the most active was the Mothers Against Drunk Driving (MADD) advocacy group. MADD's massive campaign garnered the support of United States House Representative John J. Howard from New Jersey, who proposed an amendment to the transportation bill, calling for an increase of the MLDA to 21 at the national level. The bill found strong opposition from some Senators. They argued that the bill represented a breach of the Constitution, in that it ran contrary to the principles of federalism, whereby states' power supersedes the federal government's. Moreover, these Senators felt that denying alcohol to 18–20-year-olds discriminated against them, since the age of majority was 18. Then-President Ronald Reagan played an important role in this debate. A proponent of "less government" in politics, the president initially opposed the bill, as it strengthened central government and took power away from the states. He began changing his mind, however, after being shown a significant body of research that demonstrated a dramatic increase in fatal accidents following the less restrictive alcohol policies (Grant 2011). More specifically, as described by Wagenaar (1993), Reagan's support for the bill came after MADD's president persuaded Nancy Reagan that the legislation would be instrumental in avoiding the "blood border" problem, whereby youths drive across state lines to obtain alcohol in adjacent states with lower MLDAs, increasing the chances of car crashes (Wagenaar 1993). After the release of a Gallup poll confirming the strong support among Americans for an increase in MLDA to 21 at the national level, the president passed the National Minimum Drinking Age Act, urging states to raise their MLDAs to 21 or forego 10 percent of their federal highway funds (Grant 2011).

Most LAC countries have age restrictions on alcohol sales, at least on premise. Generally, the minimum age for on-premise sale of alcohol is 18 years in the region, except in Paraguay, where the age limit is 20. Other than a handful of countries for which data was not available as of 2011, El Salvador is the only country in the region that has no age restrictions on alcohol sales (WHO 2011a).

Setting Limits on Blood Alcohol Concentration Levels—Indirect Regulation

In 1989, blood alcohol concentration (BAC) legislation was enacted in Maryland. The law prohibited from driving those 21 years old or younger with a BAC of

0.02 or greater, measured as grams of alcohol per 100 mL of blood, or a breath alcohol concentration of 210 liters of breath. Violations can be penalized through license suspension, revocation, and/or fines of up to US$ 500. In February 1990, a TV, radio, and print public information and education campaign was launched to coincide with the passage of the legislation. This campaign was launched based on a survey conducted among Maryland youth that examined the extent of their knowledge about the sanction. The campaign ran public service announcements (PSAs) on TV and radio, using local police officials as spokespersons; pamphlets and posters were also distributed. The campaign's central message: "You don't have to be drunk to lose your license in Maryland." An evaluation found that the law was effective and that the sanction was associated with a statistically significant, statewide reduction of accidents involving drivers under the age of 21 who had been drinking. The positive effects of the sanction were enhanced by the public information and education campaign, which emphasized the penalties for violation of the law (Blomberg 1992).

But the effectiveness of BAC legislation depends on the type of enforcement used. Most countries use breath tests at sobriety checkpoints. The "Checkpoint Tennessee" program was particularly effective in decreasing drinking and driving. In 1994, a statewide impaired-driving checkpoint program was initiated across the state. Four sets of three checkpoints were set up throughout the state every weekend, using vans with generators, lights, cones, signs, videotaping, and breath test equipment. The initiative was accompanied by a statewide billboard campaign, press releases announcing the program, and reports of arrests. PSAs aired on TV and radio were used as the primary means to advertise the campaign. Television, radio, and print media covered the initiative throughout the one-year intervention. A logo was developed for the program and incorporated in all publicity material. A television series called "Unlicensed to Kill" was produced and aired in Nashville, the state capital, on the effects of the campaign on drunk drivers. The district lieutenants coordinated activities with the police and informed the local media of the checkpoints. Results of the checkpoint activities were delivered to the project managers to track the effectiveness of the program and to increase awareness among the residents.

To gauge the campaign's effect on public awareness, a series of surveys were administered in driver's license renewal offices. Survey results found that support for the program increased from 88.8 percent of respondents in March 1994 to 91.7 percent in September of that year. During the program's year, the Tennessee Highway Patrol conducted 245 sobriety checkpoints, and a 20 percent reduction in fatal crashes was observed. Monitoring of the program indicates these levels are maintained (Lacey and others 1996).

In LAC, efforts to curb deaths and disability due to alcohol-related traffic accidents have been developed piecemeal. And, although blood alcohol concentration limits are imposed regionwide, it is not clear whether they are fully enforced (table 4.2).

Table 4.2 Alcohol-Control Policies, Countries of the Americas

	Excise tax on beer/wine/spirits	National legal minimum age for off-premise sales of alcoholic beverages (selling) (beer/wine/spirits)	National legal minimum age for on-premise sales of alcoholic beverages (serving) (beer/wine/spirits)	Restrictions for on- or off-premise sales of alcoholic beverages: time (hours and days)/location (places and density)/specific events/intoxicated persons/petrol stations	National maximum legal blood alcohol concentration (BAC) when driving a vehicle (general population/youth/professionals) in %
Argentina	n.a.	18/18/18	18/18/18	Yes/n.a./Yes/NA/NA	0.05/0.05/Zero tolerance policy
Bahamas, The	Yes/No/Yes	18/18/18	18/18/18	Yes/Yes/Yes/No/No	0.08/0.08/0.08
Barbados	Yes/Yes/Yes	18/18/18	18/18/18	No/No/No/No/No	No/No/No
Belize	NA		18/18/18	n.a	n.a
Bolivia	Yes/Yes/Yes	18/18/18	18/18/18	No and Yes/Yes and No/Yes/No/No	No/No/No
Brazil	Yes/Yes/Yes	18/18/18	18/18/18	No and Yes/Yes and No/Yes/No/No	0.02/0.02/0.02
Canada	Yes/Yes/Yes	Subnational	Subnational	No/No/No/No/No	0.08/0.04/0.08
Chile	Yes/Yes/Yes	18/18/18	18/18/18	NA	0.05/0.05/0.05
Colombia	Yes/Yes/Yes	18/18/18	18/18/18	No/Yes and No/Yes/No/No	0.04/0.04/0.04
Costa Rica	Yes/Yes/Yes	18/18/18	18/18/18	Yes/Yes/Yes/Yes/Yes	0.05/0.05/0.05
Cuba	Yes/Yes/Yes	18/18/18	18/18/18	Yes/Yes/Yes/Yes/Yes	No/No/No
Dominica	Yes/Yes/Yes	18/18/18	18/18/18	Yes/Yes/Yes/Yes/Yes	n.a
Dominican Republic	Yes/Yes/Yes	18/18/18	18/18/18	Yes/No/No/Yes/Yes	No/No/No
Ecuador	Yes/Yes/Yes	18/18/18	18/18/18	No/Yes/Yes/No/No	0.08/0.08/0.08
El Salvador	Yes/Yes/Yes	n.a.	n.a.	Yes/n.a./n.a./n.a./Yes	0.05/0.05/0.05
Guatemala	No/No/No	18/18/18	18/18/18	Yes/No/Yes/No/No	No/No/No
Guyana	Yes/Yes/Yes	16/16/18	18/18/18	Yes and No/Yes/Yes/Yes/No	0.08/0.08/0.08
Honduras	Yes/Yes/Yes	18/18/18	18/18/18	Yes/Yes and No/No/Yes/Yes	0.07/0.07/0.07
Jamaica	Yes/Yes/Yes	No/No/No	18/18/18	No/No/No/No/No	0.08/0.08/0.08
Mexico	Yes/Yes/Yes	18/18/18	18/18/18	Yes/Yes and No/Yes/n.a./Yes	0.08/0.08/0.08
Nicaragua	Yes/Yes/Yes	No/No/No	18/18/18	Yes and No/No/No/Yes/No	0.05/0.05/0.05
Panama	Yes/Yes/Yes	18/18/18	18/18/18	Yes/Yes/No/No/No	0.08/0.08/0.08
Paraguay	n.a.	20/20/20	20/20/20	No/No/Yes/No/No	0.05/0.05/0.05
Peru	n.a.	18/18/18	18/18/18	Yes/Yes/Yes/n.a./n.a.	0.05/0.05/0.05
St. Vincent and the Grenadines	Yes/Yes/Yes	18/18/18	18/18/18	Yes/Yes and No/Yes/Yes/Yes	0.05/0.05/0.05
Suriname	Yes/Yes/Yes	18/18/18	18/18/18	No/No/No/No/No	0.05/0.05/0.05

table continues next page

Table 4.2 Alcohol-Control Policies, Countries of the Americas (continued)

	Excise tax on beer/wine/ spirits	National legal minimum age for off-premise sales of alcoholic beverages (selling) (beer/ wine/spirits)	National legal minimum age for on-premise sales of alcoholic beverages (serving) (beer/ wine/spirits)	Restrictions for on- or off-premise sales of alcoholic beverages: time (hours and days)/location (places and density)/ specific events/ intoxicated persons/ petrol stations	National maximum legal blood alcohol concentration (BAC) when driving a vehicle (general population/youth/ professionals) in %
Trinidad and Tobago	Yes/Yes/Yes	18/18/18	18/18/18	Yes/Yes/Yes/Yes/No	0.08/0.08/0.08
United States	No/No/Yes	21/21/21	21/21/21	No/No/No/No/No	0.08/0.02/0.04
Uruguay	Yes/Yes/Yes	18/18/18	18/18/18	Yes and No/Yes and No/Yes/Yes/No	0.08/0.08/0.08
Venezuela, RB	Yes/Yes/Yes	18/18/18	18/18/18	Yes/Yes and No/Yes/ No/No	0.08/0.08/0.08

Source: WHO 2011c.
Note: n.a. = not applicable; NA = not available.

Notes

1. WHO considers an intervention to be a "best buy" if it is "cost effective, is low cost, and can be implemented in low resource settings" (WHO 2011c).
2. To view New York City Board of Health's response to the suit brought against it by the New York State Restaurant Association (NYSRA), view: http://www.cspinet.org /new/pdf/nyc_frieden.pdf.
3. New York City Board of Health. Declaration of Thomas R. Frieden. United States District Court Southern District of New York. July 5, 2007. http://www.cspinet.org /new/pdf/nyc_frieden.pdf.
4. To view the official notice of adoption of the resolution specifying these changes to the Health Code issued by New York City's Board of Health, visit http://www.nyc .gov/html/doh/downloads/pdf/public/notice-adoption-hc-art81-50-0108.pdf.
5. To view the MERCOSUR technical regulation on nutrition labeling, please visit http://www.temasactuales.com/assets/pdf/gratis/GMCRes_044_03.pdf.
6. For additional details on the Children's Food and Beverage Advertising Initiative, please visit this Better Business Bureau website. http://centralohio.bbb.org/storage/0 /Shared%20Documents/Aug_Product_List_final1.pdf.
7. Additional detail about this study is found at http://www.naos.aesan.msps.es/naos /ficheros/estrategia/IV_Convencion/Miranda_Watson.pdf.
8. A 2011 *New York Times* article on this subject can be found at http://www.nytimes .com/2011/07/24/opinion/sunday/24bittman.html?_r=3.
9. For a piece discussing the pluses and minuses of taxing bad food and subsidizing good food that ran in in *The Economist* in 2011, visit http://www.economist.com /node/21524522.
10. For a report on Denmark's repeal of the tax on the fat content of food that appeared in 2012 in *The Copenhagen Post* visit http://cphpost.dk/news/politics /fat-tax-repealed.
11. See: http://www.thecommunityguide.org/pa/campaigns/index.html.

12. For a description of the traffic calming strategy put in place in New York city, visit the city's Department of Transportation site: http://www.nyc.gov/html/dot/html/about /stratplan.shtml.

13. To view a copy of the New York City Office of the Mayor response to an article that appeared in *New York* magazine regarding bike lanes, visit http://www.nyc.gov/html /om/pdf/bike_lanes_memo.pdf.

14. For additional information on WHO's "Healthy Cities" project, visit http://www.euro .who.int/en/what-we-do/health-topics/environment-and-health/urban-health /activities/healthy-cities.

15. For additional information on WHO's healthy municipalities and communities in the Americas, visit http://www.who.int/healthy_settings/types/hmc/en/.

16. To read the paper "Illegal Pathways to Illegal Profits: The Big Cigarette Companies and International Smuggling," Issued by the National Center for Tobacco-free Kids as part of its Campaign for Tobacco-free Kids, visit http://www.tobaccofreecenter.org/files /pdfs/en/Illegal_profits_to_illicit_profit_en.pdf.

17. For a report on the Best Practice: Tobacco Control Program, updated July 12, 2011, issued by the NYC Global Partners' Innovation Exchange website, visit http://www .nyc.gov/html/unccp/gprb/downloads/pdf/NYC_Health_TobaccoControl.pdf.

18. For additional information, visit the website of New York State's Department of Health http://www.health.ny.gov/regulations/public_health_law/section/1399/.

19. For additional information for business owners and employers on New York City's 2002 Smoke-Free Air Act of 2002, visit http://www.nyc.gov/html/doh/downloads /pdf/smoke/tc5.pdf. Updated December 2006.

20. To read the press release on Quinninnipiac University's poll on New York City's ban on smoking in bars, "Ban The Butts In Bars, New York City Voters Tell Quinnipiac University Poll; Let's Have The Olympics, But Not If We Have To Pay," published on November 22, 2002, visit http://www.quinnipiac.edu/institutes-centers /polling-institute/new-york-city/release-detail?ReleaseID=463.

21. The three instruments were a 1993–2001 annual New York State Behavioral Risk Factor survey, a telephone-survey surveillance system, and a community health survey to determine the number of smokers and the intensity of smoking, classifying smokers as "heavy" and "light" smokers.

22. For an analysis of this opposition, from the viewpoint of the American Nonsmokers' Rights Association, visit http://www.no-smoke.org/pdf/esrta.pdf.

Bibliography

Adamo, K. B. 2007. *Community-based Interventions Targeting Healthy Weights among School-aged Children*. Report written on behalf of the Champlain Healthy School-aged Children Committee.

Anderson, P., D. Chiholm, and D. C. Fuhr. 2009. "Effectiveness and Cost-effectiveness of Policies and Programmes to Reduce the Harm Caused by Alcohol." *Lancet* 373: 2234–46.

Armstrong, K. 2008. *Menu Labeling Legislation: Options for Requiring the Disclosure of Nutritional Information in Restaurants*. St. Paul, MN: Tobacco Law Center.

Asaria, P., D. Chishol, C. Mathers, M. Ezzati, and R. Beaglehole. 2007. "Chronic Disease Prevention: Health Effects and Financial Costs of Strategies to Reduce Salt Intake and Control Tobacco Use." *Lancet* 370: 2044–53.

Bennett, G. G., L. H. McNeill, K. Y. Wolin, D. T. Duncan, E. Puleo, and K. M. Emmons. 2007. "Safe to Walk? Neighborhood Safety and Physical Activity among Public Housing Residents." *PLoS Med* 4 (10): e306.

Blomberg, R. D. 1992. *Lower BAC Limits for Youth. Evaluation of the Maryland .02 Law.* Washington, DC: National Highway Traffic Safety Administration.

Brownell, K. D., and T. R. Frieden. 2009. "Ounces of Prevention—The Public Policy Case for Taxes on Sugared Beverages." *New England Journal of Medicine* 360: 1805–1808.

Caballero, B., T. Clay, S. M. Davis, B. Ethelbbah, B. H. Rock, T. Lohman, J. Norman, M. Story, E. J. Stone, L. Stephenson, J. Stevens, and Pathways Study Research Group. 2003. "Pathways: A School-based, Randomized Controlled Trial for the Prevention of Obesity in American Indian Schoolchildren." *American Journal of Clinical Nutrition* 78: 1030–38.

Callinan, J. E., A. Clarke, K. Doherty, and C. Kelleher. 2010. "Legislative Smoking Bans for Reducing Secondhand Smoke Exposure, Smoking Prevalence and Tobacco Consumption." *Cochrane Collaboration* The Cochrane Library (6).

Campbell, C. A. et al. 2009. "The Effectiveness of Limiting Alcohol Outlet Density as a Means of Reducing Excessive Alcohol Consumption and Alcohol Related Harm: Guide to Community Preventive Services." *American Journal of Preventive Medicine* 37 (6).

Chaban, M. 2011. "Breaking: City Prevails in Prospect Park West Bike Lane Challenge." *New York Observer.* August.

Chaloupka, F. J. 1998. "How Effective are Taxes in Reducing Tobacco Consumption?" Prepared for the International Conference on the Social Cost of Smoking. Lausanne, Switzerland, August 21–22, 1998.

Chaloupka, F. J., K. M. Cummings, C. P. Morley, and J. K. Horan. 2002. "Tax, Price, and Cigarette Smoking: Evidence from the Tobacco Documents and Implications for Tobacco Company Marketing Strategies." *Tobacco Control* 11 (Suppl I): 62–72.

Chaloupka, F. J., R. Hu, K. E. Warner, R. van der Merwe, and A. Yurekli. 1999. "The Taxation of Tobacco Products." In *Curbing the Epidemic. Governments and the Economics of Tobacco Control,* edited by Prabhat Jha and Frank J. Chaloupka. Washington, DC: World Bank.

Cohen, D. L., and R. R. Townsend. 2012. "The Salt Controversy and Hypertension." *Journal of Clinical Hypertension* 14 (4).

Coitniho, D., C. A. Monteiro, and B. M. Popkn. 2002. "What Brazil Is Doing to Promote Healthy Diets and Active Lifestyles." *Public Health Nutrition* 5(1A), 263–267.

Cooper, M. 2002. "Mayor Signs Law to Ban Smoking Soon at Most Bars." *The New York Times.* December 31, 2002.

Da Costa, L. M., and S. Goldfarb. 2003. "Government Leadership in Tobacco Control: Brazil's Experience." In *Tobacco Control Policies: Strategies Successes & Setbacks,* edited by J. de Beyer and L. W. Bringden. Washington, DC: World Bank.

Davis, K., M. Farrelly, Q. Li, and A. Hyland. 2006. *Cigarette Purchasing Patterns among New York Smokers: Implications for Health, Price, and Revenue.* Department of State, New York. March.

Douglas, M. 1998. "Restriction of the Hours of Sale of Alcohol in a Small Community: A Beneficial Impact." *Australian New Zealand Journal of Public Health* 6: 714–19.

Elliott, A. 2004. "Bars and Restaurants Thrive Amid Smoking Bans, Study Says." *New York Times*, March 29.

Fletcher, J., D. Frisvold, and N. Tefft. 2010. "The Effect of Soft Drink Taxes on Child and Adolescent Consumption and Weight Outcomes." *Journal of Public Economics* 94: 967–74.

French, S. A., and G. Stables. 2003. "Environmental Interventions to Promote Vegetable and Fruit Consumption among Youth in School Settings." *Preventive Medicine* 37 (6, pt. 1): 593–610.

Frieden, T. R., and M. R. Bloomberg. 2007. "How to Prevent 100 Million Deaths from Tobacco." *Lancet* 369: 1758–61.

Frieden, T. R., F. Mostashari, B. D. Kerker, N. Miller, A. Hajat, and M. Frankel. 2005. "Adult Tobacco Use Levels after Intensive Tobacco Control Measures: New York City, 2002–2003." *American Journal of Public Health* 95 (6): 1016–23.

FTC (Federal Trade Commission). 2008. *Marketing Food to Children and Adolescents.* Washington, DC: FTC. http://www.ftc.gov/os/2008/07/P064504foodmktingreport .pdf.

Gomez-Feliciano, L., L. L. McCreary, R. Sadowsky, S. Peterson, A. Hernandez, B. J. McElmurry, and C. G. Park. 2009. "Active Living Logan Square." *American Journal of Preventive Medicine* 37.

Goodman, J. D. 2010. "Expansion of Bike Lanes in City Brings Backlash." *New York Times*, November 22.

Gostin, L. O. 2000. "Legal and Public Policy: Interventions to Advance the Population's Health." In *Promoting Health: Intervention Strategies from Social and Behavioral Research*, edited by B. D. Smedley and S. L. Syme, 390–416. Washington, DC: National Academies Press.

Grant, D. 2011. "Politics, Policy Analysis, and the Passage of the National Minimum Drinking Age Act of 1984." Working Paper 1103, Department of Economics and International Business, Sam Houston State University, Huntsville, TX.

Griffith, G., C. Welch, A. Cardone, A. Valdemoro, and C. Jo. 2008. "The Global Momentum for Smokefree Public Places: Best Practice in Current and Forthcoming Smokefree Policies." *Salud Pública Méx* 50 (Suppl 3): 299–308.

Guthrie, J. F., J. J. Fox, L. E. Cleveland, and S. Welsh. 1995. "Who Uses Nutrition Labeling, and What Effects Does Label Use Have on Diet Quality?" *Journal of Nutrition Education* 27:163–172.

Harris, F., A. MacKintosh, S. Anderson, G. Hastings, R. Borland, G. Fong, D. Hammond, K. Cummings for the ITC Collaboration. 2006. "Effects of the 2003 advertising/promotion ban in the United Kingdom on awareness of tobacco marketing: findings from the International Tobacco Control (ITC) Four Country Survey." *Tobacco Control* 2006, Vol. 16.

Harris, J. E. 1987. "The 1983 Increase in the Federal Cigarette Excise Tax." In *Tax Policy and the Economy*, edited by L. H. Summers. Cambridge, MA: MIT Press.

Hastings, G., and G. Carins. 2010. "Food and Beverage Marketing to Children." In *Preventing Childhood Obesity: Evidence Policy and Practice.* Oxford: Wiley-Blackwell.

Hastings, G., M. Stead, and L. McDermott. 2003. *Review of Research on the Effects of Food Promotion to Children.* Report prepared for the Food Standards Agency. Glasgow, Scotland: University of Strathclyde.

Hawkes, C. 2004. *Nutrition Labels and Health Claims: The Global Regulatory Environment.* Geneva: World Health Organization.

Hawkes, C. 2007. *Marketing Food to Children: Changes in the Global Regulatory Environment 2004–2006.* Geneva: WHO.

Haworth, A., and R. Simpson. 2004. *Moonshine Markets: Issues in Unrecorded Alcohol Beverage Production and Consumption.* Policies Series on Alcohol in Society. Washington, DC: International Center for Alcohol.

Henley, N., and S. Raffin. 2010. Social Marketing to Prevent Childhood Obesity. In *Preventing Childhood Obesity: Evidence Policy and Practice,* edited by E. Waters, B. Swinburn, J. Seidell, and R. Uauy. Oxford: Wiley-Blackwell.

HHS (United States, Department of Health and Human Services). 2006. *The Health Consequences of Involuntary Exposure to Tobacco Smoke: A Report of the Surgeon General.* Rockville, MD: Public Service Office of the Surgeon General.

Hoehner, C. M., J. Soares, D. P. Perez, I. C. Ribeiro, C. E. Joshu, M. Pratt, B. D. Legetic, D. C. Malta, V. R. Matsudo, L. R. Ramos, et al. 2008. "Physical Activity Interventions in Latin America: A Systematic Review." *American Journal of Preventive Medicine* 34: 224–33.

Holder, H., ed. 2008. *Alcohol Monopoly and Public Health: Potential Effects of Privatization of the Swedish Alcohol Retail Monopoly.* Stockholm: Swedish National Institute of Public Health.

Huhman, M., L. D. Potter, F. L. Wong, S. W. Banspach, J. C. Duke, and C. D. Heitzler. 2005. "Effects of Mass Media Campaign to Increase Physical Activity among Children: Year-1 Results of the VERB Campaign." *Pediatrics* 116: e277.

Institute of Medicine (IOM). 2010. *Strategies to Reduce Sodium Intake in the United States.* Washington, DC: IOM.

Jacobson, M. F., and K. D. Brownell. 2000. "Small Taxes on Soft Drinks and Snack Foods to Promote Health." *American Journal of Public Health* 90 (6).

Jha, P., and F. J. Chaloupka. 1999. *Curbind the Epidemic: Governments and the Economics of Tobacco Control.* Washington, DC: World Bank.

Joossens, L., and M. Raw. 2000. "How Can Cigarette Smuggling Be Reduced?" *BMJ* 321 (7266).

Katan, M. 2009. "Weight-loss Diets for the Prevention and Treatment of Obesity." *New England Journal of Medicine* 360: 923–25.

Keeler, T. E., T. W. Hu, P. G. Barnett, W. G. Manning, and H. Y. Sung. 1996. "Do Cigarette Producers Price-Discriminate by State? An Empirical Analysis of Local Cigarette Pricing and Taxation." *Journal of Health Economics* 15: 499–512.

Komro, K. A., and T. L. Toomey. 2011. "Strategies to Prevent Underage Drinking" DUI Assessment Bellevue 23:20.

Kunkel, D., C. Mckinley, and P. Wright. 2009. "The Impact of Industry Self-Regulation on the Nutritional Quality of Foods Advertised on Television to Children." Paper Commissioned by Children Now.

Lacey, J., R. Jones, and J. Fell. 1996. "The Effectiveness of the Checkpoint Tennessee Program." In *Proceedings of the Association for the Advancement of Automotive Medicine, 40th, Vancouver,* 275–82. Des Plaines, IL: Association for the Advancement of Automototive Medicine.

Leon, D., L. Chenet, V. M. Shkolnikov, S. Zakharov, J. Shapiro, G. Rakhmanova, S. Vassin, and M. McKee. 1997. "Huge Variation in Russian Mortality Rates 1984–94: Artefact, Alcohol, or What?" *Lancet* 350: 384–88.

Lin, B. H., E. Frazao, and J. Guthrie. 1999. "Away-From-Home Foods Increasingly Important to Quality of American Diet." *Agriculture Information Bulletin No. AIB749,* January.

Mathios, A. 1998. "The Importance of Nutrition Labeling and Health Claim Regulation on Product Choice: An Analysis of the Cooking Oils Market." *Agricultural and Resource Economic Review* 27 (2).

———. 2000. "The Impact of Mandatory Disclosure Laws on Product Choices: An Analysis of the Salad Dressing Market." *Journal of Law and Economics* 43 (2).

Matsudo, S. M., V. R. Matsudo, T. L. Araujo, D. R. Andrade, E. L. Andrade, L. C. de Oliveira, G. F. Braggion. 2003. "The Agita São Paulo Program as a Model for Using Physical Activity to Promote Health." *Pan American Journal of Public Health* 14 (4): 265–72.

Matsudo, V., S. Matsudo, D. Andrade, T. Araujo, E. Andrade, L. C. de Oliveira, and G. Braggion. 2002. "Promotion of Physical Activity in a Developing Country: The Agita São Paulo Experience." *Public Health Nutrition* 5 (1A): 253–61.

McKenzie, T. L., P. R. Nader, P. K. Strikmiller, M. Yang, E. J. Stone, C. L. Perry, W. C. Taylor, J. N. Epping, H. A. Feldman, R. V. Luepker, and S. H. Kelder. 1996. "School Physical Education: Effect of the Child and Adolescent Trial for Cardiovascular Health." *Preventive Medicine* 25 (4): 423–31.

Meiro-Lorenzo, M., T. L. Villafana, and M. N. Harrit. 2011. "Effective Responses to Noncommunicable Diseases: Embracing Action beyond the Health Sector." HNP Discussion Paper 65132, World Bank, Washington, DC.

Mello, M. M. 2009. "New York City's War on Fat." *New England Journal of Medicine* 360 (19).

Monteiro, M. 2007. *Alcohol and Public Health in the Americas. A Case for Action.* Washington, DC: PAHO.

Müller, F., and L. Wehbe. 2008. "Smoking and Smoking Cessation in Latin America: A Review of the Current Situation and Available Treatments." *International Journal of Chronic Pulmonary Disease* 3 (2): 285–93.

Nader, P. R., E. J. Stone, L. A. Lytle, C. L. Perry, S. K. Osganian, S. Kelder, L. S. Webber, J. P. Elder, D. Montgomery, H. A. Feldman, M. Wu, C. Johnson, G. S. Parcel, and R. V. Luepker. 1999. "Three-Year Maintenance of Improved diet and Physical Activity. The CATCH Cohort." *Archives of Pediatrics & Adolescent Medicine* 153: 695–704.

Navas-Acien, A., and R. Valdes-Salgado. 2005. "Niveles de Nicotina en el ambiente de Lugares Publicos y de Trabajo del Distrito Federal." Primer Informe Sobre el Combate al Tabaquismo. Institute for Global Tobacco Control, The Johns Hopkins Bloomberg School of Public Health and the Instituto Nacional de Salud Publica.

OECD (Organisation for Economic Co-operation and Development). 2011. *Health at a Glance 2011: OECD Indicators.* Paris: OECD.

Ofcom. 2007. Ofcom Final Statement on the Television Advertising of Food and Drink Products to Children. London: Office of Communications. Available at: http://stakeholders.ofcom.org.uk/binaries/consultations/foodads_new/statement/statement.pdf.

Oommen, V. G., and P. J. Anderson. "2008 Policies on Restrictions of Food Advertising During Children's Television Viewing Times: An International Perspective." 2008. Proceedings Australian College of Health Service Executives 2008 Conference, Going for Gold in Health Motivation, Effort, Performance. Gold Coast, Australia.

Pacific Institute for Research and Evaluation. 2004. "Prevention of Murders in Diadema, Brazil. The Influence of New Alcohol Policies." http://resources.prev.org/resource_pub_brazil.pdf.

PAHO (Pan American Health Organization). 2008. *Healthy Oils and the Elimination of Industrially Produced Trans Fatty Acids in the Americas.* Washington, DC: PAHO.

———. 2011. *Recommendations from a Pan American Health Organization Expert Consultation on the Marketing of Food and Nonalcoholic Beverages to Children in the Americas.* Washington, DC: PAHO.

Puska, P., P. Pirjo, and U. Ulla. 2002. "Influencing Public Nutrition for Noncommunicable Disease Prevention: From Community Intervention to National Programme—Experiences from Finland." *Public Health Nutrition* 5 (1A): 245–51.

Puska, P., E. Vartiainen, T. Laatikaninen, P. Jousilahti, and M. Paavola, eds. 2009. *The North Karelia Project: From North Karelia to National Action.* Helsinki: Helsinki University Printing House.

Ramirez, A., and C. Ruge. 2008. "Políticas para la reducción de la violencia relacionada con el alcohol en los jóvenes. Un enfoque ambiental." Washington, DC: PAHO.

Reger, B., M. G. Wootan, and S. Booth-Butterfields. 2002. "Using Mass Media to Promote Healthy Eating: A Community-based Demonstration Project." *Preventive Medicine* 35: 285–92.

Reis, R. S., P. C. Hallal, D. C. Parra, I. C. Ribeiro, R. C. Brownson, M. Pratt, C. M. Hoehner, and L. Ramos. 2010. "Promoting Physical Activity through Community-Wide Policies and Planning: Findings from Curitiba, Brazil." *Journal of Physical Activity and Health* 7 (Suppl 2): S137–45.

Reitan, T. 2001. "The Operation Failed but the Patient Survived: Varying Assessments of the Soviet Union's Last Anti-alcohol Campaign." *Communist and Post-communist Studies* 34 (2): 241–60.

Ribeiro, I. C., A. Torres, D. Parra, R. Reis, C. Hoehner, T. Schmid, M. Pratt, L. R. Ramos, E. J. Simões, and R. C. Brownson. 2010. "Using Logic Models as Iterative Tools for Planning and Evaluating Activity Promotion Programs in Curitiba, Brazil." *Journal of Physical Activity and Health* 7 (Suppl. 2): S155-S162.

Ridgewood Economic Associates. 2004. "The Economic Impact of the New York State Smoking Ban on New York's Bar." Prepared for the New York Nightlife Association and the Empire State Restaurant and Tavern Association, May 12.

Robertson, A., T. Lobstein, and C. Knai. 2007. "Obesity and Socio-economic Groups in Europe: Evidence Review and Implications for Action." Funded by the European Commission, November.

Saloojee, Y. and E. Dagli. 2000. "Tobacco Industry Tactics for Resisting Public Policy on Health." *Bulletin of the World Health Organization* 78 (7).

Sassi, F. and J. Hurst. 2008. "The Prevention of Lifestyle-Related Chronic Diseases: An Economic Framework." Organisation for Economic Co-operation and Development Health Working Paper 32. OECD, Paris.

Sebrié, E. M., V. Schoj, and S. A. Glants. 2008. "Smoke Free Environments in Latin America: On the Road to Real Change?" *Prevention and Control* 3 (1).

Shaer, M. 2011. "Not Quite Copenhagen. Is New York Too New York for Bike Lanes?" *New York Magazine*, March 20.

Sharma, L. L., S. P. Teret, and K. D. Brownell. 2010. "The Food Industry and Self-Regulation: Standards to Promote Success and to Avoid Public Health Failures." *American Journal of Public Health* 100 (2).

Simoes, E. J., P. Hallal, M. Pratt, L. Ramos, M. Munk, W. Damascena, D. P. Perez, C. M. Hoehner, D. Malta, and R. C. Brownson. 2009. "Effects of a Community-Based, Professionally Supervised Intervention on Physical Activity Levels Among Residents of Recife, Brazil. *American Journal of Public Health* 99 (1).

Sorensen, G., A. Stoddard, K. Peterson, et al. 1999. "Increasing Fruit and Vegetable Consumption through Workplaces and Families in the Treatwell 5-A-Day Study." *American Journal of Public Health* 89 (1): 54–60.

Stender, S., J. Dyerberg, and A. Astrup. 2006. "Consumer Protection through a Legislative Ban on Industrially Produced Trans Fatty Acids in Foods in Denmark." *Scandinavian Journal of Food and Nutrition* 50 (4): 155–60.

Stewart, K. 2005. *How Alcohol Outlets Affect Neighborhood Violence.* Stamford, CT: Prevention Research Center, Pacific Institute for Research and Evaluation.

Sturm, R., L. Powell, J. Chriqui, and F. Chaloupka. 2010. "Soda Taxes, Soft Drink Consumption, and Children's Body Mass Index." *Health Affairs* 29 (5): 1052–58.

Szilagyi, T. and S. Chapman. 2003. "Tobacco Industry Efforts to Keep Cigarettes Affordable: A Case Study from Hungary." *Central European Journal of Public Health* 11 (4): 223–28.

Tarschys, D. 1993. "The Success of a Failure: Gorbachev's Alcohol Policy, 1985–88" *Europe-Asia Studies* 45 (1): 7–25.

Taubes, G. 1998. "The (Political) Science of Salt." *Science* 281: 898–901, 903–07.

Task Force on Community Preventive Services. 2001. "Recommendations Regarding Interventions to Reduce Tobacco Use and Exposure to Environmental Tobacco Smoke." *American Journal of Preventive Medicine* 20 (2S): 10–15.

Van Camp, D. J., N. H. Hooker, and D. M. Souza-Monteiro. 2010. "Adoption of Voluntary Front of Package Nutrition Schemes in UK Food Innovations." *British Food Journal* 112 (6): 580–91.

Van Schagen, I. 2003. "Traffic-Calming Schemes." Institute for Road Safety Research. Leidschendam, the Netherlands: SWOV. http://www.swov.nl/rapport/R-2003-22.pdf.

Wagenaar, A. C. 1993. "Research Affects Public Policy: The Case of the Legal Drinking Age in the United States." *Addiction* 88 (Suppl): 75S–81.

Webb, M., P. Marriott-Lloyd, and M. Grenfell. 2004. *Banning the Bottle: Liquor Bans in New Zealand.* http://www.alcohol.org.nz/sites/default/files/useruploads/ActsImagePdf/banningbottleliquorbans.pdf.

Willett, W. C., J. P. Koplan, R. Nugent, C. Dusenbury, P. Puska, and T. A. Gaziano. 2006. "Prevention of Chronic Diseases by Means of Diets and Lifestyle Changes". In *Disease Control Priorities in Developing Countries*, edited by D. T. Jamison, J. G. Breman, A. R. Measham, G. Alleyne, M. Claeson, D. B. Evans, P. Jha, A. Mills, and P. Musgrove. Washington, DC: World Bank.

Wong, F. 2004. "VERB—A Social Marketing Campaign to Increase Physical Activity among Youth." *Preventing Chronic Disease* 1 (2).

World Bank. 2003. "The Economics of Tobacco Use & Tobacco Control in the Developing World." Background Paper for the High Level Round Table on Tobacco Control and

Development Policy. Organized by the European Commission in collaboration with the World Health Organization and the World Bank, Brussels, February.

WHO (World Health Organization). 2004a. *Building Blocks for Tobacco Control: A Handbook*. Geneva: WHO.

———. 2004b. *Global Status Report: Alcohol Policy*. Geneva: WHO.

———. 2006. "Reducing Salt Intake in Populations: Report of a WHO Forum and Technical Meeting," Paris, France, October 5–7.

———. 2009. *WHO Report on the Global Tobacco Epidemic 2009*. Geneva: WHO.

———. 2011a. *Global Status Report on Noncommunicable Diseases 2010*. Geneva: WHO.

———. 2011b. *WHO Report on the Global Tobacco Epidemic 2011*. Geneva: WHO.

———. 2011c. *Global Status Report on Alcohol and Health*. Geneva: WHO.

Zatonski, W. 2003. "Democracy and Health: Tobacco Control in Poland." In *Tobacco Control Policy. Strategies, Successes, and Setbacks*, edited by J. de Beyer and L. W. Brigden. Washington, DC: World Bank.

CHAPTER 5

Multisectoral Interventions to Promote Healthy Living in Latin America and the Caribbean

María Eugenia Barbieri for the National Ministry of Health of Argentina; Olga L. Sarmiento, Adriana Díaz del Castillo, and Ethel Segura Durán; Evelyne Rodriguez; Amanda Sica, Franco González Mora, Winston Abascal and Ana Lorenzo for the Ministry of Public Health of Uruguay

This chapter documents governance issues in the design and implementation of some successful or promising population-wide interventions intended to prevent health risk factors in Latin America and the Caribbean (LAC). Specifically, these case studies examine which stakeholders participated directly or indirectly in the decision-making process; what positions they held; which incentives they faced; which strategies they pursued; how existing institutional arrangements affected the decision-making process; what lessons can be drawn from these processes; and what the successes and setbacks were.

The case studies were selected from major population-wide, multisectoral programs in the region. The first four were considered to be some of the most representative and promising examples of policies and programs that promote healthy lifestyles and reduce risk factors for noncommunicable diseases (NCDs). Each case study was included because it examined a program or policy targeting a distinct risk factor. In addition, to ensure as wide as possible a representation, the case studies were drawn from different countries. There was no case study commissioned on alcohol control. Although there are some good examples of alcohol-control policies in LAC, they are limited in their geographical focus or on the array of interventions or sectors involved.

The first four case studies deal with the following: Argentina's policies to reduce the consumption of trans fats and sodium; Bogotá's (Colombia) built environment that promotes physical activity; Mexico's National Agreements on Food Health (Strategy against Overweight and Obesity); and Uruguay's antitobacco policies. Because Argentina's and Mexico' policies are relatively new, there is no available information on their effectiveness. They have been included here because they are some of the region's most comprehensive policies in the fight against NCDs and because similar policies, or some elements of these policies, have proven to be highly cost-effective elsewhere. Uruguay's and Bogotá's policies are older, and their effectiveness has been better documented. A fifth case—Argentina's tobacco-control policies—was added to this analysis. Despite the fact that Argentina has not yet signed the Framework Convention on Tobacco Control (FCTC), the country has advanced in tobacco control, and its experience can provide important lessons for the region.

Argentina: Amending the Food Code to Regulate Trans Fats and Agreements between the Government and the Food Industry to Reduce Sodium in Processed Foods

María Eugenia Barbieri for the National Ministry of Health of Argentina

In an effort to reduce trans fats and sodium intake in diets, the Ministry of Health (MOH) initiated a dialogue with multiple actors—government agencies, food producers and distributors, universities and scientific societies, and the public. This dialogue led to agreements to amend the Food Code to regulate trans fats and meet targets for the reduction of sodium in processed foods. Of the two, the elimination of trans fats was the least problematic. It was technically feasible; experience outside Argentina, as well as research and development, had provided important models; and substitute products were available. In fact, 70 percent of the country's food manufacturing companies were already restructuring their production processes when the dialogue started. Lowering salt intake was more difficult, however—sodium is a key ingredient in processed foods and baked goods, there is less awareness about its negative health effects, and fewer alternatives are available. The governance of these policy-making processes was complex, given the participation of a wide array of stakeholders who faced different incentives. Table 5.1 presents the key stakeholders that participated in both processes, their positions, the strategies they used, their interactions, and the lessons learned.

    The MOH played a leading role in the effort to reduce trans fats and sodium in processed foods. Through its initiative, a National Commission to Eliminate Trans Fats and Reduce Salt was created. The Commission encompasses public and business organizations, scientific associations, and civil society groups, including the MOH; the Ministry of Agriculture, Livestock, and Fisheries (MoALF); the Ministry of Social Development; the Ministry of Science and Technology; the Ministry of Economy; the National Institute of Industrial Technology (INTI); the National Food Institute (INAL); the Argentine Federation of Baked Products Industry (FAIPA); the Coordinator of Food Products Industries (COPAL); the Argentine Fats and Oils Association (ASAGA); various business groups; some workers' cooperatives; universities and scientific societies;

Table 5.1 Governance of Multisectoral Activities to Promote a Healthy Diet: Argentina's Food Code Reform to Regulate Trans Fats in Processed Foods and Agreements with the Food Industry to Reduce Sodium

Key stakeholders and their positions	Strategies	Interaction among stakeholders	Lessons learned
Ministry of Health (MOH): • To protect the population against harmful effect of trans fats and excessive sodium intake. *National Food Institute (INAL); is part of the National Administration of Drugs, Food, and Medical Technology and depends on the Ministry of Health:* • Being part of the Ministry of Health, it held the same position. *National Institute of Industrial Technology (INTI):* Although it shared the Ministry of Health's position, it disagreed with it on some points: • Before participating in negotiations, it called for an institutional agreement between INTI and the Ministry of Health to clarify its responsibilities in the process. • Advocated for stricter sodium measures. • Called for greater control of the use made by the companies of these measures. • Called for greater discussion on how best to monitor the agreements. • Wanted a comprehensive education campaign on the harmful effects of sodium and trans fats to be developed with the Ministry of Education. • Called for greater efforts to contact small and medium enterprises and to disseminate information • Advocated for continuity of the policies.	*MOH* • Coordinated the process. • Linked actions with other public agencies. • Negotiated efforts with the private sector. • Disseminated information to consumers. *INAL* • Contributed regulatory, technological, and monitoring knowledge. • Presented the issue at provincial and municipal levels through the networks in which it participates. • Technical staff participated in negotiations with the companies. • Helped to design a manual about retrofitting small and medium enterprises' production processes to eliminate trans fats. *INTI* • Its technical staff participated in negotiations with the companies. • Provided training to the bakery sector on salt reduction. • Presented and disseminated evidence on the viability of replacing trans fats in food. • Helped to design a manual about retrofitting small and medium enterprises' production processes to eliminate trans fats. *MoALF* • Contributed regulatory and technological knowledge. • Disseminated information through various communication channels reporting to the Ministry that targeted to small and medium enterprises. • Technical staff participated in negotiations with companies.	The Ministry of Health led the process. Its coordination with other government agencies was key, since the latter contributed with assistance and information about food technologies, regulations, and harmonization with MERCOSUR standards on food labeling, etc. These areas are beyond the Ministry of Health's capacity. In terms of sodium, technicians from INAL and INTI participated in discussions with the food companies and chambers of commerce on salt reduction measures and ways to launch them. To support the small and medium size enterprises in the adaptation process, it was agreed that the government would support their efforts with information and assistance. In the case of trans fats, a guide on recommendations to substitute trans fats was developed with the participation of the government and the private sector. In the case of trans fats, the cost of substitution technology has been decreasing over time. Thus, it was important for industry to agree with government on the time frame needed to reach the policy goals.	*Strengths:* • Intersectoral dialogue and negotiation. • Stewardship role of the Ministry of Health. • Leadership and coordination with other public entities. • Dialogue and negotiation with the private sector. • The public-private joint effort for public health indicates the companies' respect for consumers' concerns. *Opportunities:* • An international climate fosters work on promoting healthy diets. • Increasing consumer demand for healthy food. • The creation of an intersectoral working group that led to modifying the Food Code. *Weaknesses:* • Limited resources. • Small and medium enterprises missed out on the discussion about measures. • A lack of laboratory standardization to perform the tests to monitor and evaluate the measures. • Voluntary agreements on lowering sodium content cannot be enforced.

table continues next page

Table 5.1 Governance of Multisectoral Activities to Promote a Healthy Diet: Argentina's Food Code Reform to Regulate Trans Fats in Processed Foods and Agreements with the Food Industry to Reduce Sodium (continued)

Key stakeholders and their positions	Strategies	Interaction among stakeholders	Lessons learned
Ministry of Agriculture, Livestock and Fishing (MoALF) • To promote the value added of healthy food in the market and create a regulatory framework. **COPAL (Coordinator of Food Product Industries):** • To negotiate goals and terms, avoiding the sudden implementation of measures which could be costly. • Given international trend to work on these risk factors, knew they needed to work on these issues. • To respond to growing consumer demand for healthy foods. • Claimed that small and medium enterprises would have unfair advantages as they would have low probability of being inspected. • Did not have the capacity to invest in the needed adaptations. • To define uniform criteria to monitor compliance on the agreed goals. • Their position with regards to reductions in sodium and trans fats were different because: • Sodium is an inexpensive way to give flavor to many processed foods.	• With INTI, INAL, and ASAGA, supported industry through the design a manual for retrofitting small and medium enterprises' production processes to eliminate trans fats. **COPAL** • Represented the business sector in negotiating the measures. • Organized meetings with companies to agree on the terms and goals to be discussed with the Ministry of Health. • Collected and delivered information on sodium content in food.		**Threads** • Companies will probably want extensions to achieve the goals (particularly with regard to reducing sodium). **Monitoring and evaluation:** • A limited capacity and availability of laboratories. • Limited baseline information. • Transnational companies that set their policies at the global level can hinder the agreed-upon agreements. • A potential lack of continuity due to management changes over time.

table continues next page

Table 5.1 Governance of Multisectoral Activities to Promote a Healthy Diet: Argentina's Food Code Reform to Regulate Trans Fats in Processed Foods and Agreements with the Food Industry to Reduce Sodium (continued)

Key stakeholders and their positions	Strategies	Interaction among stakeholders	Lessons learned
• It also preserves foods and its substitution is difficult, relatively lower technical know-how than in the case of trans fats to find alternatives. • Regarding trans fats, industry was already working to replace them given technical feasibility and the availability of foreign experience and R&D. However, the industry expressed concerned linked to the high cost of substitution of trans fats.			
FAIPA (Argentine Federation of Baked Products Industry): They represented bakeries in the process of sodium reduction in artisanal breads. • A commitment to health and good eating habits. • Positive image among consumers, without requiring major investments or modifications of the production processes. • Resistance of bakers to provide information on their products. • Greater dissemination of the bakeries' efforts. • Greater resources to add more bakeries to the initiative. • Continuity of the policies.	**FAIPA** • Support the Ministry of Health in disseminating information about the initiative. • Distribute and prepare materials to offer training materials to bakers. • Providing seminars to train bakers.		

table continues next page

137

Table 5.1 Governance of Multisectoral Activities to Promote a Healthy Diet: Argentina's Food Code Reform to Regulate Trans Fats in Processed Foods and Agreements with the Food Industry to Reduce Sodium *(continued)*

Key stakeholders and their positions	Strategies	Interaction among stakeholders	Lessons learned
ASAGA (Argentinean Association of Fats and Oils) • To negotiate goals and terms, avoiding the sudden implementation of measures. • To follow the international trend to work on these risk factors. • Growing consumer demand for healthy foods. • Cost of trans-fat substitution alternatives. • Large enterprises complained that they would face unfair competition from small and medium companies because smaller businesses had low capacity for investment and low probability of being inspected. • Define uniform criteria to monitor compliance on the agreed goals.	***ASAGA*** • Contribute technical know-how to replace trans fats. • Represent the business sector in negotiating the measures. • Organize meetings with companies to agree on the terms and goals to be discussed with the Ministry of Health. • Design of a manual for retrofitting small and medium enterprises' production processes to eliminate trans fats.		

Note: R&D = research and development; MERCOSUR = Mercado Común del Sur (Common Market of the South).

and consumer groups. Different working groups were set up within the commission to advance trans-fat- and sodium-reducing policies; the groups discussed the concerns of all participating agencies and developed strategies to overcome these concerns.

Amending the Food Code to Regulate Trans Fats

The consumption of trans fats increases the risk of coronary heart disease and diabetes (Brunner and others 2007; Hu and others 1997, 2001). Coronary heart disease is a leading cause of death in Argentina and, according to the 2009 National Risk Factor Survey, 9.6 percent of the population reports having diabetes.

In 2007, the Pan American Health Organization (PAHO) created the "Trans Fat Free Americas" task force to evaluate the impact of trans fatty acids on nutrition and health and to find ways to gradually eliminate them. In 2008, the task force issued the Declaration of Rio de Janeiro, whereby it recommended replacing trans fats in processed foods and using a concentration no higher than 2 percent of total fat in oils and margarines and no higher than 5 percent in processed foods; requiring the food industry to place nutrition labels on its processed foods, stating the amount of trans fats they contain; developing educational programs about different fats and the way to read labels; and forming national working groups with industry representatives, scientists, and public health authorities to address these issues.

Although Argentina's authorities launched major efforts to reduce trans fats in 2008, the MOH had already introduced some measures in 2004, as recommended by the Program to Prevent Heart Attacks in Argentina (PROPIA) at the National University of La Plata (UNLP).

The Policy

Following discussions between the government and industry, an amendment to the country's Food Code that would regulate the amount of trans fats in processed foods was prepared. The amendment was included in Article No. 155, Chapter III, which established that "The content of industrially-produced trans fatty acids in food should not exceed 2 percent of total fats in vegetable oils and margarines for direct consumption and 5 percent of total fats in other foods. These limits do not apply to fats from ruminants, including milk fat." The article was incorporated in December 2010 through Resolution No. 137 of the MOH's Secretariat of Policies, Regulation, and Institutes and Resolution No. 941 of the then Secretariat of Agriculture, Livestock, and Fisheries—now the Ministry of Agriculture, Livestock, and Fisheries (MoALF)—and these resolution set a two-year timetable beginning December 2010 for modifying vegetable oils and margarines for direct consumption and up to four years for modifying other foods.

While the terms for replacing trans fats run their course, other efforts are currently under way, such as disseminating information to small and medium industries, which have greater difficulty in meeting the standard because they lack financial and technical resources to start the restructuring process; and launching campaigns to educate consumers about healthy diets. With respect to the first, a guide on recommendations and strategies for replacing trans fats was prepared for small and medium firms.[1] Materials were also developed for consumers, with information on the damage to health from consuming trans fats and on how to read food labels. Based on Common Market of the South's (MERCOSUR) resolution GMC No. 46, adopted in August 2006, the level of trans fats is required to be stated on the products' labels.

Policy-Making Process

In 2008, the MOH took the lead by holding a national meeting to begin applying the Rio recommendations. Participants included representatives from various government agencies, academia, and industry, who agreed to set up the following working commissions: an academic-scientific commission, coordinated by the UNLP; a regulatory-legislative commission, coordinated by INAL; and a communications-consumer commission, coordinated by the MoALF (then the Secretariat of Agriculture, Livestock, and Fisheries).

The regulatory-legislative commission was made up of several public agencies and representatives from the food industry. Among the public agencies were the Ministries of Health, MoALF, INAL, and INTI. Industry representatives included COPAL, the chambers of commerce, food and beverage companies, and ASAGA. This last entity, which consists of technicians and companies involved in producing and processing fats, oils, and byproducts, was already working on ways to substitute trans fats for other products.

In 2008, the regulatory-legislative commission began to work on amending the Food Code. To that end, the group relied on international precedents. For example, in 2006, Denmark limited trans fats to 2 percent of the total content of fats in all marketed foods, and Canada recommended that trans fats should not exceed 2 percent of total fat content in vegetable oils and spreadable margarines or 5 percent in other foods.

Main Stakeholders, Their Positions, and Strategies

Throughout the process, MOH authorities sought to dialogue with all relevant actors, particularly the producers and distributors in the livestock and food sectors. The Ministry focused on issues such as producing healthier foods, using appropriate food labels, finding incentives—such as fiscal measures—to bring about sweeping changes, marketing techniques, creating interactions and partnerships, enacting laws, setting regulations and enforcement mechanisms, and providing the public with necessary information.[2]

Different participating organizations have adopted various roles. INAL, for example, which is part of the National Drugs, Food, and Medical Technology Administration and is a decentralized entity under MOH, played an important role in discussing measures to reduce trans fats; its knowledge about regulations, technology, food labeling, and analyses of trans-fat content made it particularly well suited for this position. At the MOH's request, INAL coordinated the working group that addressed regulatory issues that led to the Food Code's modification.

INAL also helped raise the issue of trans fats at the provincial and municipal levels through the National Food Protection Network (RENAPRA) and the National Network of Official Laboratories for Food Protection (RENALOA). RENAPRA has about 1,000 agents who work in provincial and municipal food regulatory entities, share information about best practices, build consensus on food controls, and provide training. Among the issues brought to the network's attention on a monthly basis was trans fats. This helped place the question of trans fats on the agenda of various jurisdictions. RENALOA promotes the exchange of information to improve the quality of the laboratories' food analyses and provides training to member laboratories; its role was to focus on food control issues to achieve consensus among the provinces and municipalities.

INAL also worked with the Ministry of Agriculture in communication activities, and with that Ministry and INTI in preparing a manual on redesigning production processes at small and medium enterprises.

The MoALF participated in these discussions in order to promote the added value of healthy food in the market and to develop the regulatory framework. It collaborated in negotiations between the public and private sectors, participated in multi-disciplinary actions to prepare trans-fat regulations and a manual for small and medium enterprises, and disseminated results through newsletters, websites,[3] publications, management reports, fairs and food and agriculture sector events.

INTI helped the MOH to disseminate evidence on the technological feasibility of replacing trans fats, participated in negotiations with companies, and helped prepare the manual to guide small and medium enterprises in retrofitting their processes concerning trans fats. Although it aligned itself with the MOH's objectives, it disagreed with some of its strategy. On the one hand, the Institute requested that the Ministry provide it with an agreement clarifying INTI's responsibilities and certifying it with the industry, to which it also provided advice. Further, it demanded that policies, discussions regarding control measures, and an education strategy negotiated with the Ministry of Education be continued. Finally, it called attention to the low participation of small and medium enterprises in the discussions.

Although COPAL was invited to participate in the elimination of trans fats, it transferred its main role to ASAGA, an association of technicians, professionals, specialists, researchers, and companies interested in the scientific and technical aspects of fats, oils, and byproducts used in food. Because ASAGA was already exploring how to replace fats in food at the time the discussions started, and was doing so with economically feasible technologies, it could allay the industries' concerns about international regulations and pressures related to adopting new technologies. It met with the food companies to discuss the feasibility of the innovations and set timetables the companies were willing to accept. Further, by understanding the difficulties that small and medium firms faced in adapting to the new processes, ASAGA worked with other commission members to develop the manual to assist them.

Early on, some companies resisted the change because they worried about costs, since the substitutes were expensive (and fats are the most costly input). To the extent that suppliers of alternate products were able to reduce their costs and pass along savings, substitution became more viable, although companies did have to adjust their productive processes, which required time and investment. The fact that the MOH was willing to discuss time frames and goals with the companies was well received.

Large companies were concerned about small and medium firms, because the smaller firms would have a difficult time meeting the new standards to eliminate trans fats. To help ease their worries, ASAGA, INAL, INTI, the Ministry of Agriculture, the MOH, and COPAL prepared a guide recommending alternatives. These efforts notwithstanding, it was difficult to bring smaller and medium producers into the discussion.

The disparity of analytical methods and the ability of laboratories to control compliance with trans-fats standards also were of concern. To offset this, ASAGA defined a standard analysis for all laboratories. INTI, the National Institute of Livestock Technology (INTA), and INAL worked with ASAGA to develop the standard. The MOH also is developing an analysis methodology.

Agreements with Industry to Reduce Sodium in Processed Foods, Including in Artisanal Breads

According to MOH data, the leading causes of death in Argentina in 2012 were cardiovascular diseases,[4] and high consumption of salt increases the risk of developing these diseases. Indeed, Argentines consume, on average, 12 g of salt daily (Ferrante and others 2011), well above the 5 g per day WHO recommends. And, according to the 2005 and 2009 national risk factors surveys, salt consumption is on the rise. In 2005, 23 percent of adults in the country added salt to cooked foods; by 2009 this figure had increased to 25.3 percent.

The "Global Strategy on Diet, Physical Activity, and Health" (WHO 2004) recommends limiting sodium consumption from any origin. PAHO, in turn, in its Political Declaration for the Reduction of Cardiovascular Diseases in the Americas recommended reducing salt intake in food—to which Argentina adhered—to under 5 g per person per day by 2020. In 2010, the MOH addressed this topic, launching the initiative "Less Salt, More Life," which aims to lower salt consumption as a way to reduce cardiovascular, cerebrovascular, and renal diseases. The strategy is based on three components: public awareness of the need to decrease salt intake; a progressive reduction of salt in processed foods through agreements with the food industry; and a reduction of salt content in artisanal bread.

An estimated 60 percent of the salt ingested in Argentina comes from processed foods.[5] The amount of salt in bread is particularly important, since bread is a key source of salt intake. Each Argentine eats an average of 190 g of bread each day, which accounts for 25 percent of his or her total salt consumption

(Ferrante and others 2011). Given the World Health Organization's goal of a total of 5 g a day, lowering salt in bakery products becomes very important.

The Policy

The Ministries of Health and of Agriculture agreed with COPAL that salt should be progressively and voluntarily reduced in processed foods. Four food groups were targeted because they were the ones consumed most, were high in salt, and could easily reduce salt in their content—meat products; baked goods and snacks; dairy products (cheese); and soups, dressings, and canned foods.

In 2004, INTI, working through the Center for Grains and Oleaginous Products and FAIPA—which represent 30,000 bakeries in the country—and with the support of VIGI+A (a MOH program financed by the World Bank to strengthen health surveillance), launched a project to reduce salt in baked goods. The project aimed to evaluate small-scale bakeries' use of salt and to transfer salt-reduction technology to them through training and information.

In 2007, FAIPA and the MOH signed an agreement to develop healthy bakery products. This agreement contemplates communication strategies, consumer education programs, technology transfer, and training for the bakery sector. It also aims to improve the nutritional value of breads and to replace trans fats. In 2008 these activities were halted, but they were renewed in 2009, with a project in the province of La Pampa intended to study the consumption of salt, trans fats, and fiber in bread products and to demonstrate their impact on health. Preliminary results are expected in 2014; the study will then be extended to other provinces.

Policy Outputs

In 2011, 20 companies and chambers of commerce agreed to meet the salt-reduction goals for specific products; additional parties joined in 2012. Further, the MOH has stated that it will design a logo that participants can use on their products to show the public that they are part of the program.

Bakeries voluntarily participate in the salt-reduction initiative, and as of this writing, 8,000 had signed onto the agreement. Although some bakeries have been reluctant to say how they prepare their products, it seems that adapting to the salt-reduction technology has not meant undue hardship for them, and their clients are usually satisfied with the bakeries' efforts to produce healthier products.

According to a research carried out by the Ministry of Health, the voluntary agreements with the food industry, considering a 3 g reduction in dietary salt intake, could generate a net savings of US$3,765 million and gain of 656,657 quality-adjusted life years (QALY) in the high-impact scenario and a savings of US$2,080 million and 401,659 QALY in the low-impact scenario. The results would be reductions in the incidence of heart disease (24.1 percent), acute myocardial infarction (21.6 percent), and stroke (20.5 percent), as well as in mortality from heart disease (19.9 percent) and all causes (6.4 percent) (Ferrante and others 2012).

The Policy-Making Process

Setting salt-reduction goals for all food categories has been a complex process, due to the wide range of products in each category. Consequently, goals differed for each set of foods, based on technical feasibility, consumer acceptance, impact on health, and the products' market importance. Progressive reductions agreed upon ranged from 5 percent to 15 percent over the maximum values measured or over higher levels than the established average. For the soup, dressing, and canned-food category, agreements were only reached for soup; for the dairy products category, agreements were only reached for cheese. Salt-reduction goals should be met within two years, and it is expected that with this voluntary, progressive strategy, WHO's goal of 5 g of average salt consumption per person per day will be achieved by 2020. Plans are under way to expand the list of products, but they have yet to be selected.

A two-part strategy has been put in place to monitor the agreements. First, a multisectoral control commission was constituted, made up of the MOH, the Ministry of Agriculture, COPAL, INAL, and INTI. The commission is charged with collecting and analyzing indirect indicators, such as which companies adhere to the agreements and how much salt has been reduced in some products (data that will come from the companies). Second, a laboratory network headed by INAL will evaluate the products. If companies fail to comply, they will be given six months to do so, with help from facilitators. Otherwise, they may withdraw from the voluntary agreement without penalty.

Regarding salt in artisanal breads, the MOH and FAIPA launched collaborative activities to produce this bread with less or no salt. FAIPA also has participated in various activities designed to foster a healthy diet, such as fortifying flour with folic acid or eliminating potassium bromate in breads. Since 2004, it has worked to reduce sodium in collaboration with INTI and the MOH. The two-pronged strategy offers technical assistance and technology-transfer help to bakeries and widely disseminates information about issues related to salt consumption. FAIPA, the MOH and INTI have also supported talks in provinces and municipalities that were interested in the issue, distributed posters about salt in bread, provided salt measurement cups to prepare the breads, launched information campaigns, developed recipes, and helped to train bakers.

Main Stakeholders, Their Positions, and Their Strategies

The MOH also had a leading role in this process. As mentioned earlier, in 2004 the Ministry began working with bakeries to reduce salt in artisanal breads. But it was not until 2008 that efforts to reduce salt in processed food were strengthened, because at the beginning it was unclear whether the Ministry's role would be to regulate or to negotiate with the companies; it was thought that the Ministry could only alert the public about healthy diets. Moreover, internal debates arose about the salt-reduction strategy; some argued that it would lead to increase goiters (due to less iodized salt intake), since salt was seen as a vehicle to incorporate other nutrients into the diet.

As was the case with trans-fat reduction, agreements with the industry to reduce sodium in processed foods were reached within the context of the multisectoral National Commission to Eliminate Trans Fats and Reduce Salt. Along with the MOH, other agencies such as the Ministry of Agriculture, COPAL, FAIPA, INAL, and INTI also played key roles.

INAL's role has been key, as its technicians discussed ways to reduce salt with food companies and chambers of commerce and explored how to implement them for each food group.

INTI worked with FAIPA to reduce salt in bread and to transfer knowledge about how to change production processes. The Institute also helped the MOH to disseminate evidence on the technical feasibility of reducing salt, trained bakers, and participated in negotiations with companies.

Although INTI adopted the MOH's objectives, it disagreed with its strategy. INTI sought stricter goals in reducing sodium and better control on how companies can use the agreements to improve their market position. It also felt that small and medium enterprises were not well represented in the discussions.

The Ministry of Agriculture, in fulfilling its goal to promote the added value of healthy food and design regulations that foster it, contributed its knowledge on the technical feasibility of reducing salt consumption and, especially, on regulations. This Ministry works within the National Food Commission (CONAL) and within the Codex Alimentarius Commission; it also participates in the definition of standards in MERCOSUR. Its communications with the industry proved to be very useful since the Ministry has experience in introducing technology changes and fostering the production of healthy foods into the food and agro-industry, especially in small and medium enterprises. The Ministry of Agriculture also offered technical assistance to small and medium enterprises.

The active participation of food-processing companies helped to start the dialogue and to reach consensus on the salt-reduction measures. To foster the participation of food-processing companies, the MOH reached out to COPAL, an association that comprises more than 35 food and beverage companies. COPAL coordinated the work of companies and chambers of commerce in this venture and organized meetings to define goals and terms in preparation to discussions with the MOH. COPAL also provided information on the sodium content in foods.

Food-processing companies were motivated to join the discussions and reach consensus on the measures because they were aware of international trends about and consumer demand for healthy food. They also understood that regulations could be rapidly introduced, which might mean that they would have little time to adapt. COPAL stressed to the companies the extent to which the MOH was willing to go in discussing the measures with the companies and creating clear rules that prevailed throughout the process.

Some companies were reluctant to participate at the beginning, particularly in salt-reduction efforts, because they feared that this measure would change the flavor of their products and they would lose customers, especially if their competitors did not participate on the agreements. They also worried about available alternatives to preserve food. Larger companies also feared that small and medium firms neither had the capital to restructure nor felt pressured to do so, because their chances of being inspected was low. This, in turn, would generate unfair competition between large companies and their small and medium counterparts.

While it was clear that smaller companies needed help, supporting them would be difficult, since these enterprises are not grouped under a single entity and do not have the time or the technical and economic resources to discuss processes and goals. Larger companies then proposed that the state help smaller enterprises, but this represented an extraordinary burden on the MOH, which did not have the resources to identify small and medium firms and invite them to participate.

Finally, some companies questioned the monitoring of compliance methods. Measuring salt content requires the testing of large samples to verify that goals are met and, because techniques are not uniform, the process has a large margin of error. In response, COPAL, in addition to a laboratory evaluation, is developing a way to measure salt. According to this mechanism, companies would provide data about their products, processes, and the way they operate to demonstrate that their work complies with the agreement. The MOH plans to meet with scientific associations so they can help define the monitoring methods.

In the case of artisanal bread, FAIPA's commitment is so strong that lowering sodium in artisanal bread is now on the Federation's activity agenda. However, FAIPA has asked for greater financial resources from the MOH to disseminate information in the mass media and travel to the provinces and municipalities to win the support of more bakeries.

Lessons Learned

The MOH spearheaded the creation of a working group of public and private entities to reduce trans fatty acids and sodium in processed foods. Argentina's experience of joint and coordinated ventures, along with multisectoral agreements, represents a pioneering effort in the region.

Argentina's experience demonstrates the importance of working with various public entities involved in food regulation and food-technology activities, as this knowledge is beyond the scope of the MOH. This multisectoral participation was essential for negotiating goals and terms with the industry, which is well organized and has the economic and technical resources to participate in the discussions and defend its interests. In this regard, the Ministry's willingness to dialogue and negotiate with industry dispelled the companies' initial fears about sudden changes and short or no adaptation timetables, and helped persuade them to work together to define the measures that benefit public health.

Negotiations were possible because there already is an international effort under way in this matter and consumers are increasingly asking for healthy food. In addition, the inclusion of different actors in the experience provided the opportunity to form a multisectoral working team that ultimately produced the amendment to the Food Code and developed the voluntary agreements, thus laying the foundation for future measures to promote healthy diets.

Argentina's experience revealed the drawbacks in having limited resources to carry out mass information campaigns and to enlist the participation of more bakeries' in "less salt, more life" practices. In addition, small and medium enterprises only participated in the discussions to a limited degree, largely because they are scattered around the country and are not organized under an umbrella association that could represent them and facilitate negotiations. Further, it is unlikely that owners or employees of these smaller firms would have the time and resources to discuss these issues, and the MOH does not have the time or budget to bring all of them into the discussions.

With regard to the monitoring and evaluation of the new trans-fat regulations and sodium agreements, a standardized method for the laboratories that will conduct the tests still must be defined. Business associations have already advanced in this regard by forming their own working groups, but the state entities must be more actively engaged. Moreover, although voluntary agreements were reached on the sodium issues (because of the technical difficulties regarding substitutes), long-term regulations should be considered. The voluntary agreement is a politically expedient effort to place the topic in the public agenda, but it has neither enforcement mechanisms nor penalties that can be applied when food producers do not comply.

The MOH also is concerned that, as the compliance date nears, companies will ask for extensions citing technical and legal issues. While this would not be a problem with trans-fat elimination (most of the industry already has begun to retrofit its procedures) it could pose a problem with sodium-reduction efforts. Questions also might be raised about the capacity of the public sector to monitor and evaluate compliance, especially with respect to the availability of testing laboratories and their ability to perform their tasks. Other issues include the limited baseline information needed to conduct monitoring and evaluation activities and the concern that the global policies of multinational companies will not align with the voluntary agreements signed in Argentina. Finally, the strategies launched by the MOH could be halted due to a change in management, as has already occurred.

Bogotá, Colombia: A City with a Built Environment that Promotes Physical Activity

Olga L. Sarmiento, Adriana Díaz del Castillo, and Ethel Segura Durán

Thanks to the efforts of local government agencies, individuals, and civil society organizations, over the years the city of Bogotá, Colombia, has developed an environment that promotes physical activity. Infrastructure and programs such as the Ciclovía, CicloRutas, the TransMilenio bus rapid transit system, and outdoor gyms make the city an example in the region. This section describes the process by which these interventions were developed and implemented.

The Recreational Ciclovía

The Ciclovía program entails temporarily closing streets to motor-vehicle traffic in order to offer safe and free spaces for recreation and physical activity (OPS 2009; Sarmiento and others 2010a). As of this writing, the Ciclovía operates every Sunday and holiday from 7 a.m. to 2 p.m. and between 600,000 and 1.4 million people (8–19 percent of the city's population) use it. Since 1999, the program has also staged a yearly event from 6 p.m. to midnight. The program cost US$1.7 million in materials, staff, operations, and maintenance, which was covered mainly from the city budget (Díaz del Castillo and others 2011). A 2010 cost-benefit study showed that for each US$1 invested in the Ciclovía, US$3–4 could be saved through health gains related to being physically active (Montes and others 2012). Of similar programs worldwide, Bogotá's is the oldest and the one with the most users, most of whom are male; 60 percent of users are 19–45 years old, and 90 percent are in low and medium socioeconomic groups (Universidad Nacional 2005).

Since 1996, additional activities have been offered during the Ciclovía's hours of operation: service stations; sites that promote physical activity and health, known as RAFI for their Spanish acronym; and Recreovía locations (table 5.2).

Policy Outcomes

The Ciclovía program is known for its potential health benefits, including promoting physical activity, enhancing a community's social capital and fostering its economic recovery, promoting quality of life, and reducing environmental pollution and street noise by decreasing the number of motor vehicles (Hoehner and others 2008; Sarmiento and Behrentz 2008; Sarmiento and others 2010b).

Based on Bogotá's population size and Ciclovías' number of users and average minutes of participation, it is estimated that the program could provide 13.64 percent of the recommended weekly minutes of physical activity at the population level (Sarmiento and others 2010a). Of Ciclovía users, 40.5 percent report participating for at least three hours (Universidad Nacional 2005) and their

Table 5.2 Activities Offered by Bogotá's Ciclovía

Activity or program	Description
Recreovía (physical activity sites)	Parks or plazas in public spaces along the route offer one-hour physical activity classes taught by instructors. There are currently 19 Recreovía areas operating during weekends; 17 on Tuesdays, Thursdays, and/or Wednesdays and 11 twice a week during the evening.
Service stations	Vendors along the route offer food and beverages, and there are bicycle-repair stations. The Secretariat of Social Integration selects vendors.
Children's activities	Recreational activities and sports.
RAFI locations	These sites promote physical activity and healthy nutrition; they provide weight and height measurements to calculate BMIs. The District Recreation and Sports Institute IDRD operates RAFI locations.

Note: BMI = body mass index; RAFI = Spanish acronym for sites that promote physical activity and health.

reported activities include cycling (46.2 percent), walking (47.9 percent), and others (5.9 percent) (Montes and others 2012).

In addition, it was estimated that 20 percent of adults who reported participating in the Ciclovía engaged in at least 30 minutes of physical activity during leisure time for at least five days a week, thus meeting physical activity recommendations (Sarmiento and others 2010a). Women who reported participating regularly in the Ciclovía also were most likely to engage in physical activity during their leisure time (Gómez and others 2004). The average number of minutes of physical activity during leisure time and of biking as a means of transport among Ciclovía users is greater than that of Bogotá's overall adult population.

Policy-Making Process

Ciclovía started in 1974, when a group of students took over some of the city's main streets to ride their bicycles. Other activists who had been organizing annual bike rides (starting in Bogotá) to promote bicycle use for recreation and well-being also participated. The city's Department of Transit and Transportation informally supported the event by facilitating street closings. The activity continued for a couple of years, although not on a regular basis (Díaz del Castillo and others 2011; Gómescásseres 2003; Alcaldía Mayor de Bogotá and Instituto Distrital de Cultura y Turismo 2007).

In 1976, the Department of Transit and Transportation conducted a study that recommended creating a temporary Ciclovía. Study results led to the issuing of Decree 577, which formally defined the Ciclovía and established four circuits on main streets located in low- and high-income neighborhoods. At this stage, the program had no defined organization, and no entity was responsible for promoting it. According to some interviewees, the program was not a government priority, which at the time focused on building infrastructure for motor vehicles, such as bridges. But user groups continued to organize events and sought official support to achieve formal status. Moreover, the public's support for the events demonstrated its desire for public recreational spaces.

In 1982, a new mayor, Augusto Ramírez Ocampo, formally inaugurated the weekly Ciclovía. The mayor's objective was to improve equity through recreation (Bushnell 2007; Dávila and Gilbert 2001; Mockus and others 1997; Ramírez 1983, 2005). In two years, the Ciclovía had stretched to 84 km, offering safe and free space for cycling, running, roller-skating, and walking. The city's Department of Traffic and Transportation and a multisectoral committee jointly managed the Ciclovía. In 1984, the city administration changed and so did priorities, however. By 1995, the routes had shrunk to 51 km, it functioned mainly in high-income areas, and fewer people participated (Gómescásseres 2003). Still, some people continued using the routes and took responsibility for closing them to traffic, even those not officially sanctioned.

In the 1990s, the Ciclovía got an important boost, which coincided with the construction of the infrastructures described later on. All these changes in the city were indirectly spurred by several factors. First, the 1991 Colombian Constitution consolidated a decentralization process that had been under way for several years, giving Bogotá greater autonomy. Further, the Constitution stated that recreation, sports, and leisure time were rights for all citizens, and that the state would be responsible for promoting and supervising such activities. In addition, a statute established a new administrative organization for Bogotá, created opportunities for citizen participation, and increased the mayor's autonomy. It also increased the city's budget, which, coupled with the other changes, gave authorities the funds and managerial autonomy that made it possible to implement urban changes, including strengthening the Ciclovía and creating other programs and infrastructures (Díaz del Castillo and others 2011). Until these changes took effect, the city's political and administrative conditions were less democratic: mayors were not popularly elected until 1988, terms of office were irregular and short, and politicians had low credibility. Moreover, the city's budget did not cover the needs associated with the rapid growth experienced by the city since the 1950s (Instituto de Estudios Urbanos 2011; Varela 1998).

Second, land-use instruments also changed, aimed at defining guidelines for short-, medium- and long-term urban planning. The two main instruments were: (a) land-use management schemes based on 9th Law/1989 on urban reform, 2nd law/1991, and Law 388/1997, that established as a mandatory requirement to adopt a territorial plan for all municipalities, effective in the long-term (9 years, later changed to 12); and (b) development plans to be prepared by each administration, that define a budget linked to specific goals.

Third, the Ciclovía's transformation and the construction of the infrastructures described below were also linked to changes in the city administration. From 1995 to 2003, the elected city administrations of Mayor Antanas Mockus (1995–97 and 2001–03) and Mayor Enrique Peñalosa (1998–2000) shared a vision of the city and its citizenry that gave priority to urban changes and to a culture of citizen participation. The Ciclovía program was a scenario where these ideas took hold (Alcaldía Mayor de Bogotá and Instituto Distrital de Cultura y Turismo 2007; Montezuma 2003; Pizano 2003). The first Mockus administration did not execute its total budget, which gave the Peñalosa administration added resources to carry out its plans. Further, Peñalosa was elected together with a city council that supported his plans, so his development plan known as "For the Bogotá We All Want" (1998–2000) was included in a 1998 council agreement. The shared priorities of these three administrations allowed the city to launch various programs, including renovating public spaces and introducing new public transportation systems.

During these three administrations, several management changes to the Ciclovía were introduced, which consolidated and expanded the program. The program's management was transferred from the transportation sector to the recreation and sports sector, under the District Recreation and Sports Institute (IDRD, for its Spanish acronym). This institutional change reinvigorated the program, as Ciclovía evolved to be a space for recreation, sports, and adequate use of leisure time, physical activity, and improved well-being.

Other changes included assigning new personnel to manage the routes and defining the program's organizational structure; establishing agreements with the police and the Secretariat of Education to bring together police and student efforts in support of Ciclovía's operation (Law 191/1995 and Resolution 4210/1996 stated that 10 percent of those doing military service with the police should do so in the Ciclovía, as should secondary school students doing compulsory social service); increasing the area from 81 km in 1996 to 121 km in 2000, reconnecting the north-south circuit to cover 70 percent of communities, and installing permanent signals; launching new activities (for example, the Recreovía, see table 5.2); promoting an image of the program that helped to consolidate it and to obtain public acceptance; extending events by two hours; and securing private financing. By 1997, the Ciclovía ran through 70 percent of Bogotá's localities and by 2000, the routes spanned 121 interconnected km (Gómescásseres 2003).

But the Ciclovía also faced opposition. In the 1990s, businesses along routes that were slated for expansion opposed these changes. Their representative, the National Federation of Businessmen (FENALCO) claimed that the Ciclovía threatened their livelihood by restricting motor-vehicle circulation. The city administration was able to counter the claim by showing evidence (based on market studies supported by the Chamber of Commerce) that businesses would not suffer. Given the program's popularity, the city continued with its plans and encouraged the private sector to open businesses along the roads—such as bicycle repair shops and food kiosks—that cyclists and pedestrians would welcome. To encourage business owners, it held workshops with those potentially affected and established alternate parking lots. The mayor also argued that expanding the Ciclovía meant putting the general public's interests ahead of private interests.

Private-vehicle owners, who claimed that street closings interrupted traffic flow, also occasionally opposed the Ciclovía. In 2007–08, a congressional representative submitted an amendment to a transportation law that included changing the program's hours of operation from the existing 7 a.m.–2 p.m. schedule to a 5 a.m.–noon schedule. Users responded by rallying in support of the original schedule through social networks, the Internet, the media, and petitions (Comité Cívico Pro Defensa de la Ciclovía 2008; Peñalosa 2008; Revista Cambio 2008). Although the bill was blocked for other reasons, the public's reaction showed the users' organizing power.

While not intended as opposition to the Ciclovía, the construction of the city's TransMilenio bus rapid system also reduced some of the Ciclovía's circuits and connections. However, as of this writing, the circuit has been reconnected and the Ciclovía is currently 121 km long.

Since 2007, the program has not experienced major transformations, although it has undergone changes. In 2007, two city councilors presented a draft proposal to the city council and two congressional representatives submitted legislation to Congress declaring the Ciclovía as a national and cultural heritage. These initiatives sought to promote and protect the program, and to guarantee resources to maintain its quality and coverage. That same year, the Ciclovía was included in the National Public Health Plan recommendations (Decree 3039) and in 2009, in the Law on Obesity (1355) as a strategy to prevent NCD risk factors.

Main Stakeholders during the Initial Phase

In contrast to other multisectoral policies reviewed in this publication, in Bogotá's Ciclovía, CicloRutas, TransMilenio, and outdoor gyms, the health sector did not spearhead their development and did not manage their operations. The Ciclovía and the infrastructure reviewed here resulted from the joint efforts of mayors, different local government agencies, and the civil society. Table 5.3 summarizes the key stakeholders that participated in these policy-making processes and outlines their positions, the strategies they used, their interactions, and the lessons learned.

Regarding the Ciclovía in particular, students and bike activists were key at the beginning, as were city residents who, by using the program, supported it. The city government, particularly mayors Mockus and Peñalosa, as well as several local-government agencies were critical for Ciclovía implementation and continue to play key roles in its maintenance. At different points during its development, the Ciclovía has been opposed by businesses and by vehicle owners.

This program is an example of a multisectoral effort. Currently it is managed by the IDRD, with help from the police and the education sector, which provide logistical support and human resources; the urban planning institute; the transportation sector; the environmental sector; the health sector, which provides emergency assistance through the local health secretariat; marketing and service companies; academia and research groups who promote the program and conduct evaluations; the public, who has mobilized support as needed over the years and who continues to use the program; and city councilors and congressional representatives who have sought to consolidate and protect it (Meisel and others in press).

Lessons Learned

The factors that bolstered the program for the promotion of PA included a multisectoral approach with clear leadership (IDRD) to promote the initiative, political will, the public's participation, and the use of social marketing. Factors that hindered the program included shifting government priorities that did not promote the program's continuity; opposition from private vehicle owners; transportation priorities which favored vehicles over bicycles or pedestrians; and opposition from business owners who thought the program would harm their interests.

CicloRutas

Bogotá's CicloRutas consist of permanent lanes dedicated to bicycle traffic that are separated from motor-vehicle roads.[6] Based on Urban Development Institute (IDU, for its Spanish acronym) data, there were 344 km of CicloRutas in 2010, the most extensive such network in Latin America.[7] The routes were originally designed for recreation, and later became an alternative transportation strategy. Their location could also allow for the exchange between one mode of transportation and another, such as between bicycles and the TransMilenio bus rapid

Table 5.3 Governance of Multisectoral Activities to Promote Physical Activity: Ciclovía, CicloRutas, TransMilenio, and Outdoor Gyms in Bogotá, Colombia

Key stakeholders and their positions	Strategies	Interaction among stakeholders	Lessons learned from the four cases
Ciclovía During its development: • Students sought city spaces for biking. • Activists and bike enthusiasts also wanted city space protected from motor vehicles for recreation and well-being. • The city government, particularly mayors Mockus and Peñalosa, had a new vision of development, and made the Ciclovía and the infrastructures aimed at promoting well-being, sustainable modes of transportation, and use of public space a priority. • The Traffic and Transportation Department supported the Ciclovía by helping close the roads from the beginning. • City residents made use of the program. • The education and security sectors provided personnel for the Ciclovía. • Some private vehicle owners opposed the Ciclovía for the inconvenience it created by closing main roads during the daytime.	• Students activists and bike enthusiasts first tried to create a Ciclovía in 1974, as students poured into the city's main streets with their bicycles, and bike enthusiasts started organizing annual bike rides to promote the use of bikes for recreation and well-being. • City residents participated enthusiastically in the Ciclovía and in the events that preceded it. • The city government initially passed a decree along with the transit, district planning, and public works sectors. Later, Mayor Ramírez Ocampo inaugurated the weekly program in the 1980s. • The program's greatest boost came later during the administrations of mayors Mockus and Peñalosa. During their administrations, the management of the Ciclovía was transferred from the transportation sector to the recreation and sports sector, under the IDRD. This change reinvigorated the program. Ciclovía was given a defined organizational and operational structure and offered new services to meet users' needs. Changes included: assigning new personnel to manage the routes (Ciclovía caretakers); creating agreements with the police and Secretariat of Education to coalesce police and student efforts as logistic personnel; increasing the length of the route (from 81 km in 1996 to 121 km in 2000); launching new activities (such as the Recreovía); promoting the program's image that contributed to its consolidation and public acceptance;[21] extending the duration of events by two hours; and obtaining private financing (a small share).	• Activists originally pressured to create an area for recreational activity and bike use, which the city's Department of Traffic and Transportation informally supported by closing the streets to motor vehicles. • Activist support has also been present whenever there is a proposal to reduce or negatively affect the Ciclovía. Such was the case of the draft amendment of the Transportation law that would have reduced the program's hours. Activists mobilized through social networks, the Internet, and the media, and filed petitions to manifest their opposition to this proposal. • Agreements between the security and the education sectors entered into laws and regulations to ensure better security in the Ciclovía. • The city administration countered the business-sector opposition by submitting evidence of the impact of the program on the businesses through market studies carried out with the support of the Chamber of Commerce of Bogotá.	• Colombia's 1991 Constitution created a favorable context for the Ciclovía and infrastructures when it consolidated a decentralization process granting greater political and administrative autonomy to the city and establishing fixed mayoral terms. The constitution also declared that recreation, sports, and leisure time were rights of every citizen; that the infrastructure would be democratic; and that the state would be responsible for supervising it. • The creation of a Ciclovía multisectoral committee (composed of bicycle activists, the police, the Traffic and Transportation Department, the Secretariat of Education, Coldeportes, and the National Cycling Federation) gave an early boost to the measure's development. • In contrast to the Ciclovía, the CicloRutas suffered from a lack of institutional coordination. There is no lead entity in charge of promoting and facilitating bicycle use as a means of transport. Nor is there a clear policy on bicycle use that includes regulations, because the CicloRutas Master Plan has not been included in any administrative act (rather, it only serves as a frame of reference). Moreover, existing regulations give priority to motor vehicles over bicycles.

table continues next page

153

Table 5.3 Governance of Multisectoral Activities to Promote Physical Activity: Ciclovía, CicloRutas, TransMilenio, and Outdoor Gyms in Bogotá, Colombia (continued)

Key stakeholders and their positions	Strategies	Interaction among stakeholders	Lessons learned from the four cases
• Businesses around the Ciclovía, represented by the National Federation of Businessmen (FENALCO), also opposed the program alleging that it caused a reduction in economic activity. During its current implementation: • City Traffic and Transportation Department. • Urban planning agencies. • City Government • District Recreation and Sports Institute (IDRD). • Security sector. • Marketing and service sectors. • Academia and research sector. • Health sector. • Education sector. • Environmental sector.	• To face the opposition, the administration relied on such strategies as workshops with those potentially affected, a search for business alternatives that would be welcomed by Ciclovía users (such as bicycle repair shops and food suppliers), and the establishment of alternate parking lots. • A congressperson submitted a draft amendment to the transportation law aimed at changing the schedule of the Ciclovía (from 7 a.m.–2 p.m. to 5 a.m.–noon) arguing that it disrupted traffic. • Businesses near the Ciclovía opposed the program, arguing that it negatively affected business.		• All four cases are good examples of successful multisectoral work, although they differ in terms of the types of agreements and number of participants involved. In all four, the role of the health sector in promoting physical activity has been secondary. Thus, the health sector needs to build on the experiences or programs of other sectors, mainly those of recreation, culture, sports, transportation and urban planning. • The Ciclovía and parallel programs (Recreovía), along with the outdoor gyms, demonstrate that it is possible to optimize resources if the existing urban infrastructure is used in a way to promote physical activity and if public-private partnerships are promoted within the city's broad objectives. • All four cases show how strategies to improve the public space can be used to enhance physical activity.

table continues next page

154

Table 5.3 Governance of Multisectoral Activities to Promote Physical Activity: Ciclovía, CicloRutas, TransMilenio, and Outdoor Gyms in Bogotá, Colombia *(continued)*

Key stakeholders and their positions	Strategies	Interaction among stakeholders	Lessons learned from the four cases
CicloRutas • The city administration originally wanted to connect water streams with metropolitan green areas for recreational purposes; subsequently it focused on providing alternative modes of transportation for the city. • The Urban Development Institute (IDU) • The Japanese International Cooperation Agency (JICA) • District Recreation and Sports Institute (IDRD) • The water supply and sewerage company. • Grass roots organizations, some of which opposed the CicloRutas constructed around waterways, arguing that they diminished the environment around the Fucha River. Others support and promote biking as an alternative means of transport.	• Several city administrations included the CicloRutas in their city models and plans. • JICA conducted a study for the Urban Transportation Master Plan and recommended diversifying the city's transportation modes. This recommendation supported the CicloRutas Master Plan creation of the route. • The urban planning sector, through IDU, supervised the work and arranged for the study that resulted in the CicloRutas Master Plan. • The water supply and sewerage company supported the measure: the first CicloRutas were constructed to integrate the water streams with the metropolitan green system. They further participated in the construction of some segments.	• Grass-roots opposition to the construction of CicloRutas around waterways was de-escalated by the city's offer to construct a linear park around the Fucha river. • Bike activists engage in advocacy.	• These programs and infrastructures also illustrate how such efforts need to be sustained under various city administrations. The administrations also must be open to new technological and state-of-the-art changes. Further, the role of the various actors and the public must be planned so the public must be planned so the construction, use, and permanence of the infrastructure and equipment are welcomed and promoted by all concerned. They further illustrate the need to strengthen and integrate existing institutions to achieve common objectives and meet the public's needs. • A strong political will and the public's participation are essential. Regarding the Ciclovía, CicloRutas, and the TransMilenio, it was the city leaders' vision, commitment, and political will that were key to start or transform the process. Plans were executed because they were an important part of city administrations' agendas and priorities, responded to the city's needs (e.g., regarding transportation, equity, and recreation), and were consistent with models pursued through several administrations.

table continues next page

Table 5.3 Governance of Multisectoral Activities to Promote Physical Activity: Ciclovía, CicloRutas, TransMilenio, and Outdoor Gyms in Bogotá, Colombia *(continued)*

Key stakeholders and their positions	Strategies	Interaction among stakeholders	Lessons learned from the four cases
TransMilenio (bus rapid transit system) Initially: • The city administration wanted to improve the transportation system. • Public transportation operators opposed the system. • Urban planning and transportation sectors • National Council for Economic and Social Policy (CONPES) provided support at national level. • Private franchises • Homeowners near the TransMilenio construction site opposed the disruption. More recently: • Residents complained about the congestion generated by the construction and their delays, about the rapid deterioration of the pavement in the system's corridors (which led to large investments in maintenance and caused delays in trip times), about overcrowded buses, about a lack of security, and about the high fares. Homeowners living near the station also complained that their properties had suffered from the construction.	• The city administration took a top-down approach to improve the city's transit. • Public transportation operators threatened with strikes.	• Public transportation operators opposition was resolved when they were offered to opportunity to participate in the bidding process for the operation of the buses.	• For its part, the public has supported the Ciclovía and the gyms by using them often. This continuous, strong support made it difficult for government officials to adopt initiatives that would be unpopular with the public. In this regard, while the public's support for the CicloRutas and TransMilenio was not obvious at the beginning of the processes (as it was with the Ciclovía), it later became an important stakeholder who used the infrastructure and made its opinion known. The overall lesson is that both governmental actors and interest groups were (and are) necessary, but none is sufficient by itself. • Bogotá's four programs further illustrate that the task of promoting physical activity must involve various dimensions—it should include strategies to promote PA during leisure time, and as a means of transportation, such as biking and walking.

table continues next page

Table 5.3 Governance of Multisectoral Activities to Promote Physical Activity: Ciclovía, CicloRutas, TransMilenio, and Outdoor Gyms in Bogotá, Colombia *(continued)*

Key stakeholders and their positions	Strategies	Interaction among stakeholders	Lessons learned from the four cases
Outdoor gyms • The District Recreation and Sports Institute (IDRD) promoted the installation of new equipment in public spaces and the renovation or existing equipment in parks to respond to the needs of the different communities and age groups. • Private company imported and installed equipment. • The community supported outdoor gyms. • The private sector (Colsanitas, Novartis Laboratories, and Athletic Colombia, S.A.) financed equipment to promote a socially responsible image (corporate social responsibility) and receive tax exemptions. Currently: • The private sector (health and education). • The recreation, culture, and sports sectors	• IDRD promoted a public-private partnership to ensure that equipment would be installed in parks and that outdoor gyms would be available to promote physical activity, health, and well-being. The partnership worked through two models: the "Adopt a Park" program, whereby the private sector donates and maintains the equipment, and a second model that only contemplated equipment donation. • The community helps to maintain the equipment and supports the program by using it. When the first equipment was removed from Tunal Park, the community protested through a mail-in campaign and demanded that it be re-installed.		

transit system. Unfortunately, there are over 90 interruptions along the circuit, which makes connections with other routes and with mass transport difficult and endangers users' safety. The network also has 1,640 bicycle racks throughout the city that are free and monitored (at connection points and at bus rapid transit system stations). However, only 40 percent of CicloRutas users report having seen bicycle racks and, of these, only 19 percent have used them (Segura 2011). Most CicloRuta users are men who reside in low- and middle-income (L&M) neighborhoods. In 2009, the estimated cost to build and maintain Bogotá's CicloRutas was US$ 3 million, with a total investment of US$ 50 million.[8]

Policy Outcome

In studies conducted in high-income countries, dedicated bicycle lanes have been associated with the promotion of physical activity (Pucher and others 2010). In Bogotá, studies of CicloRutas users show that 70 percent cycle more than five days a week, 73 percent do it because bicycles offer a rapid means of transportation, 13 percent do it for health reasons and, 14 percent cite other reasons. Nearly one-fourth reports that the CicloRutas infrastructure is an incentive to use bicycles as a means of transportation (Segura 2011). The average number of minutes spent in physical activity during leisure time and in biking for transportation by CicloRutas users is greater than that of Bogotá's adult population.

A 2010 cost-benefit study showed that for every US$ 1 invested in the CicloRutas, US$ 2.8 could be saved through health gains related to being physically active (Ricaurte 2010). This reported benefit falls below that reported for Ciclovías, due to the difference in the number of users between the two programs.

Policy-Making Process

CicloRutas were included in Bogotá's development plan, "Charting a City," during mayor Mockus' 1995–97 administration, in which public space was one of the priorities. The plan called for a permanent "Ciclovía road network" to provide recreational and environmental benefits that would link the city's water canals with metropolitan green areas.[9] In 1997, the first corridor in the Fucha River canal was constructed.[10] The CicloRutas faced opposition from some residents, however. Specifically, people who lived around the Fucha River complained that the construction negatively affected the environment. The city negotiated with these residents, offering to build a linear park (which ultimately was built), and the CicloRutas remained a priority.

In 1996, the Japanese International Cooperation Agency (JICA) conducted a study for the Urban Transportation Master Plan that recommended diversifying the city's transportation modes and providing connections among the modes (Nair and Kumar 2005; Colombia, Instituto de Desarrollo Urbano 2003). Although the recommendations were not adopted at the time, some were included as a framework for in the CicloRutas master plan three years later (Alcaldía Mayor de Bogotá, Instituto de Desarrollo Urbano 1999).

When the city administration changed, so did the CicloRutas' emphasis, and the program shifted from an environmental and recreational focus to one that emphasized alternative means of transportation. Mayor Peñalosa's development plan called for 80 km of CicloRutas along the general road network and main city parks, intended to "reduce travel times, offer a comfortable and efficient service, and respect the surrounding environment" (Consejo de Bogotá 1998). IDU contracted with a private group to develop a CicloRutas Master Plan that would promote biking for transportation; the plan laid out the concepts, actions, and policies designed to implement and maintain a 300.9 km network. Although the Master Plan's main focus was transportation, it also mentioned bicycle use as a means to foster health, recreation, and sports.[11] Thus, the CicloRutas project was developed within the land-use plan, and from 1998 to 2001, the city built 232 km, while simultaneously renovating roads and infrastructure for the TransMilenio bus rapid transit system. Between 2002 and 2004, another 67 km were added. In 2003, the World Bank provided a loan to build road connections and optimize the network. Subsequent administrations from 2004 to 2010 built another 76 km.[12]

Mayor Luis Eduardo Garzón's administration (2004–07) included the CicloRutas in the 2005–06 Transportation Master Plan as a nonmotorized strategy, and in the Public Spaces Master Plan as part of the multisectoral public space subsystem. Although both plans mention potential health benefits, those were not the main goals, nor was the health sector involved in the program's design, implementation, or promotion (Alcaldía Mayor de Bogotá 2009).

Further, the networks were not a priority in subsequent administrations (as they had been under Mayor Peñalosa), and these subsequent city governments only complied with provisions in the 2004 land-use plan (Article 174, Classification of Road Sections, Decree 430), which required all road construction to include CicloRutas on the main road grid and on the arterial grid. In 2009, this infrastructure was included in the 1355/Law on obesity as a recommended program to prevent NCDs. Despite this, the CicloRutas Master Plan has yet to be formalized through an administrative decree.

Main Stakeholders and Their Positions

City administrators, including mayors Mockus and Peñalosa, clearly took a leadership role in launching and developing the CicloRutas, first as a link between waterways and metropolitan green areas for recreation and subsequently as an alternative mode of transportation. IDU, too, was a key stakeholder in supporting the generation of this infrastructure, as were the IDRD and the Bogotá Water Supply and Sewage Company (EAAB, for its Spanish acronym). Recommendations to diversify the city's transportation modalities contained in JICA's 1996 study, conducted for the Urban Transportation Master Plan, supported the creation of the CicloRutas. City residents supported the program by using the infrastructure. Finally, some grass-roots organizations opposed the construction of CicloRutas around waterways, arguing that they negatively affected the environment.

The network is a multisectoral effort. IDU maintains it, but public utility companies are also involved, such as the EAAB, the Bogotá Telephone Company (ETB, for its Spanish acronym), and Colombia's energy company (Codensa). The transportation sector (through the Secretaría de Movilidad) also participates. In 2006, the national police signed an agreement to guarantee security and to conduct educational activities with users. University students and activists organized cycling groups to encourage university students and workers to use the CicloRutas, help enhance security, and promote bicycling as a transportation alternative. They also engaged in advocacy (Segura 2011; Universidad de los Andes 2011).

Lessons Learned

This infrastructure faced several challenges along the way, including the fact that its number of users is low (approximately 1 percent of the population, according to data from 2004 to 2008), given the size of the investment (Cámara de Comercio de Bogotá 2009). According to a 2011 study (Segura 2011) and data from Bogotá's Chamber of Commerce, low usage could be attributed, in part, to the network's lack of connection with other transportation modes, limited security, high crime, and insufficient and inadequate bicycle racks. The fact that cars are held in higher regard than are bicycles also may be a barrier for new users. In addition, the construction of the CicloRutas was not accompanied by promotion campaigns about respecting cyclists or by measures to reduce accidents and thefts; for these reasons, the network remains unattractive to some groups (i.e., to women, high-income individuals, children, and older adults) (Cámara de Comercio de Bogotá 2009). The fact that the network's management is not adequately coordinated—Bogotá does not have a single entity charged with promoting and facilitating bicycle use as a means of transportation—is also detrimental. Finally, the city does not have a clear policy on bicycle use that includes regulations, because the CicloRutas Master Plan was not included in an administrative act; it only serves as a frame of reference.[13]

There were several factors that supported the creation and extension of the CicloRutas for the promotion of PA: the city's vision that emphasized sustainable means of transportation; a development plan that considered these means as priorities and allocated sufficient resources to bring them about; and road changes that supported the new infrastructure (e.g., the construction of corridors for the TransMilenio bus rapid transit system, which involved adding sidewalks, separators, and CicloRutas, with tree planting and underground networks). Factors that hindered the initiative included interruptions in the network that discourage its use; a lack of leadership directly responsible for coordinating the infrastructure's design, implementation, and monitoring; detrimental transportation priorities that accorded greater weight to vehicles than to bicycles; road insecurity and crime; bicycles' low status as a transportation alternative; and inadequate financing for maintenance.

TransMilenio Bus Rapid Transit System

TransMilenio is a bus rapid transit system (BRT) whereby buses travel on dedicated lanes and operate in ways similar to rail-based systems with exclusive stations (Peñalosa 2002, 1–22).

TransMilenio has 84 km of main routes and 895 km of lanes, and carries 463 million passengers per year (2010 and 2011 data), with the figure steadily increasing by 5 percent annually in recent years (TransMilenio 2011a).[14] An average of 192,936 passengers ride during rush hour, 82 percent of whom are in income levels 2 and 3, and 93 percent do not own a vehicle (a profile similar to those using other forms of public transportation). The cost of a bus ticket in 2013 was US$ 0.93 (1,700 Colombian pesos) in peak hours and US$ 0.77 in non-peak hours, Sundays and holidays, which covers travel throughout the network; two daily trips for 20 days during peak hours was the equivalent of 12 percent of the minimum wage in 2013.

TransMilenio operates through a public-private partnership that functions as follows: IDU provides the infrastructure (grid system, stations, platforms, and workshops); seven private firms selected through public bidding (and which are paid per km covered) operate the system, and two private firms obtain concessions to collect fares; TransMilenio S.A. plans, manages, and controls the system and is financed through 3 percent of ticket fares and advertising at the stations (Cain and others 2006; TransMilenio 2011b).

Phase I infrastructure was estimated to cost US$ 240 million (US$ 5.9 million per km^2), financed from the gasoline tax (46 percent), the national budget (20 percent), a World Bank loan (6 percent), and local funds (28 percent). Costs for Phase II were estimated at US$ 545 million (US$ 13.3 million per km^2) and were financed by the national government (66 percent) and gasoline tax (34 percent). In the TransMilenio master plan, total capital costs were estimated at US$ 3.32 billion, which included vehicles and fare collections (Cain and others 2006; Hidalgo and others 2007; Leal and Bertini 2003).

Policy Output

Although the TransMilenio system was not planned as a means of promoting physical activity, the fact that its stations are about 500 m apart causes users to walk about 15 minutes per trip. In other forms of public transport, users can ask bus drivers to stop nearer to their destinations, and thus walk far less. TransMilenio thus increases the likelihood that adults in a neighborhood with one or two TransMilenio stations will walk more than those living in other neighborhoods (Cervero and others 2009). On average, the number of minutes that TransMilenio users walk, both as a means of transportation and for leisure activities, is greater than that of Bogotá's overall adult population.

The Policy-Making Process

The process of building the BRT system began in 1995, when the development plan "Charting a City" included projects such as the metro, the metrobus, and the grid system. In 1998–2001 the administration at the time also proposed a system that integrated a metro with dedicated bus lanes, and discussed creating a company, TransMilenio S.A., to run it. At that time the plan to build a metro was indefinitely postponed, however, because costs exceeded the country's finances and such a system would still not meet the demand (Cain and others 2006; Gilbert 2008). Despite their initial reluctance, authorities approved a BRT system project that ultimately led to TransMilenio (based on the 20-year experience with dedicated bus lanes in Curitiba, Brazil). The priority was to improve the transportation system (Gilbert 2008). TransMilenio S.A. was created in 1999 through the Council of Bogotá's Agreement 04. The project's plan, design, and construction involved local and foreign companies; feasibility studies took about 18 months (Leal and Bertini 2003).

Public transportation operators, who wield substantial political and economic power in the city, strongly opposed the new system. To resolve the conflict, authorities invited the operators to bid on contracts to operate the system. In the end, most contracts were awarded to large companies, however, which was criticized by experts and by the media (Gilbert 2008; Hidalgo and others 2007; Leal and Bertini 2003). Although the process changed somewhat in subsequent phases of the TransMilenio, the concentration of investment in a few hands is still being criticized. The new bus system also implied a change in the relationship between the city and transport operators (based on contracts for concessions) and in the economic model adopted, framed as a subsidy to infrastructure. In addition, it separated fare collection from the system's operations (Sandoval 2010).

In April 2000, four companies formed by local operators and associated with international investors, were granted the concession to operate 470 new buses. In December, Phase I of the TransMilenio officially began operations. That same year, a National Council for Economic and Social Policy (CONPES) document set guidelines for Bogotá's mass transport system, attesting to the political will at the national level. By 2002, four grid systems were completed under Phase I. One year later, the system was carrying about 792,000 passengers daily. By December 2005, three Phase II grid systems were completed and were fully operational.[15,16]

In 2004 during Phase II construction, and again during the 2007 and 2011 mayoral campaigns, TransMilenio was the subject of criticism and public debate (El Tiempo 2007; Revista Semana 2007, 2010). Residents complained that the construction had created congestion and that the pavement in the system's corridors was rapidly deteriorating, which needed large investments to fix and slowed travel times. Many also complained that buses were overcrowded, security was inadequate, and fares were high (Cain and others 2006; Gilbert 2008; Hidalgo and others 2007). Further, some claimed that their properties had been harmed by the construction of the system. Associations of architects and urban planners also criticized the incomplete works (e.g., walls of demolished properties) for aesthetic reasons (El Tiempo 2011). Also since 2007, the design for one of the corridors (Avenida Carrera 7) sparked debate among experts, politicians, the media, and the public (El Tiempo 2007; Revista Semana 2007; Revista Semana 2010b).

Initially, the plan proposed a network of 388 km, fulfilling 85 percent of the city's demand, to be constructed in eight stages by 2016, although that timetable has changed several times. The construction of the first part of Phase III suffered several delays and cost overruns, as well as corruption (El Tiempo 2011b; Revista Semana 2012; Revista Semana 2010a). Currently, additional resources are needed to finance the remaining stages and debate has resurfaced regarding the relative merits of a metro or tram system and their advantages over the TransMilenio (*Metro en Bogotá* 2012).

As with the other three interventions reviewed, the health sector was not involved in the planning, design, implementation, or maintenance of the TransMilenio system. Rather, the health sector's role, as it was with the Ciclovía, has been to respond to emergencies in the system as they arise. Researchers have explored TransMilenio's potential to generate public health benefits (Cervero and others 2009).

Main Stakeholders

The main stakeholder behind the development of the TransMilenio was the city administration through the urban planning and transportation sectors, which wanted to improve the public transportation system. At the national level, the CONPES provided support to its development. The program and its infrastructure have faced opposition since its inception from public transport operators. Some house owners around TransMilenio's construction sites also opposed it, as did some citizens and users.

Lessons Learned

Factors that promoted the TM as an infrastructure that promotes PA included the political will of national and local governments, and the location of stations about 500 m apart, which allowed for at least 15 minutes of walking. Factors that hindered the program included low user satisfaction; the cost of the fare, which is high for lower-income groups; and various problems that surfaced during implementation.

Outdoor Gyms

The outdoor gyms are located in urban parks and contain low maintenance equipment so residents can engage in physical activity free of charge.[17] These gyms have been installed in six parks (three metropolitan, two zonal, and one local) in four Bogotá neighborhoods (2011 data); some zonal parks in the Engativá site have had a few pieces of equipment installed. Each park has exercise equipment that allows several people to do warm-ups, muscular toning, stretching, and aerobic exercises (the amount of equipment depends on the park's size and condition). The aim is for people to use each piece of equipment for 10 minutes and, for parks that have 11 pieces, to do the entire cycle in 1 hour and 50 minutes.[18] The cost of the equipment at each site, land adaptation, and installation of 11 pieces of equipment was US$ 25,000–28,000; costs vary depending on the parks' conditions.

Policy-Making Process

The first outdoor gym was installed in 2009. That year, the IDRD's technical unit promoted the idea of renovating existing equipment in parks and installing new pieces to be able to cater to various age groups and community physical-activity needs. Simultaneously, a private company presented a proposal to IDRD for installing outdoor gyms in parks. That year, the company placed some equipment in Tunal Park as a sample of what it could offer. When it removed the machines eight months later, the community launched a mail-in campaign, asking that the equipment be reinstalled. Prompted by the community's demands, IDRD decided to acquire equipment (based on its own specifications) and install it using private-sector resources within the framework of Agreement 78 of 2002.[19] This agreement created a tax exemption for companies that invest in the management, maintenance, or improvement of district parks through signed contracts with IDRD.

In the following years, IDRD reached out to the private sector through two models. The first involved a modified version of IDRD's "Adopt a Park" program, an initiative that sought partnerships between the community, private enterprise, and the district to recover and maintain the city's parks through interinstitutional agreements for one to three years;[20] the change gave the private sector the opportunity to provide exercise equipment for outdoor gyms. In the second model, private companies would donate the equipment, but would not be responsible for maintaining it; Bogotá's 2002 Agreement 78 made this second option possible.

IDRD also involved communities in the process of installing the gyms; the Institute held workshops in various neighborhoods to identify residents' preferences and reviewed previous studies about their needs. It also tried to ensure that communities would take ownership of the equipment, which it accomplished; for instance, one neighborhood association monitors the equipment to prevent vandalism. Since 2009, Colsanitas (a prepaid health care company), Novartis Laboratories, Athletic Colombia S.A., and the IDRD itself have donated equipment. This equipment was installed in high-, medium-, and low-income neighborhoods and throughout variously sized parks in the metropolitan area. The first pieces of equipment were imported, but were installed by Colombian companies; later, Colombian firms began to manufacture equipment based on IDRD designs. In 2011 new equipment was installed with help from two cooperatives from the education sector and the city administration of Engativá.

Throughout, the process never faced any opposition; rather, the public has been enthusiastic. But it is difficult to raise funds for new equipment and protect it against vandalism. In an effort to protect the equipment, it was installed in larger parks, where surveillance could be guaranteed and the protection of the equipment has been promoted to the community. The only drawback is that equipment needs to be installed in hard-surface areas, which has reduced green space. IDRD is trying to find a design that uses more environmentally friendly materials.

Main Stakeholders

IDRD was the main stakeholder in promoting the installation of new equipment in public spaces and renovating existing equipment to respond to the needs of different communities and age groups. The private sector financed some of the equipment as a way to promote an image of corporate social responsibility. The community has supported outdoor gyms by using them and asking for their installation. Currently, the following sectors participate in outdoor gym use and maintenance: the private sector (health and education), and the recreation, culture and sports sectors.

Lessons Learned

Facilitating factors for the program included mutually beneficial partnerships between the public and private sectors and widespread public use. The factors that hindered the program included inadequate financing to install the new equipment and vandalism.

Lessons Learned from the Ciclovía, CicloRutas, TransMilenio, and Outdoor Gyms

The implementation of the Ciclovía and the infrastructures are all examples of multisectoral work, although they each occur through different levels of formal agreements and numbers of participants. In all four cases, the health sector's role has been secondary and limited with regard to these program and infrastructures. Thus, the health sector should build on the experiences or programs of other sectors, mainly those of recreation, culture, sports, transportation, and urban planning. This is especially important in contexts which seek to avoid inefficient replication of efforts and to optimize resources aimed at promoting physical activity. Given the potential benefits of the Ciclovía, CicloRuta, TransMilenio, and outdoor gyms in promoting physical activity and, in turn, preventing NCDs, the health sector should participate in their planning and evaluation.

The Ciclovía and parallel programs (Recreovía), as well as the outdoor gyms, demonstrate that it is possible to optimize resources if the existing urban infrastructure is used to promote physical activity and if public-private partnerships are promoted within the city's broad objectives. Since these programs' benefits involve several goals (including but not limited to physical activity), it makes it easier to create a collaborative environment involving other sectors, such as recreation, social integration, transportation, culture, and tourism sectors.

The cases reviewed here demonstrate how strategies to improve public space can be used to promote physical activity. However, such efforts must be accompanied by activities that guarantee safety, social equality, and offer opportunities for people of different age groups, including those with disabilities.

The cases described also illustrate how such efforts need to be sustained under various city administrations. Cities, which are constantly evolving, must include them in their short-, medium-, and long-term plans, as this will promote a more comprehensive and efficient approach.

These cases further illustrate the need to strengthen and integrate institutions to achieve common objectives and meet the public's needs. In the case of Bogotá, multisectoral efforts aimed at impacting the population at large, made it possible for the city to produce a significant transformation in a relatively short time.

Regarding the Ciclovía, CicloRutas, and TransMilenio, it was the city leaders' vision, commitment, and political will that were key at the beginning of the process and that ultimately led to the program and infrastructures' success. Plans were executed because they were an important part of these leaders' agendas and priorities, responded to the city's needs (e.g., of transportation, equity, and recreation), and were consistent with models pursued through several administrations. For example, administration changes made it possible to strengthen the Ciclovía program and guarantee its continuity. For its part, the public has supported the Ciclovía and the gyms by frequently using them. This sustained support makes it difficult for government officials to take stances that run counter to public opinion.

Finally, the Bogotá experience illustrates that the task of promoting physical activity must involve various dimensions—in other words, it should include strategies to promote PA during leisure time, and as a means of transportation (e.g., biking and walking).

Mexico: National Agreement on Food Health, Strategy against Overweight and Obesity

Evelyne Rodriguez

Under the leadership of Mexico's Secretariat of Health, a National Agreement on Food Health (ANSA) was signed by several government agencies and the industry; it aimed to reduce the country's high percentage of overweight and obese persons. The Technical Basis for the National Agreement on Food Health is the technical document that accompanies the Agreement; it describes the actions by Ministry and Agency. Finally, deriving from an ANSA agreement, the Secretariat of Health and the Secretariat of Public Education also signed on to the General Guidelines for the Sale or Distribution of Food and Beverages in School Consumption Facilities in Basic Education Schools. This document establishes the criteria that govern which foods and beverages are recommended for consumption and sale in schools and which should not be distributed. The policy-making process that culminated in these agreements was long and difficult. In the end, although agreed-upon measures were less ambitious than those originally proposed by the Secretariat of Health, these agreements represent some of the most comprehensive efforts in the region to fight against the overweight and obesity epidemic.

Background

Mexico has some of the highest obesity rates among LAC and OECD countries (OECD 2011). According to the 2012 National Health and Nutrition Survey (ENSANUT 2012), 9.7 percent of pre-school children (under 5 years old) are overweight or obese. Among school-age children (5 to 11 years old), 34.4 percent are overweight or obese; 19.5 percent of boys are overweight and 17.4 percent are obese, while 20.2 percent of girls are overweight and 11.8 percent are obese. Among adolescents 12–19 years old, 35 percent are overweight or obese; 19.6 percent of boys are overweight, and 14.5 percent are obese; and 23.7 percent of girls are overweight, and 12.1 percent are obese. Among adults 20 years old and older, 71.3 percent are overweight or obese: 42.6 percent of men are overweight, and 26.8 percent are obese, while 35.5 percent of women are overweight, and 37.5 percent are obese. Between 2006 and 2012 (years of the last two ENSANUT surveys), the prevalence of overweight and obesity among adolescents and adults increased (albeit at a lower growth rate than that shown from 1999 to 2006) as well as children under 5; while the prevalence among school-age children remained the same.

In 2008, the costs attributable to obesity in Mexico represented 13 percent of total health expenditure (0.3 percent of gross domestic product [GDP]). If cost-effective interventions are not implemented to prevent and control obesity and its co-morbidities (hypertension, type 2 diabetes, cardiovascular disease, breast cancer, and colorectal cancer), direct costs could double and indirect costs could triple in a decade.[22]

The Policy

Faced with these numbers, in January 2010, the Government of Mexico, under the leadership of the Secretariat of Health, launched the National Agreement for Food Health: Strategy Against Overweight and Obesity (Acuerdo Nacional para la Salud Alimentaria: Estrategia contra el Sobrepeso y la Obesidad, known as ANSA for its Spanish acronym). ANSA aimed at implementing national, multisectoral, and multidisciplinary actions to reverse the obesity epidemic and its associated chronic diseases. The Agreement was signed by public-sector secretariats and agencies and by industry representatives. It set the following main targets for 2012: reverse the rising trend in the prevalence of overweight and obesity in children 2–5 years old, bringing the rate down to the figure for 2006; halt the increase in the prevalence of overweight and obesity in the population 5–19 years old; and slow the growth in the prevalence of overweight and obesity in the adult population.

ANSA established the following specific objectives:

- Promote physical activity in the population in the school, workplace, community, and recreational environments with the collaboration of public, private, and social sectors.
- Increase the availability, accessibility, and consumption of safe drinking water.
- Decrease the consumption of sugars and fats in drinks.

- Increase daily intake of fruits and vegetables, legumes, whole grain cereals, and fiber in the diet by making these foods more available, more accessible, and by promoting their consumption.
- Improve the population's informed decision-making capacity about proper diet through nutrition labeling that is useful and easily understood, and through the promotion of literacy in nutrition and health.
- Promote and protect exclusive breast-feeding until six months of age, and promote appropriate complementary feeding beyond six months of age.
- Decrease the consumption of sugar and other caloric sweeteners added to foods, by, among other measures, increasing the availability and accessibility of food with reduced or no added caloric sweeteners.
- Provide guidance to the population on recommended portion sizes in home food preparation and make processed foods that allow for this accessible and available, including smaller portion sizes in restaurants and food outlets.
- Reduce daily intake of saturated fats in the diet and minimize trans fats from industrial sources.
- Reduce daily sodium intake by lowering the amount of sodium added and increasing the availability and accessibility of products with low or no sodium.

The Technical Basis for the National Agreement on Food Health (henceforth referred to as the Technical Basis), is a document detailing the proposed policies and actions for the prevention of overweight and obesity. The Technical Basis specifies objectives, activities, and actions each agency or entity must undertake to reach the 2012 targets; it includes 117 activities and 249 actions.

Also within the context of ANSA, in August 2010, the Secretariat of Health and the Secretariat of Public Education issued an additional document, the General Guidelines for the Sale or Distribution of Food and Drinks in School Consumption Facilities in Basic Education Schools (hereafter referred to as the Guidelines), which is a binding regulation for all public and private basic education schools. These Guidelines establish the criteria that govern the type of foods and beverages that are allowed for sale and those recommended for consumption in school facilities. It also establishes a Committee for the School Consumption Facility to monitor the preparation, handling, consumption, and sale of food and beverages in schools.

In addition to the secretariats of Health and of Public Education, the heads of the following federal government secretariats and agencies (agency names in English are followed by their Spanish acronyms) also signed ANSA: the Federal Consumer Protection Agency (PROFECO); the Institute for Social Security and Social Services for State Workers (ISSSTE); Mexican Petroleum (PEMEX); the National Commission of Physical Culture and Sport (CONADE); the National System for Comprehensive Family Development (SNDIF); the National Water Commission (CONAGUA); the Secretariat of Agriculture, Livestock, Rural Development, Fisheries, and Nutrition (SAGARPA); the Secretariat of the Economy (SE); the Secretariat of Finance and Public Credit (SHCP); the

Secretariat of Labor and Social Welfare (STPS); the Secretariat of National Defense (SEDENA); the Secretariat of the Navy (SEMAR); the Secretariat of Social Development (SEDESOL); and the Mexican Social Security Institute (IMSS).

ANSA also was signed by the National Institute of Public Health (INSP) representing academic institutions; and by the industry represented by the Business Coordination Council (CCE), the Confederation of Chambers of Industry (CONCAMIN), the National Chamber for the Transformation Industry (CONACINTRA), and the Mexican Council of Consumer Products Industries (CONMEXICO). Later on, ANSA was also endorsed by state and local governments.

The Policy-Making Process

There were different negotiation processes for ANSA, for the Technical Basis, and for the Guidelines. ANSA and the Technical Basis documents underwent three processes of negotiation—within the Secretariat of Health to reconcile the five-step strategy proposed by the Coordination of Advisors to the Secretary of Health and the comprehensive agreement proposed by the Undersecretary for Prevention and Health Promotion; within the federal government to reach consensus between the Secretariat of Health and the other secretariats and agencies; and between the Secretariat and industry regarding the wording of ANSA. Negotiations for ANSA and the Technical Basis took 10 months, ANSA was signed in January 2010 and the Technical Basis were published in February 2010. The Guidelines underwent separate negotiations between the Secretariat of Health, the Secretariat of Public Education, SE, and industry.

During this process, the H1N1 emergency started and the Secretariat of Health issued a health alert that lasted from April 2009 to June 2010. The high-level officials of the Secretariat focused its efforts dealing with the health emergency, and as a result, the negotiation process was suspended temporarily.

Within the Secretariat of Health

Of the two initiatives for dealing with the obesity and overweight epidemic within the Secretariat of Health, the Coordination of Advisors to the Secretary's approach emphasized individual responsibility; the one supported by the Undersecretary for Prevention and Health Promotion argued that, in addition to individual responsibility, overweight and obesity were multifactorial problems resulting from the environment where people live, socialize, and work. Because many of the factors affecting the epidemic were beyond the health sector, the approach of the Undersecretary for Prevention and Health Promotion also called for integrating and implementing policies through the broad participation of relevant governmental, industry, and civil society stakeholders. Proponents also felt that actions must occur at the individual, family, community, and school levels.

Within the Federal Government

The Secretariat of Health presented a national agreement against obesity proposal to the Social Cabinet. This proposal set forth actions for each agency; the proposal, which was more ambitious than the agreement eventually signed, was adopted in general terms by the Social Cabinet in March 2009. With support from the Social Cabinet, the Secretariat of Health called on the various agencies that would be involved to discuss their responsibility under the proposed actions, including the Secretariat of Public Education, and STPS, SE, SHCP, SEDESOL, and SAGARPA. According to the Secretariat of Health, only the Secretariat of Public Education showed interest in participating in the agreement, including the Secretary himself. The others viewed the issue of obesity as a responsibility of the Secretariat of Health.

According to officials from the Secretariat of Health interviewed, the following actions were in the original proposal but were not agreed upon during the negotiations, and thus were left out of ANSA: the SE for updating nutrition labels, SHCP for fiscal stimuli and taxes on soft drinks, SEDESOL-Diconsa for changing the supply of products in Diconsa stores, SEDESOL-Liconsa for substituting whole milk for skim milk in the subsidized milk sold by Liconsa, SEDESOL-Oportunidades for changes in nutritional supplements offered by the "Oportunidades" program (a conditional cash-transfer program), SEDESOL for changing the standards for construction sites, and SAGARPA for promoting reduced fat dairy products.

Between the Secretariat of Health and Industry

Because some of the interventions originally proposed in ANSA could have significantly affected industry, the Secretariat of Health began a negotiation process with industry's representative bodies. This process was long, difficult, and exhausting for both parties. In the end, industry agreed to sign ANSA and the Secretariat agreed not to publish the Technical Basis as part of the same document. Thus, neither ANSA nor the Technical Basis includes any specific industry actions. ANSA is a political document describing the targets for 2012 and the general objectives of the strategy. It established the creation of a National Forum for Prevention of Overweight and Obesity integrated by federal agencies, and representatives of industry, academia, municipalities, and civil society that was never created. During these negotiations, the INSP acted as a technical body of the Secretariat of Health, providing evidence in support of the Secretariat's proposals and sitting in at the negotiating table with the food industry, always in the presence of a Secretariat officer. All 10 ANSA goals were discussed during the negotiations, with agreement quickly reached in some of them but not in others. For example, agreement was easily reached in encouraging water consumption and physical activity, but there was disagreement on issues such as reductions in the consumption of sugar, saturated fats, and sodium.

Negotiations for the General Guidelines

Upon signing the Agreement, negotiations for the Guidelines started. INSP developed a proposal after regularly meeting with the secretariats of Health and of Public Education. Given the decentralised operation of health and education services, the two Secretariats also discussed the proposed Guidelines with the state health and education authorities through joint summons. Negotiations for these Guidelines were particularly complex. In addition to the participation of the above-mentioned secretariats and INSP's technical support, the Presidency and the SE participated at industry's request as well as SAGARPA. The food and beverage industry participated through corporate organizations such as CONMEXICO, the National Agricultural Council (CNA), the Confederation of Employees of the Mexican Republic (COPARMEX), and CCE; CONMEXICO led the process.

The Secretariats of Health and of Public Education sent their proposed guidelines to the Federal Commission for Regulatory Improvement (COFEMER) prior to publication; this proposal had not been agreed upon with industry, but it had gradual implementation mechanisms. COFEMER is an agency of the SE whose mandate is to assess the regulations that the federal government's agencies want to issue to ensure that their social benefits are greater than their costs. To this end, agencies must submit their draft regulations to the Commission, undergo a public-consultation process, and await COFEMER's decision. As soon as it receives these regulations, COFEMER is required to make public the regulations, the opinions it issues, and the authorizations and exemptions it grants. In the approval process for the Guidelines, COFEMER received some 900 comments, to which the Secretariats of Health and Public Education responded. Discussions with the industry started after the guidelines were sent to COFEMER. As occurred during the ANSA negotiations, INSP and experts from other institutions, such as the Salvador Zubirán National Institute of Medical Sciences and Nutrition (INNSZ) and the Ibero-American University, supported both secretariats. International evidence and recommendations, particularly from WHO, also were very helpful. On the down side, at the negotiating table industry was represented by officials largely responsible for regulatory aspects and for liaisons with the government, with nutritional experts participating only sporadically.

Industry's main concerns during the negotiations were that the measures' economic impact had not been estimated, that the Guidelines did not include provisions about the measures' implementation, evaluation, monitoring and enforcement, that the proposal did not discuss the sale of food prepared to be sold in the schools or sold in the vicinity of the schools, and that no other complementary or alternative measures, such as physical activity, closing the food outlets in the schools and providing box lunches and/or providing full availability of drinking water in schools had been considered. Also, they were concerned about a stigmatization of their products. In response, the secretariats of Health and of Public Education argued that industry already was prepared to deal with possible economic consequences, since it was technically able to make the needed changes to its processes and since some of the acceptable products were already available in the market, and that there would not be a high economic cost; the Mexico's Technological Autonomous Institute (ITAM) was hired to evaluate the economic impact of the proposal. The secretariats also contended that the school environment limited the students' possibilities of buying foods outside the schools while they were attending school and that they would work with local authorities to prevent food sales in the area around the schools. Finally, the secretariats also argued that other existing measures already promoted physical activity.

As a result of the negotiations, the original proposal was modified and some elements, such as the limitation of food based on energy density, were eliminated and the wording was changed to avoid the stigmatization of products. Upon COFEMER's approval, the secretariats of Health and of Public Education jointly issued the Guidelines in August 2010. These guidelines have been highly publicized.

Main Stakeholders

Table 5.4 shows the main actors and their roles in this initiative. In the public sector, the Secretariat of Health spearheaded the design and negotiations, relying heavily on the INSP. The Social Cabinet, by gathering all relevant federal agencies for discussion and signing the Agreement, played an important role. In terms of the Guidelines, the main government negotiators were the secretariats of Health, of Public Education, and of the Economy. For industry, the leading role was played by CONMEXICO, an umbrella organization that brings together 43 leading companies, mainly from the food and beverage industry, including Coca Cola, PepsiCo, Nestle, Bimbo, Danone, Alpura, Barcel, and Kellogg's.

Lessons Learned

Of the three documents reviewed, the Guidelines is the most visible and the strongest legally; it also contains more substantive actions than the other two. ANSA and the Technical Bases are broad policy documents that set goals only through 2012. The activities and actions included in these two instruments only pertain to the federal government, and few of these activities represent substantive changes from the normal work of the agencies and programs. The greatest changes rest with the secretariats of Health and of Public Education, and deal with improving the quality of school breakfasts. Some relevant programs and actions were excluded from the Agreement, such as preventive health programs within the Secretariat of Health, IMSS, and ISSSTE. Further, most activities related to programs that distribute food support were also excluded, with the sole exception of the milk composition sold by SEDESOL-Liconsa. According to an official from the Secretariat of Health, ANSA is only an "acceptable minimum," while the Guidelines represent a "successful international experience." Table 5.5 summarizes the key stakeholders that participated in these policy-making processes, their positions, the strategies they used, their interactions, and the lessons learned.

Table 5.4 Roles and Responsibilities of Participating Institutions during ANSA Negotiations

Institutions and departments or units	Roles and responsibilities
Secretariat of Health • The Secretary • Undersecretariat for Prevention and Health Promotion • General Directorate of Health Promotion • Strategy and Development Directorate of Healthy Environments • Coordination of Advisers of the Secretary • Coordinating Unit for Vinculation and Social Participation	Design the proposed Agreement; conduct its negotiations within the executive branch and with industry. Responsible for monitoring.
Secretariat of Public Education • The Secretary • Secretariat for Basic Education • General Directorate of Development Management and Educational Innovation	Negotiation of the Guidelines with the Secretariat of Health. Responsible for implementation.
National Institute of Public Health • Center for Research in Nutrition and Health	Design of specific recommendations to the Agreement. Generation of technical evidence for the design and negotiation of the Agreement. Participation in negotiating tables with industry; providing technical support to the Secretariat of Health.
Secretariat of the Economy • Undersecretariat of Industry and Trade	Participated in the negotiation of the Guidelines with industry, along with the secretariats of Health and of Public Education.
Federal Commission for Regulatory Improvement (COFEMER)	Responsible for approving federal regulations that impact the private sector. It approved the Guidelines.
Presidency of the Republic • Social Cabinet	Called on federal government secretariats and agencies to discuss the Agreement.
Mexican Council of Consumer Products Industry (CONMEXICO)	Leader of the industry's position in the negotiation of the ANSA and the Guidelines.

Note: ANSA = National Agreement on Food Health.

Among the strengths of this experience, the effort effectively positioned the issue of obesity within the government's agenda and generated a greater consciousness of the industry; it issued a public document based on international evidence that provides guidance in the fight against overweight and obesity; it was a learning experience about overweight and obesity and how to confront the epidemic; it generated a multisectoral dialogue and negotiation around the issue; it demonstrated the Secretariat of Health's leadership and coordination capabilities in working with other public agencies and with the private sector and strengthened its relationship with the Secretariat of Public Education to position the issue in the school agenda; and exemplified what can be accomplished through a joint public-private effort toward a public health goal; and the process of public consultation of the Guidelines allowed for discussion of all relevant issued posed by the industry and other stakeholders.

Table 5.5 Governance of Multisectoral Activities to Prevent Risk Factors for Overweight and Obesity: Mexico's National Agreements on Food Health (Strategy against Overweight and Obesity [ANSA])

Key stakeholders' positions	Strategies	Interaction among stakeholders	Lessons learned
Secretariat of Health (SS): Led the processes with the aim of reducing the prevalence of overweight and obesity in the population. **National Institute of Public Health (INSP):** Had the same position as the Health Secretariat **Secretariat of Public Education (SEP):** Participated in the discussions with the aim of reducing overweight and obesity among school age children. **Secretariat of Economy (SE)** Participated in the discussions with the industry related to the Guidelines. **The Federal Commission for Regulatory Improvement (COFEMER):** Its objective was to ensure that the net social impact of the Guidelines was positive; in other words, that their social benefits were larger than the costs, through a public consultation process.	**Secretariat of Health** • Coordinate the process. • Articulate actions with other public agencies. • Negotiate actions with the private sector. • Disseminate information. **INSP** • Provided technical expertise to draft the Agreement, the Technical Basis, and the Guidelines. • Technically supported the SS during negotiations with Industry. • Used existing international evidence to draft the proposals and support negotiations with the industry. **SEP** • Was one of the agencies that showed support and commitment to the Agreement besides the Secretariat of Health. • It negotiated the Guidelines and is currently implementing it.	There were four negotiation processes involved. The first one took place within the SS, between those that wanted a strategy based on individual responsibilities and those that wanted a more comprehensive multisectoral agreement. Once the decision was taken on the strategy to use, a proposal was presented to the Social Cabinet. This proposal was accepted and then the Social Cabinet called all relevant Federal Government agencies to discuss the proposed agreement. In this negotiation, the SEP was the agency that was most supportive of the SS proposal. In this negotiation instance, some of the original activities of the proposal were rejected by the agencies that would be responsible for implementing them. As a result, a less ambitious proposal was then negotiated with the industry. The industry only agreed and signed on to the general objectives and targets of ANSA; therefore, the document with the actions by agency had to be published in a different document, the Technical Basis. In neither one are there specific compromises by the industry.	**Strengths** • It positioned the issue in the government agenda; • It generated a multisectoral dialogue and negotiation around the issue; • Was supported on a good diagnosis of the issue. • It showed the leadership and coordination capacity of the SS with other public agencies and with the private sector; • Joint public-private work toward a public health goal. • It strengthened the relationship between SS and SEP. • Greater consciousness of the industry on the issue. • Public consultation process of the Guidelines. **Weaknesses** • The cost of actions was not estimated and no budgetary resources were allocated to the actions of government committed to. • No system to monitor and evaluate the Agreements was established; • No assessments have been made of the Agreement or its specific measures;

table continues next page

Table 5.5 Governance of Multisectoral Activities to Prevent Risk Factors for Overweight and Obesity: Mexico's National Agreements on Food Health (Strategy against Overweight and Obesity [ANSA]) (continued)

Key stakeholders' positions	Strategies	Interaction among stakeholders	Lessons learned
Presidency of the Republic – Social Cabinet: Call main responsible agencies and discuss what could be done to reduce the obesity epidemic.	**SE** • Participated in the negotiations for the Guidelines. **COFEMER** • It approved the Guidelines.	In the context of ANSA the Guidelines were drafted and agreed between the SS and the SEP. The Guidelines had to be submitted to COFEMER for its approval. During the process of approval, SS and SEP with the intervention of SE negotiated with the industry. Once they were approved, they were issued.	• The National Forum for Prevention of Overweight and Obesity integrated by federal agencies, and representants of industry, academia, municipalities and civil society established in ANSA was never created. Instead the responsibility to monitor the Agreement was given to the National Council for the Prevention and Control of Chronic, Noncommunicable Diseaes (CONACRO) but this monitoring is currently not taking place;
Mexican Council of Consumer Products Industries (CONMEXICO): Defend industry interests in the negotiations for the ANSA and the Guidelines.	**Social Cabinet** • Supported the SS by calling all relevant Government agencies to participate in the discussions for the ANSA. **CONMEXICO** • Main industry representative that participated in the negotiations of ANSA and Guidelines. • Did not agree to the specific activities per agency, therefore only signed ANSA that contains the general objectives and the specific actions were published as a separate document in the Technical Basis.		• ANSA and the Technical Basis are not binding nor enforceable;

175

The current context provides many opportunities to continue the work begun by ANSA: there is an international climate inclined to work on healthy lifestyles and consumers are increasingly demanding healthy foods.

The initiative also had some weaknesses. Drawbacks included the fact that the cost for federal agencies and industry of Agreement activities and actions was not estimated; no budgetary resources were allocated to the actions the government had committed itself to (e.g., the availability of drinking water in schools); no system was established to monitor and evaluate the Agreements; no assessments were made of the Agreement or its measures; the National Forum for Prevention of Overweight and Obesity integrated by federal agencies, and representatives of industry, academia, municipalities and civil society established in ANSA was never created, instead the responsibility for monitoring the Agreement was assigned to the National Council for the Prevention and Control of Chronic, Noncommunicable Diseases (CONACRO, for its Spanish acronym), a council integrated only by federal agencies, which has not operated; and the Agreement is not binding or enforceable.

Uruguay: Tobacco-Control Policies

Amanda Sica, Franco González Mora, Winston Abascal and Ana Lorenzo for the Ministry of Public Health of Uruguay

Uruguay's tobacco-control policies, which are among the strongest in the region, have come about through a long and continuous process characterized by a strong partnership between civil society organizations, international organizations, parastatals, and government agencies, as well as by the strong leadership and commitment of policymakers. Uruguay was the first South American country to ratify the WHO Framework Convention on Tobacco Control and the first middle-income country to enact legislation on creating 100 percent smoke-free environments. As a result of its strong anti-tobacco policies, between 2006 and 2009, daily tobacco consumption among adults decrease in 10 percentage points.

Background

In Uruguay, 14.5 percent of all deaths (around 13 a day) are attributed to tobacco use: 34.9 percent from cancer, 28.7 percent from respiratory diseases, 28 percent from cardiovascular diseases, and 8 percent from second-hand smoke (Sandoya 2011).

The Policy

In pursuit of its early commitment to tobacco control, Uruguay developed policies to promote public health for over a decade. Most importantly, since ratifying the FCTC the country has worked steadily to adopt the measures included in the Convention, focusing on creating smoke-free environments nationwide.

Outcome

While it cannot be stated definitively that daily tobacco consumption dropped from 2001 to 2006, there has been a 10 percentage point decline between 2006 and 2009 (table 5.6).

Policy-Making Process

Uruguay's anti-tobacco efforts started much before the country's signing and ratification of the FCTC. In the 1950s, pioneers like Dr. Joseph Saralegui and Prof. Helmut Kasdorf began working on tobacco-control activities. And since 1988, the first Tobacco Addiction Polyclinic started operations in the Medical Clinic "A" of the Faculty of Medicine of the University of the Republic. In the 1990s, with the support of the PAHO and the Latin American Coordinating Committee on Tobacco Control (CLACCTA), educational activities were organized for primary and secondary school teachers to decrease tobacco prevalence and its onset in children and young people. In 1994, the first postgraduate course on tobacco and health was developed, and the Faculty of Medicine of the University of the Republic was declared a smoke-free building. That same year, the Honorary Commission to Fight Cancer (CHLCC) began to inform the public and to work with various institutions in the implementation of 100 percent smoke-free environments, to conduct research on youth and smoking, and to teach courses on tobacco control. Simultaneously, the Honorary Committee for Cardiovascular Health worked on educational activities and coordinated the first "Stop and Win" competitions.

In 2000, at the request of the Ministry of Public Health's Directorate General of Health (DIGESA), an unofficial organization, the National Alliance for Tobacco Control (ANCT, for its Spanish acronym), was established. The alliance comprised government agencies, parastatals, international agencies, academic organizations, and nongovernmental organizations (NGOs). The Alliance was the first entity to put forth the issue of tobacco control

Table 5.6 Prevalence of Daily Tobacco Smoking among the Population 15–64 Years Old, Urban Areas, Uruguay, 1998–2011

Source	Incidence (%)	Confidence intervals	
		Low (%)	High (%)
Third National Drug Consumption Prevalence Survey, 2001	30.7	28.8	32.7
Fourth National Drug Consumption Prevalence Survey, 2006	33.5	32.3	34.7
Global Adult Tobacco Survey (GATS 2009)	23.5	21.8	25.4
Continuous household surveys, 2011	22.8	21.7	23.9

Source: Estimates using information from the source surveys.

as a public health issue in the media, and gave visibility to the organized movement on tobacco control in Uruguay. The partnership created a greater understanding of the magnitude of the problem among smokers and nonsmokers, with the latter becoming aware of their right not to be exposed to tobacco smoke from others. The process of cohesion and empowerment in Uruguay's tobacco-control movement began with a broad educational and information campaign, followed by advocating for the signing and subsequent ratification of the FCTC.

The ANCT was instrumental in the ratification of the FCTC and in making progress on national anti-tobacco legislation. In 2002, the senate's Public Health Committee met the members of the newly formed ANCT. During the meeting, members introduced the Alliance to the senate and presented their concerns about the tobacco epidemic in the country. In 2003 and 2004, parliament received members of different health organizations, including the Medical Union (SMU), the Ministry of Public Health, and ANCT; this was a joint effort of state institutions and civil society to promote the ratification of the FCTC.

At that time, several workshops were conducted with journalists, human resource managers of public agencies, and managers of health services. In addition, all available scientific evidence on the tobacco epidemic was widely distributed. Of great strategic importance were the activities aimed at informing and sensitizing policymakers in parliament and representatives of different political parties. As a result of all this work, in 2005 the Alliance received a special recognition during PAHO/WHO's World No Tobacco Day.

Uruguay ratified the FCTC through Law No. 17,793 in July 2004, becoming one of the first 40 countries that ratified the FCTC worldwide and the first one to do so in South America.

In addition, in 2004 the Ministry of Public Health created the National Advisory Committee for Tobacco Control, an official entity reporting to this Ministry to advise it in all aspects of tobacco control.

In 2005, the new President Dr. Tabaré Vázquez, an oncologist committed to tobacco control, assumed office. That year, the National Program for Tobacco Control was created within the Ministry of Public Health, and was to become the focal point for tobacco control at the national level. This program has been responsible for planning, developing, and implementing all the tobacco-control policies that the country has carried out since then. It also represents the country at the regional and international levels.

In the first months of the new administration, the country fast-tracked the adoption of FCTC policies through executive orders (Executive Decrees). The new government issued seven tobacco-control-related decrees in under five months, which focused on reducing exposure to second-hand smoke. The executive use of fast-track regulations on tobacco control gave a boost to congress, which started to work on these measures and make them into laws.

The smoke-free spaces regulation (Decree 268/05) was enacted on 5 September 2005 and took effect six months later, on 1 March 2006. These intervening six months were used to provide information, raise awareness, and prepare for implementation. The public was informed about the benefits of smoke-free environments and was sensitized about the rights of nonsmokers. Campaigns always struck a positive note without stigmatizing the smoker, and offered treatment to people who wanted to stop. The first campaign, "1 Million Thanks," collected the signatures of people thanking smokers because on 1 March 2006 they would quit smoking in closed spaces. The 1-million-signature target was exceeded by 300,000 additional signatures collected in 45 days. In addition to reaching the target, the entire population and the communications media were effectively mobilized, amply demonstrating the extent of the population's involvement and acceptance of smoke-free environments. The second campaign, "Tobacco-Smoke-Free Uruguay," spread the word on the benefits of smoke-free air, raised awareness of the rights of nonsmokers, and offered treatment to those who decided to quit tobacco consumption.

Because the bar, restaurant, and commercial associations adamantly opposed the smoke-free regulation, it became essential to reach consensus with these entrepreneurs. At all times it was made clear that the policy was a high-level policy and that it would not change. Therefore, the measure itself was never in question, just the best way to implement it. Business associations worried that the measure could have negative economic impacts for them. To counter this, the government provided scientific evidence that showed the policies' potential positive effects. The business associations themselves took opinion polls among their customers about the possible effects of the measure—results showed that over 80 percent of respondents supported the measure, including smokers. Over the course of many meetings between businesses, civil society, and the government an agreement was reached to ensure transparency in enforcement cases that resulted in punitive measures. Since then, business associations lent strong support to the implementation of the measures and have become partners in the process.

Health advocates also worked hand in hand with businesses and the public transportation union. In particular, a major effort was made to win the support of bus drivers' unions, which opposed the changes. Authorities stressed the issue of occupational health and agreed to provide treatment for all smokers who requested it through public health agents. Authorities also emphasized that penalties would be imposed on drivers who smoked inside the vehicles.

In 2005, two other executive decrees were added to the smoke-free measure: the tobacco excise tax was raised, which resulted in an increase in tobacco prices, and health warnings would now take up to 50 percent of the larger sides of the cigarette package and would include images. The selection of these images was done after a careful analysis of various proposals; the final images were chosen by focus groups and later approved by the Ministry of Public Health. Further, misleading terms such as light, ultralight, or soft were banned from tobacco advertising, and tobacco advertising and sponsorships of sports events were prohibited.

A 2007 tax reform imposed a 22 percent value-added tax (VAT) on tobacco products, which had been exempt up to that point, and this tax was added to existing excise taxes. That same year, the parliamentary debate on a comprehensive bill on tobacco control began, which culminated in the approval of Law 18,256 on March 6, 2008.[23] To measures already in place, this law added a comprehensive ban on advertising, promotion, and sponsorship of tobacco products, and a requirement to provide diagnosis and treatment of tobacco addiction at the first level of care in all health services. These new measures constituted a comprehensive package of convergent measures.

To circumvent the ban on using terms such as "light" or "ultralight" on cigarette packages, the tobacco industry linked these terms to colors, letting consumers know the association between a color and its associated term. To eliminate this practice, a regulation was approved in 2009, allowing the tobacco industry only a single cigarette brand; in addition, the size of the health warning was increased to 80 percent of both larger sides of tobacco packages, in accordance with Article 11 of the FCTC and its guidelines. In 2010, the price of tobacco products rose again due to the tax increase. The price of tobacco products in effect rose far more than the consumer price index (CPI).

Between 2004 and 2010, the political climate was favorable to tobacco control: the party in power held a majority in both chambers, and a key lawmaker promoting the process (a physician) was in the main opposition party. Other parties also supported the measures.

On the other hand, the tobacco industry's reaction to tobacco-control measures was to avoid them or weaken them. When Uruguay became a smoke-free country in 2005, the industry claimed the controls limited "freedom" and smokers' "rights." It published articles in the local press citing practices in countries such as Chile, the Netherlands, and Spain, where smoking areas were designated within closed sites.

The industry and some groups, such as advertising agencies and kiosk owners, resisted the ban on publicity, promotion, and sponsorship in certain venues. The industry also disregarded the ban by delivering free cigarette samples to young people, launched publicity without including the warnings required by the regulations, or simply ignored the ban.

Further, when parliament debated the tobacco law, the industry lobbied lawmakers to reject it. It argued that the law would limit individual rights, negatively affect tourism, and hurt the national industry's competitiveness vis-à-vis multinational companies, which it claimed could advertise in other countries.

Finally, the industry used litigation at the national and international levels. Beginning in 2008, it filed judicial and administrative lawsuits in Uruguay against all the regulations. Abal Hermanos, representing Philip Morris in Uruguay, British American Tobacco (BAT), and Monte Paz filed lawsuits against different regulations, including the Tobacco Control Law of March 2008; the law's regulatory decree of June 2008; an August 2008 ordinance (514/2008) that provides for a single presentation for each commercial brand of tobacco products and the size of the pictograms on 50 percent of the total surface of both package sides;

the decree that increased the size of the pictograms to 80 percent of the total surface of both package sides; and 2009 and 2011 ordinances that provide for new graphic designs.

In their first legal action, BAT and Abal Hermanos filed appeals for infringement of fundamental rights and freedoms in ordinance 514/2008. They argued that it was illegal because it would restrict companies' rights to use their brands and designs and would infringe on the right to work and the right of trade and industry, causing serious economic damage to tobacco companies and their workers. But the courts of first instance and the appellate courts recognized the Ministry of Public Health's prerogative to regulate health policies, and deemed the regulations justified and not excessive.

Abal Hermanos also filed a suit in Uruguay's Supreme Court of Justice, claiming that Articles 9 and 24 of Law No. 18256 violated the principles of legality and separation of powers, because the legislative branch must handle the limitation of rights. They also argued that the brand was being indirectly expropriated without compensation, based on the required size of the graphics, and that the rights to work, trade, brands, industry, and production would also be limited.

All of the tobacco companies questioned the legality of other decrees and ordinances using the same arguments. The tribunal, as did the Supreme Court, recognized the Ministry of Public Health's regulatory power with regard to health, however. It also found that the country was complying with the FCTC, which had been ratified by law, and that the Ministry should protect public health to avoid the thousands of deaths caused by smoking each year.

At the international level, Philip Morris Brands Sarl (Switzerland), Philip Morris Products S.A., and Abal Hermanos S.A. requested arbitration to the International Centre for Settlement of Investment Disputes (ICSID) in February 2010 (Switzerland and Uruguay have an investment protection agreement and are part of the ICSID).

Throughout the legal process, Uruguay has claimed its sovereign right to establish public health policies to protect its population from the threat to health from tobacco use. Further, it argued that the right to health, which is closely related to the right to life, should be regarded as a fundamental human right, and that measures must be put in place to regulate the marketing of harmful products.

Main Stakeholders

Among the proponents of the initiatives, national, international, public, and private institutions and groups supported tobacco-control measures. From 2000 to 2004, many of these proponents were coordinated under an umbrella organization created by the Ministry of Public Health—the ANCT. The Alliance included PAHO's Country Office in Uruguay, the Montevideo Municipality (Health Division), the Honorary Committee to Fight against Cancer, the Honorary Commission for Cardiovascular Health, the Medical Union of Uruguay, the Medical Federation of the Interior (outside Montevideo) (FEMI), the University of the Republic's School of Medicine, Uruguayan Passive Smokers, and

Uruguayan Society of Family Physicians (SUMEFA). This broad range of organizations, many with excellent track records and social recognition, helped secure funds and build public understanding about the issues. The Ministry of Public Health served as the Alliance's headquarters and was the link to the executive and legislative branches in the promotion of tobacco control. Table 5.7 summarizes the key stakeholders that participated in these policy-making processes, their positions, the strategies they used, their interactions, and the lessons learned.

The National Program for Tobacco Control, created by the Ministry of Public Health in 2005, has played a leading role since its inception. It has operated as a national focal point for the development and implementation of the tobacco control policies.

More recently, institutions outside the Ministry of Public Health and Alliance also played a role, including the National Resources Fund. The Fund became active in smoking-addiction treatment and trained health professionals to decentralize the services and improve access to free treatment nationwide; it also launched a program offering free medications at clinics. Other institutions that participated at this juncture included the Smoking Epidemic Research Center (CIET), which conducted research to promote and strengthen capacities for tobacco control and to monitor the effects of policies, and the Uruguayan Tobaccology Society (SUT), a scientific society offering continuous vocational training, academic activities, and conducting research.

A key player in the enactment of the smoke-free spaces decree was the President of the Republic, whose firm conviction about tobacco control persuaded all members of his party to endorse the tenets of the FCTC, and subsequently led to the law's approval. The law had the support of all political parties. The President of the Republic's staunch support helps explain the fact that the executive branch, together with the organized tobacco-control movement, issued, beginning in 2005, a series of tobacco control measures that included Uruguay becoming a smoke-free country.

Among the ranks of the opposition to the measures, the tobacco industry led the charge against tobacco control. For many years, three companies have manufactured and marketed tobacco in Uruguay—Monte Paz, S.A., the national company, and BAT and Philip Morris (Abal Hermanos), two multinationals. Since the 1980s, Monte Paz S.A. has had the largest market share. Businesses such as bars and restaurants also opposed the smoke-free environment decree at the beginning of the process since they argued these would negatively affect them.

Factors that Supported the Implementation

Several factors fostered the implementation of the tobacco-control measures, including the six leading ones described below.

The creation of the ANCT may well be one of the most important factors in the successful implementation of tobacco-control measures. The Alliance's multidisciplinary composition and its independence from party politics were critical to its success. Many of the groups that gathered under its umbrella already had excellent track records and social recognition, which helped secure funds and

Table 5.7 Governance of Multisectoral Activities to Prevent Tobacco Use: Uruguay's Tobacco-Control Policies

Keys stakeholders' positions	Strategies	Interaction among stakeholders	Lessons learned
The presidency supported tobacco control.	**The presidency issued** several executive decrees for tobacco control, which started the process. Provisions in these decrees were later enacted into law and approved by parliament.	• After many meetings with bar, restaurant, casino, and business trade associations, health authorities agreed on control procedures and ensured transparency when penalties were imposed. From then on, business associations lent much support to the smoke-free measure.	• Uruguay was able to carry out tasks through a government–civil society partnership that sought and reached consensus on the issues.
The Ministry of Public Health. At its insistence the National Alliance was formed in 2000. Starting 2005 the work was carried out through the National Program for Tobacco Control.	**The Alliance** • Its lobbying efforts brought the health aspects of tobacco use and control into the news. • It worked toward the ratification of the FCTC. • It held workshops with journalists, administrators of health services, and those responsible for human resources in government agencies.		• The partnership used information campaigns to alert the public about the hazards of smoking. However, it was careful not to stigmatize smokers, and thus get the attention of both smokers and nonsmokers. Ultimately, this led to greater acceptance of the controls.
The National Alliance for Tobacco Control (the Alliance) advocated and worked toward tobacco-control policies. The institutions that were part of the Alliance were:	• It launched a comprehensive media campaign to ensure the public's support for the smoke-free environment decree—the "1 million thanks campaign."		
• The Ministry of Public Health, which acted as the lead agency in the effort and the institution that formed the National Alliance.	• It provided lawmakers with scientific evidence on the extent of the tobacco problem.	• In discussions with the bus drivers union, health authorities also stressed the issue of occupational health and agreed to provide treatment for all smokers who requested it through public health agents. Also, it stressed that penalties would be imposed on drivers who smoked inside the vehicles.	• Partnership members adopted the common theme of creating smoke-free environments, which proved an effective strategy that allowed them to later focus on other interventions.
• The Municipality of Montevideo. • The Honorary Committee to Fight Against Cancer • The Honorary Commission for Cardiovascular Health. • The Pan American Health Organization (through its Country Office in Uruguay). • The Medical Union of Uruguay. • The Medical Federation of the Interior (outside Montevideo).	**The Ministry of Health through the National Tobacco Control Program (since 2005)** • Launched a comprehensive media campaign to ensure the public's support for the smoke-free environment decree ("Tobacco-Smoke-Free Uruguay"). The campaign was based on the benefits of smoke-free spaces, raising awareness of the rights of nonsmokers.		• Policies focused on the issue of smoke-free environments. Through this approach, public opinion shifted from accepting smoking as a normal habit to one that was harmful. Thus, authorities were able to approve programs to stop smoking, and prevent nonsmokers from starting.
• The University of the Republic. • Uruguayan Passive Smokers. • Uruguayan Family Doctors Society.	• The Program was responsible for the development and implementation of tobacco-control policies at the national level, coordinating efforts with the other groups that were developing policies.	• Interaction with the tobacco industry has been confrontational; as of this writing, the international arbitration at the ICSID is pending.	
Other stakeholders outside the Alliance that also supported Tobacco Control: • National Resources Fund. • Smoking Epidemic Research Center (CIET) • Uruguayan Tobaccology Society (SUT)	• It assumed the task of checking compliance with the regulations using inspectors trained to carry out the task country-wide.		

table continues next page

Table 5.7 Governance of Multisectoral Activities to Prevent Tobacco Use: Uruguay's Tobacco-Control Policies *(continued)*

Keys stakeholders' positions	Strategies	Interaction among stakeholders	Lessons learned
The tobacco industry—Monte Paz S.A., the national company, along with British American Tobacco (BAT) and Philip Morris (Abal Hermanos), two multinationals. **Trade associations of bars, restaurants, casinos, and businesses** originally opposed the smoke-free environments, believing that they would diminish their profits. They also wanted to ensure transparency in the implementation of penalties for noncompliance with smoke free environments. **The bus-drivers union** opposed the smoke-free environment decree.	**The tobacco industry:** • When Uruguay became a smoke-free country in 2006, the industry claimed the measure limited "freedom" and infringed on smokers' "rights." It published articles in the local press citing practices in countries such as Chile, the Netherlands and Spain, where designated smoking areas were permitted within closed sites. • Further, when parliament debated the tobacco law, the industry lobbied lawmakers to reject it: It argued that the law would curtail individual rights, harm tourism, and damage the national tobacco industry's competitiveness with respect to multinational companies, which, it argued, could advertise in other countries. • Finally, the industry used litigation at the national and international levels. Since 2008, it filed judicial and administrative lawsuits nationally against all the regulations. At international level, Philip Morris Brands Sarl (Switzerland), Philip Morris Products S.A., and Abal Hermanos S.A. requested that the ICSID–World Bank arbitrate in their favor against Uruguay in February 2010 (Switzerland and Uruguay have an investment protection agreement and are part of the ICSID). **Bar, restaurant, casino, and business trade associations** conducted their own opinion survey to determine their clients' views on smoke-free environments; the results showed that over 80 percent of respondents—including smokers—supported the measure.		• Clear, transparent controls were created, along with enforcement procedures. These included severe economic penalties on violators, since it was understood that if regulations were not enforced, they would be ineffective. • Health warnings on cigarette packages had to include large graphics along with the texts. Also, the images chosen were based on results from studies of the target population. It was found that images that included people had a greater impact than those with just symbols. • Comprehensive measures were adopted at the same time, which increased the effectiveness of the individual measures.

build public understanding about the issues. And, because they worked as a group, no delegate could be singled out for holding anti-smoking positions was also beneficial. The Alliance's lobbying efforts also brought the health aspects of tobacco use and control into the news. The Alliance held workshops with journalists, administrators of health services, and those responsible for human resources in government agencies. Further, it provided lawmakers with scientific evidence on the extent of the problem.

A second key factor was the creation of the National Program for Tobacco Control within the Ministry of Public Health. This entity developed and launched the country's tobacco controls, prepared prevention strategies, established treatment for those addicted to tobacco, and coordinated national efforts with the other groups that were developing policies. The Program also took charge of checking compliance with the regulations nationwide, using specially trained inspectors. Inspection results are recorded in a computer program that classifies the information by geographical area, activity, and type of violation. Based on the data and upon consultation with the Program and the National Advisory Committee for Tobacco Control, the Ministry of Public Health levies penalties. At the regional and international levels, the National Program represents Uruguay in the Inter-governmental Commission for Tobacco Control of MERCOSUR and Associated States and at WHO and FCTC Secretariat meetings. The Program also shares information with other Latin American and Caribbean countries and some countries outside the region.

The existence of the Honorary Committee to Fight Against Cancer and the Honorary Commission for Cardiovascular Health also was critical; the fact that both entities are autonomous and committed to preventing disease clearly helped implement these measures.

The country's international commitment, in its ratification of the FCTC, also had a hand. Uruguay was committed to complying with the FCTC, which focused on controlling consumption and reducing demand and supply through price increases (with taxes); regulating the contents of products and emissions; requiring health warnings on labels; promoting public education campaigns; banning ads and sponsorship of tobacco products; and treating tobacco addiction.

The political context, too, fostered the change and helped bring about the new national policies. The country's political organization, where all political parties participate in agreements that lead to national policies also helped, as did the active participation of lawmakers from the opposition parties throughout the process.

Finally, then-President Tabaré Vázquez's commitment also was critical in bringing about the measures.

Lessons Learned
Uruguay was able to successfully carry out tasks thanks to a partnership between governmental and civil society organizations that sought and reached consensus on tobacco-control issues.

The various groups relied on information campaigns to alert the public about the hazards of smoking. They were careful not to stigmatize smokers, however, which allowed them to capture the attention of smokers and nonsmokers alike. The sensitization of the population through positive messages led to greater public acceptance of all tobacco-control measures.

The adoption of smoke-free environments as the policy's linchpin, not only proved to be an effective strategy that allowed proponents to subsequently focus on other interventions but also represents a significant change in social behavior.

Thanks to this multifaceted strategy, public opinion shifted from accepting smoking as a normal habit to viewing it as a harmful one. Thus, authorities were able to approve programs to stop smoking, and prevent nonsmokers from starting.

Clear, transparent control procedures were created, along with enforcement procedures. The latter included severe economic penalties on violators, since it was understood that if regulations were not enforced, they would be ineffective. Health warnings on cigarette packages also were required to include large graphics along with text. Moreover, the images were chosen based on results from studies of the target population. Studies concluded that images that included people had a greater impact than those with just symbols.

The national clinical guidelines to address smoking covered all health workers, not just physicians; all health personnel were subject to these guidelines in accordance with the regulations in effect. The provision of free and universal access to tobacco-dependence treatment in both public and private health care services at the primary care level was considered to be both important and fair.

Once the measures were adopted, two groups in particular, needed to be targeted—those at low socioeconomic and cultural levels, and adolescents. The first group was chosen because it has higher rates of smoking than the general public. The second group was important because it is at those ages that the smoking epidemic propagates, and there is always the risk that a new generation of adolescents will start smoking.

The simultaneous application of a comprehensive package of measures ensured that there was synergy and that the impact of each measure was enhanced.

Pending Issues

First, authorities must intensify supervision to ensure compliance with the tobacco-control measures. Second, efforts must redouble to obtain passage of the draft bill that health authorities submitted to parliament in May 2012, and which seeks to eliminate the only remaining tobacco publicity (where tobacco is sold). Third, price increases of tobacco products should reflect economic conditions, such as improved income levels and inflation. Under such considerations, increases should be periodic. Fourth, since young people continue to consider smoking, health authorities must run frequent information campaigns targeting them. Fifth, health institutions should carry out programs to evaluate the scope, quality, and results of health of their tobacco cessation treatments. Sixth, authorities should move forward with strategies to promote smoke-free homes. Seventh, more research must be conducted to determine the burden of disease and death caused by smoking, as well as on the years of healthy life lost due to disability. The research should be accompanied by studies of the economic burden the diseases impose on the health care and social security systems. And finally, more research is needed to determine factors related to tobacco consumption among lower socio-economic groups and adolescents.

Argentina: Tobacco-Control Policies

María Eugenia Barbieri for the National Ministry of Health of Argentina

Even though Argentina has not ratified the FCTC, the country's Ministry of Health (MOH) and civil society groups have worked effectively over several years in the fight against tobacco: they have built coalitions, disseminated information, and helped deliver services. In particular, they played a key role in getting the National Law No. 26687 on tobacco control approved, despite much opposition from a powerful tobacco industry.

Background

In Argentina, tobacco consumption is responsible for 40,591 deaths a year—almost 13.6 percent of them among persons over 35. Cancers account for 31 percent of total deaths, followed by cardiovascular diseases (30 percent) and respiratory diseases (27 percent). Also, it is estimated that 111 people die every day due to tobacco-related diseases (Pichon-Riviere and others 2013).

In addition, an estimated 824,804 disability-adjusted life years (DALYs) are lost to tobacco consumption, with 35.5 percent representing premature mortality and 64.5 percent representing persons living with different degrees of disability. Males bear the greatest burden (67 percent of DALYs lost), but increased smoking among women, especially younger women, may change these figures (Rossi and others 2005). Also, an estimated 926,878 QALY are lost to tobacco consumption (Pichon-Riviere and others 2013). It is estimated that diseases associated with tobacco consumption represent 15 percent of national health expenditures, far greater than tobacco taxes collected in any one year (Bruni 2005). New information reveals that the direct cost of tobacco related diseases represents 1 percent of the Gross National Product (GNP) and 12 percent of national health expenditures (Pichon-Riviere and others 2013).

In the last 14 years, tobacco consumption in Argentina has dropped overall: in 1999, for example, the Secretariat for the Prevention of Drug Abuse and Drug Trafficking (SEDRONAR) estimated that 39.8 percent of the population between ages 16 and 64 smoked. According to the 2005 and 2009 National Risk Factors Surveys, tobacco consumption among adults (18 years and older) decreased from 29.7 percent to 27.1 percent between those two years.

The Global Adult Tobacco Survey (GATS), carried out in 2012, showed that the prevalence of tobacco consumption decreased to 21.4 percent in 2012, representing 700,000 fewer smokers than in 2009. Although tobacco use has decreased overall, there is a concern about its use among adolescents. According to the 2012 Global Youth Tobacco Survey (GYTS), 22 percent of students between ages 13 and 15 years smoke.

The Policy

Tobacco-control policies in Argentina have evolved over time. One of the most significant milestones was the approval of Law No. 26687 in 2011, which regulates ads, promotion, and consumption of tobacco products. Its key aspects include a ban on smoking in all public or private closed spaces, including casinos, bingos, bars, restaurants, theaters, museums, libraries, public transport, covered stadiums, and workplaces; a ban on ads, promotion, and sponsorship of cigarettes or tobacco products in the media and on public thoroughfares; health warnings with graphics on cigarette packages and a ban on misleading words like light, smooth, low-tar content or similar terms; and a ban on cigarette sales to minors, loose or in packs, in educational, health, or recreational establishments. At the provincial and local levels, many controls have been introduced since the 1990s; in 2005, some provinces began approving anti-smoking laws with technical support from the MOH. Altogether, 21 out of 24 provinces have such laws.

While the laws vary, generally they promote smoke-free environments and ban ads, promotion, and sponsorship of tobacco products or sales to minors. Some provinces have strict laws on smoke-free areas, as does the city of Buenos Aires, but 14 others added exceptions, such as gambling rooms and casinos, entertainment areas that do not admit people under 18, mental health centers, prisons, reserved areas in bars, restaurants or coffeehouses, and smokers' clubs. To a lesser extent, some laws also allow establishments to define their smoking areas (for example, Santa Cruz allows industrial, commercial, or service establishments to choose whether or not they will apply the smoking ban).

Fourteen provinces have enacted articles covering advertising, promotion, and sponsorship: for example, direct or indirect ads and sponsorship of sports or cultural events are prohibited, as is the use of clothing at such events that advertise the names of tobacco companies. But three provinces allow some ads, if they state that consuming tobacco harms health. In provinces that have not passed smoking controls, some municipalities have introduced their own laws.

A basic legal principle is that standards from higher-level jurisdictions take precedence over those from lower ones; if standards are incompatible, the national standard prevails over the provincial law, and the provincial one prevails over the municipal one. If the standard protects a human right, as with regulations that protect health, the more protective norm is applied. Thus, the national law sets the standards for 100 percent smoke-free spaces. Where provinces or municipalities have already enacted laws, the highest standard regarding public health will prevail, whether national, provincial, or municipal.

Outcome

Public health has clearly benefitted from these laws and actions. For example, the city of Neuquén recorded a significant reduction in exposure to second-hand smoke, respiratory symptoms (from 57.5 percent to 28.8 percent), and irritation (from 86.3 percent to 37.5 percent) after the law was introduced (Schoj and others 2010), and in Santa Fe province, hospitalizations for acute coronary syndrome were reduced by 28.3 percent after the smoke-free law was passed.[24] Moreover, the 100 percent smoke-free laws in the City of Buenos Aires, Córdoba, Santa Fe, and Tucumán did not negatively affect business in bars and restaurants (González-Rozada and others 2008).

According to a study carried out by the Ministry of Health, in the period 2012–20, 7,500 coronary heart disease (CHD) deaths, 16,900 myocardial infarctions, and 4,300 strokes could be avoided with the full implementation and enforcement of the National Law No. 26687. Annual percent reduction would be 3 percent for CHD deaths, 3 percent for myocardial infarctions and 1 percent for stroke (Konfino and others 2012).

Policy-Making Process

Argentina has yet to ratify FCTC, even though the president has signed it and 31 bills have been introduced in the national congress to ratify it. Some studies suggest that this delay is due to the tobacco industry's lobbying of lawmakers and officials within the Ministry of the Economy (Mejia and others 2008; Barnoya and Glantz 2002). Industry spokespersons claim that reducing tobacco consumption would have a significant economic impact on tobacco producers, employment, and the collection of the Special Tobacco Fund (FET), a cigarette tax they say is the mainstay of small producers (box 5.1) (Mejia and others 2008). There are studies that refute these arguments, however. For example, research conducted by the Torcuato Di Tella University (Buenos Aires) found that FET funds do not necessarily benefit small producers, because funds are distributed based on the amount produced by each province. For example, Salta and Jujuy, which are the two provinces with the highest production, receive two-thirds of the funds. But in these two provinces, a few major producers account for most of the tobacco farming, and so FET funds benefit them, not the small farmers (Alonso and González-Rozada 2010). According to the most recent data from the Ministry of Agriculture, in 2011, 65.4 percent of FET resources were allocated to Salta (35 percent) and Jujuy (30.4 percent). These provinces account for 15.1 percent of total tobacco producers, with an average of 17.2 hectares planted per producer (13.0 in Salta and 21.4 in Jujuy), the highest of the country.

In December 2009, the Coalition to Ratify the FCTC was formed, bringing together almost 70 NGOs and scientific associations that promote tobacco control. The Coalition works closely with the MOH's National Tobacco Control Program (for more details on the development and goals of this program, see the section on main stakeholders below) and is developing a strategy to get the FCTC ratified. The Coalition pursues its goal through advocacy, mass media campaigns,

Box 5.1 The Special Tobacco Fund (FET)

Decree-law No. 19800 of 1972 created the Special Tobacco Fund (FET). The FET is financed through a tobacco excise tax, approximately 7 percent of the retail price of each cigarette pack.

According to the law, 80 percent of the tax collected is for price support to tobacco producers, which represents a subsidy; the remaining 20 percent goes to retrofitting and diversification efforts in the tobacco-growing provinces. Argentina began to reduce the subsidy in 1997, when it signed the World Trade Organization's Agricultural Agreement, an agreement that mandates that internal assistance must be reduced by 13 percent within 10 years, beginning in 1995. At present, Argentina cannot provide more than US$ 75 million a year in direct subsidies to tobacco-growing activities.

The funds collected are allocated to the tobacco-growing provinces based on quantity of tobacco produced. The Fund's revenues increased 214 percent from 2006 to 2011, amounting to a bit more than 1 billion Argentine pesos in 2011. Most of the resources go to Jujuy and Salta, which receive more than 60 percent.

The Ministry of Agriculture, Livestock, and Fisheries (MoALF) enforces the FET[a]. The Ministry pegs the price of the varieties of tobacco and transfers collected FET funds to the provinces, which, in turn, pay the surcharge directly to producers. The Ministry also uses the remaining balances to finance the sector's retrofitting plans. These plans include credit to tobacco producers, technological inputs, market studies, retention of payment systems, purchase of capital goods, technical assistance, training courses and institution building.

On many occasions between 1984 and 2004, the executive branch has tried to reduce the FET transfers. For example, Decree 455 of 1999 provided for a 12 percent reduction, and the 2001 budget stipulated a 50 percent reduction—none went into effect. On the contrary, in 2008 Law 26467 was passed, creating measures to compensate the agro-industrial complex, the regional economies that depend on tobacco production, and the fiscal collection for the potential damage caused by the tobacco control measures, *increasing* the amount of the FET. The law was submitted along with another regulation on health measures (file 0039-EP-2008, presented to the chamber of representatives) signed by the president and the MOH. However, the latter was not approved.

Source: Alonso and González-Rosada 2010.

a. Argentina, Ministerio de Agricultura, Ganadería y Pesca. 2008. Ejecución mensual del presupuesto del FET – Ejercicio. Law 26467: Modificaciones a la Ley Nº 24,674 de Impuestos Internos y a la Ley Nacional del Tabaco Nº 19,800. Establézcanse medidas económicas para desalentar el consumo de productos elaborados con tabaco.

the training of journalists, holding of public events (such as marches to the national congress to demand ratification), and dissemination of materials to lawmakers explaining why smoking issues are critical. Initially, coalition strategies were effective. For example, the senator for the City of Buenos Aires, Daniel Filmus, included the tobacco issue in his agenda and held two hearings to which he brought civil society groups, persons affected by tobacco (addicts or those with health problems), representatives of the National Program for Tobacco Control, physicians, economists, lawyers, and tobacco companies. In February 2010, he proposed legislation to ratify the FCTC. However, industry again prevented the bill from being approved, using the same arguments as before—ratifying the FCTC would harm regional economies, eliminate the FET, and ban tobacco production. The Coalition then warned against such delays and lobbied officials to ratify the FCTC and approve a strong national law. Aware that the FCTC would not be approved in its entirety, the Coalition proposed the enactment of a national law that included some of the FCTC measures: establishing 100 percent smoke-free environments; banning tobacco ads, promotions, and sponsorships; and providing health warnings, with graphics, on cigarette packs.

Subsequently (and when it was clear that tobacco subsidies would remain), cigarette producers and sellers broke ranks with tobacco producers. In June 2010, a new law for tobacco control was drafted (file 1950/10), which the National Tobacco Control Program supported and that included some provisions of previous laws drafted by the MOH in 2006 and 2008. Four more draft bills were presented (three from lawmakers representing tobacco provinces) that included concessions such as separate smoking areas, ventilation requirements for closed spaces (bars and restaurants), small warnings on cigarette packs (without graphics), and partial bans on ads. Negotiations continued between smoking-control advocates and those who backed the weaker laws. Coalition representatives worked with legislators, insisting that smoke-free environments and warnings on the packages that included graphics were nonnegotiable. However, they ultimately yielded on the issue of ads (allowing for exceptions in commercial publications read by those that grow, manufacture, import, export, distribute, deposit, and sell tobacco products and in direct communications with those over 18, when prior consent is obtained and their age is confirmed). However, this last exception makes the law open to interpretation.

This legislation is an initial step that, combined with other measures, is designed to comply with the National Program. However, it was only until 2011, after various attempts and the support of the MOH and civil society, that the national congress approved Law No. 26687, which regulates ads, promotion, and consumption of tobacco products. As mentioned earlier, many controls have been introduced at the provincial and local levels since the 1990s.

Although this legislation represents an important step forward in smoking control, advocates insist that it is not a substitute for the ratification of the FCTC. First, it does not comply with all the health-protection recommendations in that Convention. Further, it is not an international treaty that commits participating states to certain obligations. Finally, its provisions are not incorporated into Argentina's Constitution, which is above any national or provincial law. It should be noted, however, that even without ratification of the FCTC, Argentina after many national and subnational laws has lowered smoking prevalence by 18 percent between 1999 and 2012, a drop that is equivalent to more than 1 million fewer smokers. There was also a decrease in smoking prevalence among the youth as reflected by the GYTS. The enactment of smoke-free laws decreased the exposure to second-hand smoke, especially in restaurants and public places. Additionally, a strong tobacco surveillance system was developed in the Ministry of Health that gave the opportunity to implement the GYTS four times and be among the four countries that implemented GATS in Latin America. All of this was achieved without having the FCTC ratification and provides an idea of the additional benefits that the FCTC ratification would have in improving health in Argentina.

Main Stakeholders, Their Positions, and Strategies

The MOH and its National Tobacco Control Program played leading roles in spearheading Argentina's tobacco-control policies and measures. Civil society coalitions also worked steadfastly in support of tobacco control. On the other hand, the country's powerful tobacco industry—including tobacco growers, as well as cigarette producers and sellers—waged serious opposition to the passage of these measures. Table 5.8 summarizes the key stakeholders that participated in these policy-making processes, their positions, the strategies they used, their interactions, and the lessons learned.

In Argentina, tobacco-control policies have been limited, and the market for trading in and advertising tobacco products was virtually unrestricted. So, in 2003, the MOH began to work actively to launch some of the measures in the FCTC. To that end, through the 2003 Ministerial Resolution 236 and funding from the VIGI+A Program, the National Smoking Prevention and Control Program was established to sensitize and empower the population, promote the FCTC's ratification, and approve national laws. Later, through the 2006 ministerial Resolution 1124, it became the National Tobacco Control Program, with funds from the MOH.

The National Program targeted the main drivers behind the tobacco epidemic, including easy access to tobacco products, broad positive images associated with smoking, high exposure to second-hand smoke, and the health services' limited capacity to help individuals stop smoking. The Program's activities address the tobacco problem in three coordinated dimensions: primary prevention, cessation, and protection of passive smokers. Activities include regulating access to tobacco, promoting a lifestyle without tobacco, promoting and regulating smoke-free environments, and developing services and incentives to help smokers stop. Since 2011, it is also responsible for the application of the national tobacco control law, having the obligation of creating a national registry of allegations and offenders.

The MOH also supports economic studies that estimate the price elasticity of cigarette consumption and the effects on tax revenues. For example, a 2004 study found that a 10 percent increase in the price of cigarettes would reduce consumption by 2.65 percent, a result similar to that found in high-income countries. In terms of fiscal revenues, taxes could increase up to 102 percent and, thus, raise revenues (González-Rozada 2006). The Ministry also promotes studies to draft and follow up on legislative bills.

The MOH's message is designed to discourage consumption and prevent people from starting. Specifically, it attempts to set standards that restrict ads (as much as possible) or promotion and sponsorship of tobacco products; stop

Table 5.8 Governance of Multisectoral Activities to Prevent Tobacco Use: Argentina's Tobacco-Control Policies

Key stakeholders' and their positions	Strategies	Interaction among stakeholders	Lessons learned
The Ministry of Health (national) through the Tobacco Control Program, as well as provincial ministries of health and municipalities sought to reduce the harmful effects of tobacco by: • Regulating access to tobacco; • Promoting lifestyles without tobacco; • Promoting and regulating smoke-free environments; • Developing services and incentives to help smokers quit. • Building capacity in and providing technical assistance to municipalities to help them become 100 percent smoke free. **Civil society organizations** sought to reduce the harmful effects of tobacco use. The leading organizations are: • The Coalition for the Ratification by Argentina of the FCTC. • The Argentinean Anti-Smoking Union (UATA) • The Argentinean Tobacco Association (AsAT) • The Smoke-Free Partnership – Argentina (ALIAR) • The Inter-American Heart Foundation–Argentina (FIC Argentina) **The Ministry of Agriculture, Livestock and Fisheries and the Ministry of the Economy:** • Were concerned about the impact that these policies and the ratification of the FCTC could have on producers.	**The Ministry of Health** created the Tobacco Control Program, which has developed a comprehensive policy to address the main issues in tobacco control, such as: • Generate public awareness and empowerment. • Promote Framework Convention on Tobacco Control (FCTC) ratification and approval of national and provincial laws as well as municipal ordinances. • Generate information to guide and evaluate decision-making on tobacco control. • Foster the creation of a network of civil society organizations and the scientific community, media, and provincial and health municipal agencies to support and expand program activities; **Civil society organizations:** Advocacy. • Forming coalitions. • Disseminating information, including mass media campaign, training of journalist, disseminating information to lawmakers. • Monitoring compliance. • Delivering services. • Promoting the ratification of FCTC and national or provincial tobacco control laws through such strategis as public events, public marches to the National Congress. **The Ministry of Agriculture, Livestock and Fisheries** • Disseminated information about the negative effects that the ratification of the FCTC could have on producer provinces.	Argentina's tobacco-control achievements clearly are due to the leadership and efforts of the Ministry of Health and its Tobacco Control Program, as well as the sustained efforts of numerous civil society organizations that have advocated, provided information, trained, and provided technical assistance to lawmakers and other policy makers to promote tobacco control legislation at national and provincial level. This process has not been easy, the staunch and orchestrated opposition of tobacco-producer provinces and the tobacco industry. The national law for tobacco control was partly due to proponents generating a 'rupture' in the cooperation between the industry and tobacco producers by focusing on the health aspects of the legislation and clarifying that the tobacco subsidy the provinces receive would not be eliminated.	• The creation of the National Tobacco Control Program boosted tobacco control in Argentina. This Ministry of Health Program has led much of the tobacco control effort in the country. • The coordinated efforts of government and civil society organizations to pressure lawmakers to pass tobacco control measures, disseminate information on the harmful effect of tobacco and support smoke free initiative all over the country have also been key in the success so far. • The development of tobacco-control policies in Argentina are a good example of the difficulties inherent in the developing and implementing these laws, in countries where there are powerful players that oppose them, in this case the tobacco industry, several producer provinces, and sometimes government agencies, which were concerned about possible negative effects on producers and on fiscal revenue.

table continues next page

Table 5.8 Governance of Multisectoral Activities to Prevent Tobacco Use: Argentina's Tobacco-Control Policies (continued)

Key stakeholders' and their positions	Strategies	Interaction among stakeholders	Lessons learned
• Were concerned about the possible revenue losses from tobacco taxation. **Provincial and local governments (particularly governments in nonproducer provinces)** • were concerned about the harmful effects of tobacco use **Producer provinces and tobacco producers:** The provinces of Jujuy (37 percent of production); Salta (34.5 percent), Misiones (22 percent) and Tucumán (42 percent) were against the policies, including the ratification of the FCTC, on the grounds that they: • did not want to lose employment and economic activity. • did not want to lose resources from the Special Tobacco Fund (7.35 percent of final cigarette price). **The tobacco industry:** Nobelza Piccardo (representatives of British American Tobacco) and Massalin Particulares (Phillip Morris subsidiary) were against the policies.	**The Ministry of the Economy** • Established annual tax collection goals with the tobacco industry, at the expense of not levying or increasing any tax, contribution, fund, or surcharge on tobacco. **Provincial and local governments (particularly governments in nonproducer provinces)** • Several provinces have approved tobacco control laws with technical support from the national Ministry of Health. Córdoba, Santa Fe, Tucumán, the City of Buenos Aires, Río Negro, Chaco, Corrientes, Tierra del Fuego, San Juan, and San Luis were the first to do so. Several municipalities also have been approving tobacco control ordinances, such as Bahía Blanca. Even in provinces without smoking laws (mainly producer provinces) some municipalities have introduced their own, such as Tala (Salta), San Salvador de Jujuy (Jujuy), and Jardín América (Misiones). **Producer provinces and tobacco producers** • They have often, but not always, cooperated with the tobacco industry to block ratification of the FCTC and other tobacco control laws. • They have promoted weaker tobacco laws in congress to avoid the ratification of the FCTC and stronger national laws. **The tobacco industry** (Sebrié and others 2005): • Created a weak voluntary self-regulating code that eliminated television ads since 2003. • Proposed less stringent draft legislation that neutralized or diverted attention from stronger initiatives • Promoted programs such as "Courtesy of Choice" in order to avoid the 100 percent smoke-free environments • Conducted prevention programs for young people, to avoid stricter measures. • Disseminated the negative economic effects of such policies.		• This example also shows that even in such adverse circumstances, the concerted and committed efforts of health advocates both within and outside government and at the national and local levels can succeed in passing legislation to reduce the harmful effects of tobacco. • The country's federal nature also adds a layer of complexity, as national laws would need the support of all provinces. This has impeded the ratification of the FCTC, because producer provinces have opposed this. However, under the leadership of the Ministry of Health, working through the states and municipal governments (the bottom up strategy), obtaining the cooperation and support of other social groups, and launching public awareness campaigns over 10 years resulted in significant gains. It shows that even without ratifying the FCTC, measures can be adopted and laws can be passed to create 100 percent smoke-free environments in many locales.

industry's use of misleading terms such as "light" or "smooth" cigarettes; require strong health warnings on cigarette packs; disseminate messages to counter tobacco ads; redefine smoking as an addiction; and incorporate the themes of smoking prevention and control of second-hand smoke into the educational system. While some of these issues were addressed in the national law enacted in 2011—such as banning misleading words and placing graphic health warnings on cigarette packs—the Ministry continues to evaluate various national, provincial, and municipal laws to completely ban tobacco ads, promotions, and sponsorships. It also distributes information and teaching materials, conducts studies on tobacco marketing and ads, and organizes school competitions on the topic.

The MOH has also worked extensively to promote 100 percent smoke-free environments in public and private institutions, collective-use spaces, transport, and homes, and sets standards that ban smoking in work environments and closed public areas. To these ends, it created a national registry of smoke-free companies and institutions, which in 2012 listed 1,252 private enterprises, municipalities, public agencies, schools, hospitals, and national universities; trained staff in institutions that wanted to become 100 percent smoke-free and prepared good practices guides, and other training materials to get more institutions to create smoke-free spaces; offered technical assistance to provinces and municipalities on how to introduce laws on smoke-free areas; distributed information to the general public; and undertook studies and evaluations on smoke-free areas and the public's acceptance, as well as on their health benefits. The National Program, too, has worked to promote smoke-free urban areas through its cooperation with the Argentine Network of Healthy Municipalities. It develops training courses and offers technical and economic assistance to municipalities so they can meet the requirements to be considered 100 percent smoke-free, distributes materials at events, and devotes part of its website to this issue.

The MOH also participates in various efforts designed to help people stop smoking, such as a free telephone service to help smokers quit; "Quit and Win" contests; a web page to support smokers who want to stop;[25] the development of national guidelines on treating tobacco addiction, endorsed by more than 35 national scientific institutions, academia, and professionals; training health teams on treating tobacco addiction; and disseminating information on how to quit to the general public.

The MOH's monitoring activities include a tobacco module in the 2005 and 2009 National Survey of Risk Factors; a smoking survey among school adolescents in 2000, 2002, 2003, and 2007; and smoking surveys in large cities.

Civil-society groups, too, have been key in getting tobacco controls approved. They have formed coalitions, disseminated information, monitored compliance, delivered services, and worked collaboratively to counteract the industry's lobbying. These groups include the Coalition to Ratify the FCTC, the Argentine Anti-Smoking Union (UATA), the Argentine Tobacco Association (AsAT), Smoke-Free Partnership–Argentina (ALIAR), and Inter-American Heart Foundation-Argentina (Mercet and others 2010).

ALIAR, created in 2007, is a coalition of over 100 groups working to pass tobacco control laws and, particularly, to establish 100 percent smoke-free areas countrywide. ALIAR includes medical, human rights, and environmental associations; groups of health professionals; the restaurant sector; and communication organizations. The partnership supports legal projects at the municipal and provincial levels as a way to counter industry's actions to prevent the enactment of a national law. It also works with the media and human rights or gender organizations, and has contributed scientific evidence about the economic and health impacts of smoke-free areas, evaluated compliance by monitoring air quality and public opinion, and positioned itself as a reliable source of information.

UATA, created in 1987, has over 300 members that coordinate education activities and programs.

AsAT is a scientific group that was created in 2006; it consists of health professionals, journalists, educators, and public opinion makers, among others. It participates on commissions focused on education, the press and media, youth, Web pages, bulletins, policies, and inter-institutional relations.

The Inter-American Heart Foundation-Argentina, created in 2009, addresses projects with a multi-disciplinary perspective (medicine, law, economy, and social work): it promotes laws and public policies; develops education and training activities for the general public and specific audiences such as the health sector, the media, and civil society organizations; and is involved in research projects.

Argentina's powerful tobacco sector, both tobacco producers and cigarette manufacturers and sellers, pursued a sustained and multi-pronged opposition to the tobacco-control measures. In contrast to the situation in Uruguay, Argentina's tobacco producing sector is important to the country's economy and employment, particularly in the provinces of Jujuy, Salta, and Misiones, where 94 percent of the nation's tobacco is produced. Argentina exports almost 80 percent of its tobacco which, in 2011, totaled US$ 392.9 million and 82 million kg (MoALF 2011). The country produces 2 percent of the world's tobacco and accounts for 4 percent of the international trade of this product (Corradini and others 2004).

The country's tobacco industry (cigarette production and sales) is highly concentrated and privately owned. It consists of only two companies—Nobleza Piccardo (linked to BAT) and Massalin Particulares (a Philip Morris subsidiary), representing 37.2 percent and 62.8 percent, respectively, of the market's invoiced amount (González-Rozada 2006). It is estimated that in 2009, tobacco-growing contributed 0.2 percent to the country's GNP.[26] Regarding employment, tobacco-growing as a whole (primary and secondary activities) employed 170,754 workers, or 1 percent of the employed population at the national level. In the seven tobacco-growing provinces, tobacco-related employment represents an estimated 1.9 percent of employment—5.1 percent in Misiones, 4.3 percent in Jujuy, and 2.5 percent in Salta (MoALF 2011).

In general, the strategies the tobacco industry has used to block controls in Argentina are similar to those the industry has used in the United States and elsewhere. For example, it has pushed for a weak, voluntary self-regulation code that eliminated television ads since 2003; has drafted less stringent laws that neutralized or diverted attention from stronger initiatives; have promoted programs such as the "Courtesy of Choice" to avoid the establishment of 100 percent smoke-free environments, prevention programs for youth, and stricter measures; and has spread false claims about the policies' negative economic effects (Sebrie and others 2005).

Lessons Learned

Argentina's tobacco-control policy moved forward once the National Tobacco Control Program was established in 2003. Since then, much progress has been made: smoke-free environments have been created; studies have been conducted on the health and economic impacts and results from the interventions, which have provided valuable information for policy making; laws have been approved in most of the provinces and in several municipalities. At the national level, "stop smoking" services have been strengthened, and many activities to raise awareness of the issue have been developed.

This progress has been due to the MOH's strategy to lead and coordinate the interests of several actors (civil society organizations, scientific associations, provincial and municipal health ministries, and the public). These players, once aware of the tobacco-related problems, could then demand action from the state to stop the advance of the epidemic. Further, Argentina's civil society organizations have pressured lawmakers to pass tobacco-control measures, disseminated information on the impact of smoking and the myths associated with economic consequences from tobacco controls, and supported different initiatives such as smoke-free environments and national and provincial programs. Also, provincial and municipal authorities have introduced many regulations to control the tobacco epidemic even before the approval of the national law. The MOH, through the National Tobacco Control Program, has an important position to coordinate the actions of these many actors involved in the implementation of tobacco control measures.

The main lesson learned is that progress can be made in tobacco-control policies, even in a country where the tobacco industry is powerful and resists such measures. Working through state and municipal governments (the bottom-up strategy), obtaining the cooperation and support of various social groups, and launching public awareness campaigns over 10 years resulted in significant gains, despite the roadblocks. It also shows that, even without ratifying the FCTC, laws could still be passed to reduce the harmful effects of tobacco.

While many issues are still pending, efforts to date have led to multisectoral and multidisciplinary networks (such as the Coalition for the Ratification of the FCTC); the empowerment of actors who can generate greater demands for action; and the approval of provincial, municipal, and national laws.

Notes

1. The Ministry of Health's guidelines for small and medium enterprises are found at http://www.msal.gov.ar/argentina-saludable/pdf/Guia%20de%20 Recomendaciones%20PyMEs%20marzo%202011.pdf.

2. An example of a poster providing the public with such information is available at http://www.msal.gov.ar/argentina-saludable/media/Afiche%20grasas%20trans.pdf.

3. For an example of such a website, please visit www.alimentosargentinos.gob.ar.

4. Argentina, Dirección de Estadísticas e Información de Salud. 2010. Estadísticas vitales-2010. Serie 5-Número 54.2011. Buenos Aires: Ministerio de Salud de la Nación.

5. Argentina, Ministerio de Salud de la Nación. 2011. – Sal + Vida: Disminuí el Consumo de Sal para Tener una Vida Más Saludable. Hoja Informativa.

6. Colombia, Alcaldía Mayor de Bogotá and Instituto de Desarrollo Urbano. 1999. Plan Maestro de CicloRutas.

7. Colombia, Instituto de Desarrollo Urbano. 2011a. CicloRutas. http://www.idu.gov.co /web/guest/espacio_CicloRutas.

8. Colombia, Instituto de Desarrollo Urbano. 2009. Programas desarrollados en función de la promoción y uso de las CicloRutas.

9. Colombia, Instituto de Desarrollo Urbano. 2011a. CicloRutas. http://www.idu.gov.co /web/guest/espacio_CicloRutas.

10. Colombia, Instituto de Desarrollo Urbano 2003. Ciclorrutas. Sistema de transporte alternativo. http://www.itdp.org/documents/Seminar/3%20Andres%20Trujillo.pdf.

11. Colombia, Alcaldía Mayor de Bogotá, Instituto de Desarrollo Urbano. 1999. Plan Maestro de CicloRutas.

12. Colombia, Instituto de Desarrollo Urbano 2003. Ciclorrutas. Sistema de transporte alternativo. http://www.itdp.org/documents/Seminar/3%20Andres%20Trujillo.pdf.

13. Colombia, Cámara de Comercio de Bogotá. 2009. Movilidad en bicicleta en Bogotá. http://camara.ccb.org.co/documentos/5054_informe_movilidad_en_bicicleta_en _Bogotá.pdf.

14. Colombia, Cámara de Comercio de Bogotá and Universidad de Los Andes. 2011. Observatorio de movilidad. Comportamiento de los indicadores de movilidad de la ciudad a diciembre de 2010.

15. Colombia, Instituto de Desarrollo Urbano 2011b. Infraestructura Transmilenio. http:// www.idu.gov.co/web/guest/construcciones_transmilenio.

16. Bogotá, Colombia, Departamento Nacional de Planeación. 2000. Documento Conpes 3093. Sistema de servicio público urbano de transporte masivo de pasajeros de Bogotá.

17. Colombia, Secretaría de Cultura, Recreación y Deportes. 2011. "Bogotá cuenta con seis Parques Biosaludables para todo el público."http://www.culturarecreacionydeporte .gov.co/portal/node/2059.

18. Colombia, Instituto Distrital de Recreación y Deporte. 2010. Adopta un Parque. http://www.idrd.gov.co/htms/seccion-adopta-un-parque_128.html.

19. Colombia, Concejo de Bogotá. 2002. Acuerdo 78 de 2002 (Accord No. 78 of 2002). http://www.alcaldiaBogotá.gov.co/sisjur/normas/Norma1.jsp?i=6824.

20. Colombia, Instituto Distrital de Recreación y Deporte. 2010. Adopta un Parque. http://www.idrd.gov.co/htms/seccion-adopta-un-parque_128.html.

21. Even today, those interviewed remember the slogan "Bogotá may not have an ocean, but it has the Ciclovía," something that in their view was a very successful marketing strategy.

22. Mexico, 2012. Encuesta Nacional de Salud y Nutrición 2012, Evidencia para la Política Pública en Salud. Obesidad en adultos: los retos de la cuesta abajo. Available at http://ensanut.insp.mx/doctos/analiticos/ObesidadAdultos.pdf.

23. Text available in http://www.parlamento.gub.uy/Leyes/AccesoTextoLey.asp?Ley=18256&Anchor. Last accessed on: March 26, 2013.

24. Argentina, Ministerio de Salud de la Nación. 2009. Reducción de los Ingresos Hospitalarios por Síndromes Coronarios Agudos Luego de la Implementación Exitosa de la Legislación 100% Libre de Humo. Boletín de Vigilancia de Enfermedades No Transmisibles y Factores de Riesgo No. 1.

25. To view the web page, please visit www.dejohoydefumar.gov.ar.

26. In 2002, three multinational tobacco companies (Japan Tobacco, Philip Morris, and British American Tobacco) held the greatest share of the tobacco market, with income exceeding US$ 121 million. This figure is greater than the combined GDP of Albania, Bahrain, Belize, Bolivia, Botswana, Cambodia, Cameroon, Estonia, Georgia, Honduras, Jamaica, Jordan, the former Yugoslav Republic of Macedonia, Malawi, Malta, Moldova, Mongolia, Namibia, Nepal, Paraguay, Senegal, Tajikistan, Togo, Uganda, Zambia, and Zimbabue (PAHO 2004).

Bibliography

Alcaldía Mayor de Bogotá D.C., Instituto Distrital de Cultura y Turismo. 2007. La ciclovía: laboratorio para el futuro: Alcaldía Mayor de Bogotá D.C. Bogotá, Colombia.

Alonso, C., and M. González-Rozada. 2010. *Algunas consideraciones para el tratamiento del Convenio Marco de Control de tabaco.* http://www.utdt.edu/ver_contenido.php?id_contenido=5595&id_item_menu=11594.

Barnoya J., and S. Glantz. 2002. "Tobacco Industry Success in Preventing Regulation of Secondhand Smoke in Latin America: The 'Latin Project.'" *Tobacco Control* 11:305–14.

Blanco-Marquizo, A., B. Goja, A. Peruga, M. R. Jones, J. Yuan, J. M. Samet, P. N. Breysse, and A. Navas-Ancien. 2010. "Reduction of Secondhand Tobacco Smoke in Public Places Following National Smoke-Free Legislation in Uruguay." *Tobacco Control* 19: 231–4.

Bruni, J. M. 2005. *Costos directos de la atención médica de las enfermedades atribuibles al consumo de tabaco en Argentina.* Buenos Aires: Ministry of Health.

Brunner, E., K. Rees, K. Ward, M. Burke, and M. Thorogood. 2007. "Dietary Advice for Reducing Cardiovascular Risk." *The Cochrane Collaboration.* http://www.cochrane.org.

Bushnell, D. 2007. *Colombia. Una nación a pesar de sí misma.* Bogotá: Editorial Planeta.

Cain, A., G. Darido, M. R. Baltes, P. Rodríguez, and J. C. Barrios. 2006. *Applicability of Bogotá's Transmilenio BRT System to the United States.* Washington, DC: Federal Transit Administration.

Cámara de Comercio de Bogotá. 2009. "Movilidad en bicicleta en Bogotá." Available at http://camara.ccb.org.co/documentos/5054_informe_movilidad_en_bicicleta_en_bogota.pdf (last accessed on March 27, 2013).

Cervero, R., O. L. Sarmiento, E. Jacoby, L. F. Gomez, and A. Neiman. 2009. "Influences of Built Environments on Walking and Cycling: Lessons from Bogotá." *International Journal of Sustainable Transportation* 3: 203–26.

Champagne, B. M., E. Sebrié, and V. Schoj. 2010. "The Role of Organized Civil Society in Tobacco Control in Latin America and the Caribbean." *Salud Pública de México* 2 (S330–9): 10–52.

Colombia, Alcaldía Mayor de Bogotá, Instituto de Desarrollo Urbano. 1999. Plan Maestro de CicloRutas.

Colombia, Instituto de Desarrollo Urbano 2003. Ciclorrutas. Sistema de transporte alternativo. http://www.itdp.org/documents/Seminar/3%20Andres%20Trujillo.pdf.

Colombia, Universidad Nacional (National University). 2005. Resultados del estudio de Ciclovía y Recreovía. Estudio Universidad Nacional. Convenio inter administrativo N0311 entre el IDRD y la Facultad de Ciencias de la Universidad Nacional.

Colombia, Alcaldía Mayor de Bogotá and Instituto Distrital de Cultura y Turismo. 2007. La ciclovía: laboratorio para el futuro.

Comité Cívico Pro Defensa de la Ciclovía. 2008. Defendamos nuestra ciclovía (*Let's Defend Our Ciclovía*). http://www.defendamoslaciclovia.blogspot.com/.

Concejo de Bogotá 1998. "Acuerdo 6 de 1998. Por el cual se adopta el Plan de Desarrollo Económico, Social y de Obras Públicas para Santa Fe de Bogotá, D.C., 1998-2001 – Por la Bogotá que queremos." Available at http://www.alcaldiabogota.gov.co/sisjur/normas/Norma1.jsp?i=535 (last accessed March 27, 2013).

Corradini, E., H. Zilocchi, R. Cuesta, R. Segresso, M. Jiménez, and J. Musco. 2004. *Caracterización del Sector Productor Tabacalero en la República Argentina.* Segunda versión. Serie Documentos de Investigación. Universidad Católica Argentina.

Dávila, J., and Gilbert, A. 2001. "Los alcaldes mayores y la gestión de Bogotá, 1961–2000." *Territorios* 5: 15–34.

Díaz del Castillo, A., O. L. Sarmiento, R. Reis, and R. C. Brownson. 2011. "Translating Evidence to Policy: Urban Interventions and Physical Activity Promotion in Bogotá, Colombia, and Curitiba, Brazil." *Translational Behavioral Medicine* 1: 350–60.

El Tiempo. 2007. "Arrancó Campaña por Alcaldía de Bogotá con Polémica por TransMilenio en la Carrera Séptima." http://www.eltiempo.com/archivo/documento/CMS-3412063.

———. 2011a. "Así Van las Troncales de TransMilenio en la Calle 26 y la Carrera 10a." http://www.eltiempo.com/colombia/Bogotá/ARTICULO-WEB-NEW_NOTA_INTERIOR-10843124.html.

———. 2011b. "Revelan sobrecostos en TransMilenio de Soacha, la 26 y la 10a." Available at http://www.eltiempo.com/archivo/documento/CMS-9965966 (last accessed March 27, 2013).

Ferlay, J., H. R. Shin, F. Bray, D. Forman, C. Mathers, and D. M. Parkin. 2008. *GLOBOCAN 2008 v2.0, Cancer Incidence and Mortality Worldwide.* International Agency for Research on Cancer CancerBase No. 10 http://globocan.iarc.fr/.

Ferrante, D., J. Konfino, R. Mejía, P. Coxson, A. Moran, and L. Goldman. 2012. "Relación costo-utilidad de la disminución del consumo de sal y su efecto en la incidencia de enfermedades cardiovasculares en Argentina." Rev Panam Salud Pública 32(4): 274–80.

Ferrante, D., N. Apro, V. Ferreira, M. Virgolini, V. Aguilar, M. Sosa, P. Perel, and J. Casas. 2011. "Feasibility of Salt Reduction in Processed Foods in Argentina." *Revista Panamericana de Salud Pública* 29 (2): 69–75.

Gilbert, A. 2008. "Bus Rapid Transit: Is Transmilenio a Miracle Cure?" *Transport Reviews* 28(4): 439–67.

Gómescásseres, T. 2003. "Deporte, Juego y Paseo Dominical: la Recreación en Espacios Públicos Urbanos, el Caso de la Ciclovía de Bogotá." Tesis para optar por el título de socióloga. Universidad Nacional de Colombia.

Gómez, L. F., J. C. Mateus, and G. Cabrera. 2004. "Leisure-Time Physical Activity among Women in a Neighborhood in Bogotá, Colombia: Prevalence and Socio-Demographic Correlates." *Cadernos de Saúde Pública* 20(4): 1103–9.

González-Rozada, M. 2006. *Economía del Control del Tabaco en los Países del MERCOSUR y Estados Asociados. Argentina 1996–2004.* Washington, DC: OPS.

González-Rozada, M., M. Molinari, and M. Virgolini. 2008. *The Economic Impact of Smoke-Free Laws on the Sales in Bars and Restaurants in Argentina.* Buenos Aires: Universidad Torcuato Di Tella and Minsiterio de Salud de la Nación.

Hidalgo, D., P. Custodio, and P. Graftieaux. 2007. *A Critical Look at Major Bus Improvements in Latin America and Asia: Case Studies of Hitches, Hiccups, and Areas for Improvement; Synthesis of Lessons Learned.* Washington, DC: World Bank.

Hoehner, C. M., J. Soares, D. P. Perez, I. C. Ribeiro, C. E. Joshu, M. Pratt, B. D. Legetic, D. C. Malta, V. R. Matsudo, L. Ramos, E. J. Simões, and R. C. Brownson. 2008. "Physical Activity Interventions in Latin America: A Systematic Review." *American Journal of Preventive Medicine* 34(3): 224–33.

Hu, F., J. Manson, and W. Willett. 2001. "Types of Dietary Fat and Risk of Coronary Heart Disease." *Journal of the American College of Nutrition* 20(1): 5–19.

Hu, F., M. Stampfer, J. Manson, E. Rimm, G. Colditz, B. Rosner, C. Hennekens, and W. Willett. 1997. "Dietary Fat Intake and the Risk of Coronary Heart Disease in Women." *New England Journal of Medicine* 337: 1491–9.

Instituto de Estudios Urbanos. 2011. Evolución urbana de Bogotá. Bogotá, Colombia. Available in http://institutodeestudiosurbanos.info/endatos/0100/0140/01411.htm (last accessed on: March 27, 2013).

Konfino J., D. Ferrante, R. Mejía, P. Coxson, A. Moran, L. Goldman, and E. Perez-Stable. 2012. "Impact on Cardiovascular Disease Events of the implementation of Argentina's National Tobacco Control Law." *Tobacco Control* 2012;0: 1–8.

Leal, M. T., and R. L. Bertini. 2003. "Bus Rapid Transit: An Alternative for Developing Countries." Paper presented at the Institute of Transportation Engineers annual meeting, August 24–27, Seattle, Washington.

Ministerio de Salud de la Nación. 2013. "Encuesta Mundial de Tabaquismo en Adultos. Argentina 2012." Resumen ejecutivo. Buenos Aires, Argentina.

Meisel, J. D., O. L. Sarmiento, F. Montes, E. O. Martinez, P. D. Lemoine, J. A. Valdivia, R. C. Brownson, and R. Zarama 2013. "Network Analysis of Bogotá's Ciclovía Recreativa, a Self-Organized Multisectorial Community Program to Promote Physical Activity in a Middle-Income Country." *American Journal of Health Promotion* (in press). doi: http://dx.doi.org/10.4278/ajhp.120912-QUAN-443.

Mercet Champagne, Beatriz, and Ernesto Sebrié y Verónica Schoj. 2010. "The Role of Organized Civil Society in Tobacco Control in Latin America and the

Caribbean." *Salud Pública de México* Vol. 10(52supl2): S330–39. Available at http://bvs.insp.mx/rsp/articulos/articulo_e4.php?id=002536 (last accessed on April 8, 2013).

Mejia, R., V. Schoj, J. Bernoya, L. Flores, and E. Pérez-Stable. 2008. "Tobacco Industry Strategies to Obstruct the FCTC in Argentina." *CVD Prevention and Control* 3(4): 173–9.

Metro en Bogotá. 2012. "Se abre la discusión sobre la posibilidad de tener un tranvía por la 7a." http://www.metroenBogotá.com/movilidad-Bogotá/carrera-7/se-abre-la-discusion-sobre-la-posibilidad-de-tener-tranvia-por-la-7a.

MoALF (Ministry of Agriculture, Livestock, and Fisheries). 2011. *Impacto Regional del Convenio Marco para el Control de Tabaco. Cuantificación del Impacto Económico y Social en las Provincias Productoras de Tabaco.* Buenos Aires: MoALF.

Mockus, A., J. Castro, J. Ruiz, J. Silva, and N. Cordoba. 1997. *Descentralización. Modernización de la gestión en Santa Fe de Bogotá.* Bogotá: Fundación Corona.

Montes, F., O. L. Sarmiento, R. Zarama, M. Pratt, G. Wang, E. Jacoby, T. Schmid, M. Ramos, O. Ruiz, O. Vargas, et al. 2012. "Do Health Benefits Outweigh the Costs of Mass Recreational Programs: An Economic Analysis of Four Ciclovía Programs." *Journal of Urban Health: Bulletin of the New York Academy of Medicine.*

Montezuma, R. 2003. *La Transformación de Bogotá. Redefinición Ciudadana y Espacial 1995–2000.* Quito Programa de Gestión Urbana. UN/HABITAT, Fundación Ciudad Humana.

Nair, P., and D. Kumar. 2005. "Transformation in Road Transport System in Bogotá: An Overview." *ICFAI Journal of Infrastructure* (September): 20–8.

OECD (Organisation for Economic Co-operation and Development). 2010. *Obesity and the Economics of Prevention: Fit or Fat.* Document prepared by Franco Sassi. OECD: Paris.

———. 2011. *Health at a Glance 2011: OECD Indicators.* OECD: Paris. http://dx.doi .org/10.1787/health_glance-2011-en.

OPS (Organización Panamericana de la Salud). 2009. *La Vía RecreActiva de Guadalajara, Facultades de Medicina e Ingeniería de la Universidad de los Andes BC, Centros para el Control y la Prevención de Enfermedades. Manual para implementar y promocionar la Ciclovía Recreativa.* Bogotá: OPS.

PAHO (Pan American Health Organization). 2004. *Tobacco Increases the Poverty of Countries.* Fact Sheet. Washington, DC: PAHO.

Peñalosa, E. 2002. "The Role of Transport in Urban Development Policy." In *Sustainable Transport: A Sourcebook for Policy-Makers in Development Cities.* Eschborn, Germany: GTZ.

Peñalosa, E. 2008. "La Ciclovía es un Patrimonio Cultural de los Bogotános." http://www .caracol.com.co/oir.aspx?id=578955.

Pichon-Riviere, A., A. Alcaraz, A. Bardach, F. Augustovski, J. Caporale, and F. Caccavo. 2013. "Carga de Enfermedad atribuible al Tabaquismo en Argentina." Documento Técnico IECS N° 7. Mayo 2013.

Pitarque, R., P. Perel, and G. Sanchez. 2000. *Mortalidad Anual Atribuible al Tabaco en Argentina, Año 2000. Programa Vigia.* Buenos Aires: Ministerio de Salud de la Nación.

Pizano, L. 2003. *Bogotá y el Cambio. Percepciones sobre la Ciudad y la Ciudadanía.* Bogotá: Universidad Nacional de Colombia y Universidad de los Andes.

Pucher, J., J. Dill, and S. Handy. 2010. "Infrastructure, Programs, and Policies to Increase Bicycling: An International Review." *Preventive Medicine* 50: S106–25.

Ramírez, A. 1983. "La Ciudad para El Ciudadano." In *Ciclovías, Bogotá para el Ciudadano*, edited by B. Villegas. Bogotá: Benjamín Villegas.

Ramírez, A. 2005. "Todos los Ombligos son Redondos." (unpublished paper).

Revista Cambio. 2008. Posibilidad de Cambio de Horario de la Ciclovía ha Puesto en Alerta a Sus Usuarios. No. 775. Bogotá, Colombia.

Revista Semana. 2007. TransMilenio Destrozaría la Séptima. http://www.semana.com /enfoque-principal/transmilenio-destrozaria-septima/100700-3.aspx.

———. 2010a. "Líos en TransMilenio III." Available at http://www.semana.com/enfoque /lios-transmilenio-iii/134065-3.aspx (last accessed March 27, 2013).

———. 2010b. "Procuraduría Recomienda Suspender la Licitación de Obras de TransMilenio por la Séptima." http://www.semana.com/nacion/procuraduria -recomienda-suspender-licitacion-obras-transmilenio-septima/143525-3.aspx.

Ricaurte, A. M. 2010. "Cost Benefit Analysis of the CycloRoute in Bogotá: A Health and a Willingness to Pay Approach." Thesis for a master's degree in economics, Faculty of Economy, Universidad de los Andes.

Rossi, S., M. E. Roger, J. Leguiza, and A. Irurzun. 2005. *Carga Global de Enfermedad Atribuible al Tabaquismo en Argentina. Programa Vigia.* Buenos Aires: Ministerio de Salud de la Nación.

Sandoval, E. 2010. "¿A dónde Van los Recursos de TrasnMilenio?" In *Hace 10 años. La Historia de la Ciudad que Cambió.* Bogotá: Subdirección Imprenta Digital.

Sandoya, E., and E. Bianco. 2011. "Mortalidad por tabaquismo y por humo de segunda mano en Uruguay." *Revista Uruguaya de Cardiología* 26: 201–06.

Sarmiento, O. L., and E. Behrentz. 2008. *La Ciclovía, Un Espacio sin Ruido.* Nota Uniandina.

Sarmiento, O. L., T. Schmid, D. Parra, A. D. del Castillo, L. Gómez, M. Pratt, E. Jacoby, J. D. Pinzon, and J. Duperly. 2010a. "Quality of Life, Physical Activity and Built Environment Characteristics among Colombian Adults." *Physical Activity and Health* 7: S181–95. Bogotá, Colombia.

Sarmiento, O. L., A. Torres, E. Jacoby, M. Pratt, T. Schmid, and G. Stierling. 2010b. "The Ciclovía-Recreativa: A Mass Recreational Program with Public Health Potential." *Journal of Physical Activity and Health* 7: S163–80.

Schoj, V., M. Alderete, E. Ruiz, S. Hasdeu, B. Linetzky, and D. Ferrante. 2010. "Impacto de Legislación 100% Libre de Humo en la Salud de los Trabajadores Gastronómicos de la Ciudad de Neuquén, Argentina." *Tobacco Control* 19 (2): 134–7.

Sebrie, E., J. Barnoya, E. Perez-Stable, and G. Stanton. 2005. "Tobacco Industry Successfully Prevented Tobacco Control Legislation in Argentina." *Tobacco Control* 14 (5).

Segura, E. 2011. "Movilidad y Espacio Público en el Planeamiento Urbano para Promover Ciudades Más Saludables: El Caso de las CicloRutas y TransMilenio en Bogotá D.C.-Colombia." PhD thesis, Bogotá: Escuela de Gobierno, Universidad de Los Andes.

TransMilenio. 2011a. Sistema TransMilenio. Cifras (Data). http://www.transmilenio.gov .co/WebSite/Contenido.aspx?ID=TransmilenioSA_TransmilenioEnCifras_Estadisticas Generales.

———. 2011b. Sistema TransMilenio. Componentes (Components). http://www .transmilenio.gov.co/WebSite/Contenido.aspx?ID_REDIRECT=TransmilenioSA _QuienesSomos_SistemaDeTransporte _Componentes.

Universidad Nacional (National University). 2005. Resultados del estudio de Ciclovía y Recreovía. Estudio Universidad Nacional. Convenio inter administrativo N0311 entre el IDRD y la Facultad de Ciencias de la Universidad Nacional. Colombia: Universidad Nacional

Universidad de Los Andes. 2011. "A los Andes en bici." 2011. Available at http://www .uniandes.edu.co/component/content/article/276-a-los-andes-en-bici (last accessed: March 27, 2013).

Varela, C. 1998. La Ciudad Latinoamericana en Nuestros Días. *Revista Austral de Ciencias Sociales* (2): 19–27.

WHO (World Health Organization). 2004. *Global Strategy on Diet, Physical Activity and Health*. Geneva: WHO.

CHAPTER 6

Lessons Learned and Agenda for the Future

María Eugenia Bonilla-Chacín and Claudia Trezza

Latin America and the Caribbean (LAC) have been experiencing a rapid demographic and epidemiological transition, with important health and economic consequences. Not only is the population in the region aging fast, but it is also experiencing major changes in lifestyle, including dietary changes and a more sedentary way of life. This, in turn, has resulted in changes in the region's disease and mortality profiles that is reflected in the increasing weight that noncommunicable diseases (NCDs)—such as heart disease, stroke, cancer, and diabetes—have in the regional burden of disease. These conditions also represent an increasing economic and development threat to households, health systems, and economies in LAC.

Much of this health and economic burden can be avoided, since many NCDs are due to exposure to preventable risk factors, such as an unhealthy diet, physical inactivity, tobacco use, and alcohol abuse. An unhealthy diet represents an important health risk for the LAC population. Dietary patterns in several of the region's countries are dense in energy—high in sodium, refined sugar, and fat; and low in fruits and vegetables. These energy-dense diets, combined with a sedentary lifestyle, are responsible for the high rates of overweight and obesity among adults in the region, particularly among women. The 2010 Burden of Disease Study ranked a high body mass index (BMI) as the leading health risk factor in Argentina, Chile, and Uruguay; the second in the Caribbean and in Mesoamerica, and in Colombia and República Bolivariana de Venezuela; and the third in the rest of the region (Lim and others 2012). Tobacco use remains among the first five leading health risk factors in the region, given the disability-adjusted life years lost (DALYs) attributed to it (Lim and others 2012). And alcohol abuse is the leading health risk factor in most of LAC. Indeed, in 2010 alcohol abuse was estimated to be the main health risk factor in all LAC subregions, save for the Caribbean and Argentina, Chile, and Uruguay, where alcohol ranks among the first five risk factors (Lim and others 2012). Alcohol abuse not only increases the risk of developing several NCDs, but it also raises the risk of injuries, particularly those resulting from traffic accidents and violence.

International and Regional Experiences with Multisectoral Interventions to Prevent Health Risk Factors—Lessons for LAC

Health policies are shaped not just by public officials, but also by an array of other actors and by broader contextual social and political processes (Roberts and others 2008). These processes, in turn, are shaped by the interaction of stakeholders, their relative power, their positions, and the public perception of a given health policy reform. The interplay between the different stakeholders, their power to shape policies, and the strategies they use inevitably affects the short- and long-term outcomes of any reform (Roberts and others 2008). These factors are not fixed and can be influenced through political strategies that the players adopt.

In the case of policies aiming to improve diet, increase physical activity, and reduce tobacco use and alcohol abuse, these processes tend to be even more complex. In contrast to secondary-prevention and control interventions that occur within the health system, these population-based interventions involve a multitude of actors and opposing forces within and outside government (table 6.1). They also require the active participation of several stakeholders in sectors outside of health, although the health sector's involvement is key to ensure that these interventions take place. Given this complexity, policymakers and other health advocates must cope with various challenges in the governance of the decision-making process of these interventions.

Despite these challenges, there are multiple examples of successful or promising multisectoral interventions to promote healthy living. Some of these examples were reviewed in chapters 4 and 5 and summarized in table O.2. To learn from these international examples, it is important to understand the processes whereby they were developed and implemented. To that end, it is important to examine: the major stakeholders who influenced and shaped policy decisions, their positions, incentives they faced and strategies they used, and the institutional arrangements that framed the decision-making process.

Main Stakeholders

In policies aimed at improving diet, ministries of health and local health authorities have not been the only governmental entities playing a role, with ministries of agriculture, institutes of industrial technology, consumer protection agencies (such as the U.S. Food and Drug Administration [FDA]), and others (table 6.1) also participating in important ways. The food industry has also actively participated, sometimes opposing the government's actions and sometimes working with it to advance public health goals. In addition, the restaurant and advertising industries have also played important roles in these processes. For instance, the amendment to Argentina's Food Code to regulate trans fats in processed foods was made possible thanks to the participation of the Ministry of Health (MOH); the Ministry of Agriculture, Livestock, and Fisheries (MoALF); the Argentine Fats and Oils Association (ASAGA); the Coordinator of Food Product Industries

Table 6.1 Cost-Effectiveness and Key Sectors Involved in Multisectoral Interventions Designed to Reduce Noncommunicable Disease Risk Factors

Risk factor	Cost-effectiveness	Intervention	Key sectors involved
Unhealthy diet	Best buys[a]	Salt-reduction strategies Replacing trans fats	Agriculture, health, food industry, food retail industry, advertising industry, restaurant associations, city governments, the legislature, others.
	Other cost-effective[b]	Regulating advertising on marketing of foods and beverages high in salt, fat, and sugar, especially to children Taxes and subsidies	
Physical inactivity	Effective with insufficient evidence on cost-effectiveness[c]	Modifying the built environment to increase physical activity	City governments, urban planning, transport, health, civil society organizations, and the media.
Community-based programs to improve nutrition and increase physical activity	Effective with insufficient evidence on cost-effectiveness[c]	Work-based programs School-based programs Other community-based programs	Agriculture, health, food industry, food retail industry, schools, work places, food retailers, others.
Tobacco use	Best buys[a]	Fiscal measures Banning smoking in public places. Raising awareness and increasing knowledge about dangers of tobacco use. Bans on tobacco advertising, promotion and sponsorship	Finance, health, agriculture, legislature, international organizations, tobacco industry, civil society organizations
Alcohol abuse	Best buys[a]	Fiscal policies Restrictions on availability and access to alcohol Limiting the hours of alcohol sales Age restrictions on alcohol purchase and sale	Federal and state governments, city governments, health sector, police, and civil society organizations.
	Other cost-effective efforts[b]	BAC[d]	

Source: Author, based on WHO 2011a.

Note: The table includes most of the programs reviewed for this study.

a. "Best buys" are interventions that the World Health Organization (WHO) considers as "cost-effective, low cost, and can be implemented in low resource settings" (WHO 2011a).

b. These are other cost-effective interventions that are not among WHO's "best buys."

c. These are effective interventions for which there is insufficient evidence on their cost-effectiveness.

d. Blood alcohol concentration.

(COPAL); the National Institute for Industrial Technology; the National Food Institute; and others.

In many policies to promote physical activity, local authorities (e.g. cities, municipalities, and communities) had leading roles in their design and implementation, particularly local transportation, sports and recreation, and urban planning agencies. For instance, in the current management and implementation of the Ciclovía in Bogotá the following sectors and actors participate: the City Department of Traffic and Transportation, urban planning agencies, the District Recreation and Sports Institute (IDRD), security agencies, marketing and service sectors, academia and research, health, education, and the environment.

In tobacco- and alcohol-control policies, different government entities have played important roles, including agencies in the health, agriculture, commerce, economy, and finance sectors, as well as agencies in the executive branches of government. In the efforts to control tobacco use and alcohol abuse, the role of civil society organizations has been particularly strong and effective in advocating and supporting policies. Particularly in the case of tobacco control, the tobacco industry and tobacco producers have been engaged as powerful stakeholders opposing control efforts.

Sometimes, the mobilization toward a public health goal does not originate in the government, but rather comes from external interest groups that advocate for reform. These groups can be provider groups, such as doctors or nurses; consumer groups; or groups that advocate for specific issues, such as preventing underage drinking in the United States, reducing tobacco use in Uruguay and Argentina, or temporarily closing roads to motor vehicles for recreational activities in Bogotá, Colombia. The legislative success of these groups depends on various factors, including their ability to convince and mobilize enough political players and to develop sound and well-based solutions to public health challenges.

Governments and health advocates face no shortage of difficulties in promoting healthy living. Not only do private companies and businesses tend to resist measures they view as overly intrusive or that could shrink their profits, citizens, too, often oppose measures if they feel that these infringe on their personal liberties or lifestyles, or that tell them how to live. Some of these stakeholders can be very powerful in terms of the resources they can mobilize to oppose these policies. This is particularly the case of the transnational tobacco, alcohol, and food and beverage industries. Efforts to improve public health through reductions of salt intake, the elimination of trans fats from processed foods, the imposition of taxes on alcohol, the addition of bike lanes, or the banning of smoking in public places, are far from immune to such opposition.

Governments also may face internal hurdles: often, policymakers differ on which public goals are valid and on how best to pursue them. For instance, in the case of tobacco control in producer countries, health ministries might disagree with agriculture and finance ministries. The establishment and subsequent removal of the Gorbachev era alcohol-control policies in the USSR is another example of policies that faced strong opposition within the government. Legislative or regulatory success often depends on the effectiveness of a government's strategy to align the interests of political parties and agencies, civil society groups, private businesses, and the public toward a common public health goal.

Stakeholder Strategies

International experience has shown that in order to overcome the challenges involved in multisectoral policies to promote healthy living, intense dialogue and negotiation with all parties is required, as are strong coordination mechanisms and institutional arrangements that favor such coordination, effective gauging and mobilizing of public opinion, available information and research to mobilize public opinion and important stakeholders, strong leadership from politicians and policymakers, and taking advantage of favorable conditions for the design and implementation of these policies.

For the dialogue and negotiation with different stakeholders to be successful, the incentives each actor faces must be clearly understood by policymakers. There are promising examples of agreements between the government and industry that aim at improving the population's health. Two of these examples are the agreements between the food industry and the Government of Argentina to reduce sodium in processed foods and the amendment of the Food Code to regulate the amount of trans fats in processed foods. In both instances policymakers clearly understood the incentives and limitations that industry faced, worked with it to overcome some of the challenges, and ultimately reached an agreement with it.

As a result of the government's initiating a dialogue, companies often have developed their own guidelines and standards to improve their impact on public health. In the United Kingdom, for example, food companies came up with their own standards for nutritional labels (Traffic Light System [TLS]).

These voluntary actions can be ineffective, however, forcing policymakers to impose regulations to replace them. In Europe, Canada, and the United States, early voluntary nutrition labeling actions failed to meet government standards and expectations, leading governments to switch to mandatory guidelines. In New York City, encouraging restaurants to voluntarily provide nutrition information in plain sight to customers proved ineffective, and the city government resorted to mandatory regulations (Mello 2009). Industry guidelines restricting inappropriate advertising—such as promoting unhealthy foods to children—proved weak and resulted in low levels of adherence across the industry. This led the Government of the United Kingdom to impose statutory regulations that restricted advertising for unhealthy foods by limiting the times during which ads for foods high in fat, sugar, and salt content could be aired on television (Hawkes 2007).

Sometimes the interplay between a government and the sector it seeks to regulate can be highly confrontational, and the government should be prepared for this. The regulation of the tobacco industry is such an example. Even countries that have successfully reduced tobacco prevalence through strong control policies still face hurdles, as is the case of Uruguay. In 2010, Phillip Morris International requested to the International Centre for Settlement of Investment Disputes (ICSID) an arbitration procedure against the Government of Uruguay for its tobacco-control policies, specifically for the requirement that 80 percent of the packages must display health warnings and for forbidding companies to differentiate their brands across products.

Most successful efforts also require strong coordination among the many stakeholders involved. Often, the MOH's leadership has been key to an effective coordination, as have institutional arrangements that favor it. Such was the case in Argentina, where the MOH coordinated the negotiations that led to the agreements to reduce sodium and to revise the country's Food Code in order to reduce trans fats in processed food. At the Ministry's behest, a National Commission to Eliminate Trans Fats and Reduce Salt was created, which includes several public and business organizations, scientific associations, and civil society groups. This also occurred in Uruguay, where at the request of the MOH, the National Alliance for Tobacco Control (ANCT), a coordination agency comprising government agencies, parastatals, international organizations, academic institutions, and nongovernmental organizations (NGOs), was established.

Policymakers and health advocates in general often gauge and mobilize public opinion as a strategy to gain support for these health promotion policies and ensure that their design and implementation actually occur. For instance, while the regulation to reduce trans fats was being discussed in New York City, the city's government delivered constant and persuasive messages to the public on the links between trans fats and coronary heart disease, a campaign that helped to generate consensus among the public in favor of the regulation. In Uruguay, too, the policy to promote smoke-free environments was coupled with vigorous communication campaigns to ensure the public's support. And similarly, in the city of Diadema, Brazil, education campaigns and discussions with alcohol retailers, quickly turned the public's opinion in favor of the alcohol-restriction policies.

In many of the successful instances, research played a critical role in the adoption of population-wide preventive interventions. A solid, independent, and convincing research base is indispensable in shaping public opinion and raising support for policies. In the United Kingdom, the decision to create a statutory regulation on advertising foods to children was influenced by research that found an association between advertising and children's food preferences, as well as a study showing that a large percentage of food advertising during children's air time targeted foods high in fat, sugar and salt (Hastings and Carins 2010). Research still needs to be communicated effectively to policymakers and the public. In many cases, civil society groups played a crucial role in publicizing data and raising awareness among the population.

At the heart of many of the successful cases has been the leadership and political commitment of a few key political figures. In Uruguay, a group of committed politicians and policymakers, including then-President Tabaré Vázquez, supported by strong advocacy groups successfully fought tobacco industry lobbying and installed comprehensive and effective tobacco-control policies. In Bogotá, the continuous efforts of two mayors, Antanas Mockus and Enrique Peñaloza, were behind the consolidation of the city's built environment. And in New York City, Mayor Michael Bloomberg's leadership has been one of the main drivers behind the different healthy lifestyles initiatives in the city.

Often policymakers' engagement is shaped by the advocacy and persuasion efforts of civil society groups. Such was the case in the minimum legal drinking age (MLDA) policies in the United States. Mothers Against Drunk Driving (MADD) in particular, an organization founded by the mother of a victim of a repeat drunk driver, was fundamental in convincing politicians and policymakers, including then-U.S. President Ronald Reagan, into passing a bill that awarded highway funds to states with anti-drunk-driving measures.

Taking advantage of favorable conditions or moments has also been key in the enactment and implementation of some of these policies. In terms of tobacco control, the Framework Convention on Tobacco Control (FCTC) has generated an international context that has facilitated the adoption of tobacco-control policies globally. The signing and ratification of the FCTC in Uruguay was a strong driver of that country's tobacco-control policies. Similarly, the decentralization process in Colombia made it possible for elected mayors to independently pursue policies that changed the built environment in Bogotá.

Unfinished Agenda for LAC

Given the region's disease profile, strengthening multisectoral efforts to reduce health risk factors, particularly those aimed at reducing tobacco use and alcohol abuse, should be of top importance in the region. Fortunately, there already are several cost-effective interventions designed to decrease exposure to tobacco use and alcohol abuse. There are fewer cost-effective interventions to improve diet and promote physical activity, however, except for those aimed at decreasing the intake of sodium and trans fats. Thus, controlling tobacco use and, particularly, alcohol abuse, which is the main health risk factor in most of the region, should be a priority. That said, given the importance of overweight and obesity as a risk factor, LAC countries also should experiment with different programs and policies aimed at stopping and even reversing the increasing prevalence of these conditions.

The region also has witnessed several examples of promising and some successful interventions to promote healthy living, including agreements between the government and the food industry in Argentina to reduce sodium and reforms to the Food Code to reduce trans fats in processed foods; a built environment in Bogotá, Colombia, that promotes physical activity; Academia das Cidades in Brazil also designed to promote physical activity; the National Agreements for Food Health in Mexico (Strategy against Overweight and Obesity); and tobacco-control policies in Uruguay. In these and other instances, groups of motivated and deeply committed policymakers and health advocates have worked diligently and successfully at the local and national levels to counter opposition and put in place effective and long-lasting policies to prevent NCDs.

And yet, with the exception of tobacco-control initiatives, there is relatively little and widely scattered evidence about ongoing activities to fight NCDs at the population level in LAC. In fact, much remains to be done in the region to improve diet, promote physical activity, and reduce tobacco use and alcohol abuse.

Ongoing efforts to reduce the intake of sodium and trans fats in Argentina, Brazil, Chile, Costa Rica, and Mexico are the exception. But these efforts need to be consolidated and evaluated. And the region's countries are only starting to design and implement community-based interventions to prevent and control overweight and obesity. Changing the rising trend in the percentage of overweight and obese people has proven difficult across the globe, but some policies have proven to be effective in improving diet and promoting physical activity. Further, since nutrition habits start very early on in life, and since the number of overweight children in the region is growing, school-level interventions are particularly important to consider and evaluate.

A promising blueprint in the fight against obesity was Mexico's National Agreement for Food Health. In response to the country's high rates of obesity, the government set up a comprehensive strategic plan that included the collaboration of multiple actors, including various government agencies, the private sector, civil society, and academia. The government intended to reduce overweight and obesity by increasing opportunities for physical activity and improving the population's diet. According to the plan, increased physical activity was to be pursued in the schools, workplaces, and neighborhoods and communities. Trans fats were to be banned, and programs were to be implemented across different sectors of society to encourage a greater intake of fruits, vegetables, and grains.

In an effort to counter the increase in sedentary lifestyles, some of the region's cities have put in place policies that encourage and facilitate physical activity. Many of the region's cities have Ciclovías,[1] sustainable public transportation systems, and/or bike routes, for example, but most of these efforts have centered in major urban centers in upper-middle-income countries. For instance, although most countries have at least one Ciclovía, most are in one or two large urban centers; only Brazil, Colombia, Mexico, and Peru have several functioning ones.[2] One of the best examples of a built environment is that in Bogotá, Colombia.

While almost all countries have signed the FCTC and have passed laws and regulations accordingly, often these are not fully enforced. And much remains to be done in terms of fiscal policies, as many countries still have room to increase taxes. In 2010, in only 4 of 32 countries for which information was available, did taxes represent more than 70 percent of the price of the most frequently sold brand of cigarettes (WHO 2011b).

Regarding policies on alcohol, most countries have some cost-effective interventions in place for controlling alcohol abuse, but, again, these are not necessarily enforced (WHO 2011c; Monteiro 2007). For instance, while most of the region's countries have laws setting caps on blood alcohol concentration levels while driving and restrictions on hours of alcohol sales, these regulations are not always enforced. In addition, because these laws have many gaps, particularly legislation restricting alcohol sales, there is much room to strengthen them. As mentioned earlier, alcohol abuse is the main health risk factor in most of the region, as it increases the risk of injuries and of developing NCDs. Despite this, information on comprehensive strategies to control alcohol abuse in the region remains scarce. The literature review done for this study found only two good examples of comprehensive strategies—interventions in the cities of Diadema and Paulina in Brazil—both at the local level.

Since some multisectoral interventions to prevent health risk factors are more effective at the regional level, it is important to develop regional and subregional approaches to promote healthy living. This is true for fiscal policies, particularly those dealing with tobacco and alcohol taxation. Harmonizing tobacco and alcohol pricing (through tax levels) would reduce the incentive for smuggling, for example. And standardizing tobacco advertising bans would also make these policies more effective. There are some subregional efforts to this end, such as the work of the Intergovernmental Commission for Tobacco Control (part of MERCOSUR).

The strengthening of surveillance systems should be part of any strategy to prevent and control NCDs, as this would improve the information base on these diseases. For example, to date there is very little data on some health risk factors, and when information is available, it is not standardized, which makes it very difficult to compare across countries or through time. This is particularly so for sedentary lifestyle, overweight and obesity, high blood glucose, high blood pressure, and abnormal blood lipids. Some countries do not even have data available on tobacco use and alcohol abuse. Information on the prevalence of NCDs, although available for most countries, is usually based on administrative data, which makes it difficult to disaggregate it across socioeconomic groups, rural or urban residence, or educational levels. Without this level of breakdown it is difficult to target interventions to those most in need.

Existing policies and interventions in LAC countries have been little researched and evaluated. Such assessment is particularly important in the case of policies aimed at improving diet and promoting physical activity, as there is less international evidence on cost-effective interventions targeting this issue. Project GUIA (Guide for Useful Interventions for Physical Activity in Brazil and Latin America),[3] is attempting to fill this void for the physical inactivity risk factor. As important as this Centers for Disease Control and Prevention (CDC)-funded project is in shedding light on current physical-activity interventions in the region, it is certainly not enough. If the region's governments are to execute meaningful plans to reduce NCDs, they must develop an overview of the current situation that demonstrates the strengths and weaknesses of ongoing programs and identifies where more action is needed. In addition, international experience and experience in the region has shown the importance of research not only for evidence-based policy making but also to gather public opinion in support of health promotion policies.

Notes

1. A Ciclovía program temporarily closes streets to motor-vehicle traffic, offering safe and free spaces for recreation and physical activity.

2. For additional information on other ciclovía programs in the Americas, visit http://www.cicloviasrecreativas.org/en/map.

3. Project GUIA is an effort whose goal is to identify, test, and disseminate effective interventions that promote physical activity in the Americas. This multidisciplinary partnership includes Brazil's Ministry of Health, several Brazilian universities, the Centers for Disease Control and Prevention (CDC), and the Pan American Health Organization (PAHO).

Bibliography

Hastings, G., and G. Carins. 2010. Food and Beverage Marketing to Children. In *Preventing Childhood Obesity. Evidence Policy and Practice*, edited by E. Waters, B. Swinburn, J. Seidell, and R. Uauy. Oxford, U.K.: Wiley-Blackwell.

Hawkes, C. 2007. *Marketing Food to Children: Changes in the Global Regulatory Environment 2004–2006*. Geneva: World Health Organization.

Lim, S., A. D. Lopez, C. J. L. Murray, M. Ezzati, T. Vos, A. D. Flaxman, G. Danaei, K. Shibuya, H. Adair-Rohani, M. Amann, H. R. Anderson, K. G. Andrews, M. Aryee, C. Atkinson, L. J. Bacchus, A. Bahalim, et al. 2012. "A Comparative Risk Assessment of Burden of Disease and Injury Attributable to 67 Risk Factors and Risk Factor Clusters in 21 Regions, 1990–2010: A Systematic Analysis for the Global Burden of Disease Study 2010." *Lancet* 380 (9859): 2224–60.

Mello, M. M. 2009. "New York City's War on Fat." *New England Journal of Medicine* 360 (19).

Monteiro, M. 2007. *Alcohol and Public Health in the Americas. A Case for Action.* Washington, DC: PAHO.

Roberts, M., W. Hsiao, P. Berman, and M. Reich. 2008. *Getting Health Reform Right: A Guide to Improving Performance and Equity.* New York: Oxford University Press.

Van Camp, D. J., N. H. Hooker, and D. M. Souza-Monteiro. 2010. "Adoption of Voluntary Front of Package Nutrition Schemes in UK Food Innovations." *British Food Journal* 112 (6): 580–91.

Weiler, T. 2010. *Phillip Morris vs. Urugay. An Analysis of Tobacco Control Measures in the Context of International Investment Law.* Report #1 for Physicians for a Smoke Free Canada, 28 July.

WHO (World Health Organization). 2008a. *The Global Burden of Disease: 2004 Update.* Geneva: WHO. Available at HYPERLINK "http://www.who.int/evidence/bod" www.who.int/evidence/bod

———. 2008b. *Global Health Observatory Data Repository, Noncommunicable Diseases Risk Factors.* Geneva: WHO.

———. 2011a. *Global Status Report on Noncommunicable Diseases 2010.* Geneva: WHO.

———. 2011b. *Report on the Global Tobacco Epidemic 2011.* Geneva: WHO.

———. 2011c. *Global Status Report on Alcohol and Health.* Geneva: WHO.

Survey Sources, Health Status Surveyed, and Information on NCDs and Disability, for Brazil, Chile, Colombia, El Salvador, and Honduras, Various Years

Country	Survey	Self-reported health status	NCD	Disability
Chile	Encuesta de Caracterización Socioeconómica Nacional (CASEN), 2009	—	Has [a household member] been treated for any of the following diseases in the past 12 months ..... [possible answers include hypertension, diabetes, depression, and asthma]	Do you suffer from any of these long-term conditions? [a maximum of three per person]: blindness or difficulty seeing, deafness or difficulty hearing, muteness or speech impairments, physical impairments, mental or intellectual impairments, Psychic or psychiatric impairments.
Colombia	Encuesta de Condiciones de Vida (ECV), 2008	In general ... is your health status [very good, good, average, poor]	... Do you suffer from a chronic disease (long-term disease, prolonged treatment, etc.)?	(Surveyed only at the household level) Does this household include someone who, due to a disease, accident, or birth condition, permanently experiences any of the following: total blindness; total deafness; mutism; difficulty moving or walking on his own; difficulty bathing, dressing, or feeding himself; difficulty going out by himself; difficulty understanding or learning.
Brazil	Pesquisa Nacional Amostra Domicilios (PNAD), 2008	In general [individual],do you consider your health status to be: very good, good, average, poor, very poor.	Has a physician or health professional told you that you have [a condition that affects your spine or ribs; arthritis or rheumatism; cancer; diabetes; bronchitis or asthma; high blood pressure; heart disease; kidney failure; depression; tuberculosis; tendonitis; cirrhosis]?	As a rule, because of a health problem, do you have difficulty in [feeding yourself; bathing yourself or going to the bathroom; lifting heavy objects; playing sports or doing physically demanding work, moving furniture or performing domestic chores, climbing stairs or ladders; bending down, kneeling, or curling up; walking for more than 1 km; walking for about 100 m; shopping for groceries, clothes, or medicines without help?

table continues next page

Country	Survey	Self-reported health status	NCD	Disability
El Salvador	Encuesta de Hogares de Propósitos Multiples (EHPM), 2007	—	In the month before the survey, which was the most recent symptom, disease, accidental injury that (name) had? [asthma/difficulty breathing; kidney failure; cancer/tumor; high blood pressure; heart failure/heart attack; diabetes] Question 107. Do you have diabetes?	—
Honduras	Encuesta Nacional de Condiciones de Vida, 2004 (ENCOVI 2004)	—	In the 30 days before the survey, did you have a disease or condition such as [high blood pressure; diabetes]? Question 116a, In the last five years, has anyone in this household been diagnosed with cancer?	—

Source: Author, based on information from the listed source surveys.
Note: — = not available.

Biases in any analysis using these data may arise from a person's subjective perception of "disease" (e.g., "do you have a given illness"?), or from compounding factors such as health-care utilization (e.g., "sought medical care due to a specific disease?") that are affected by perception and by physical and financial access to providers. Surveys can also vary in terms of the specificity of their questions, which can go from general (e.g., "any permanent health condition") to specific health problems (e.g., diabetes). The recall period can also vary depending on the type of question, since some ask about the month prior to the survey (e.g., "sought treatment in the last 30 days") or an existing diagnostic (e.g., "had been diagnosed with illness?"). Finally, questions can also vary in terms of the source of the information. Brazil's National Household Sampling Survey (PNAD), for example, asks whether a "medical professional has diagnosed specific illnesses," compared to Colombia's or Chile's survey that ask whether the person "has any chronic disease." Information about disability also varies. Most commonly used measures of disability are indicators of activities of daily living (ADL) that can also range from specific to general and from temporary to permanent. Because these differences in information about noncommunicable diseases (NCDs) are common in studies about these diseases, the findings and interpretations in this section should be considered carefully. As questions vary in the time frame the interviewee is asked to consider for his/her answers (a month, a year) and type of diagnosis (medical or self), the resulting NCD indicators are not fully comparable across countries.

Dietary Analysis Methodology

The dietary analysis presented in this paper uses the Living Standard Measurement Surveys (LSMS), the Income and Expenditures Surveys, and the nutritional database of the U.S. Department of Agriculture (USDA). The LSMS and the Income and Expenditure Surveys provide consumption information at the household level. USDA's National Nutrient Database for Standard Reference provides food composition information at the product level.

Three types of data are commonly used to evaluate food availability and consumption patterns in the world (Serra-Majem and others 2003). The first is data on food supply and utilization that form the basis of food balance sheets. These data allow for an assessment of food availability at an aggregate level, not of food actually consumed. In addition, these data would not allow any examination of the patterns of consumption or food availability across different socioeconomic groups. The second type of information is data from household income and expenditure surveys, which is the type used in this study. Although these data only provide information at the household level, they allow for evaluations to be made of socioeconomic variations across population groups. Finally, the third are data from individual food consumption surveys. This is the most reliable source of data for this type of analysis; however, individual nutrition surveys are expensive and time consuming and, thus, not many countries have them. For example, none of the Central American countries included in this study have nationally representative individual nutrition surveys. Table E.1 presents results using the three types of data for the early 1990s for Canada, Poland, and Spain. As seen in the table, results using household budget surveys, although higher, are similar to those using individual surveys.

Two years of detailed nutrition information from Guatemala and Panama and three years from Nicaragua have been analyzed for this study (table E.2). In most countries the years analyzed are close to each other, with most of the information coming from the first half of the 2000s. In Nicaragua, although data from the first two years come from comparable surveys, the sample frame slightly changed between the two surveys,[1] which renders the results not fully comparable. In addition, the 2009 data might reflect the effects of the economic and financial crisis and thus its results will also need to be assessed with caution. Finally, in Panama the years are 2003 and 2008, when the food crisis started, which might make comparisons across those two years problematic. Only in Guatemala are the data from the two years fully comparable.

In order to estimate the nutritional profile of households in Central America, the food items in the surveys were identified and matched with items in the USDA nutritional database. Most fruits, vegetables, beverages, and meats were matched at this stage. Products that were not matched were mainly local and traditional meals, some fruits or vegetables whose names could not be translated, and unusual foods. Then the meals in the surveys were matched with equivalent items in the USDA database. The list of Latino foods in the USDA database helped in matching several items in the surveys.[2]

Once the matching was done, the various foods were converted into their nutritional equivalent. First, the amount of food was converted into grams, using the typical presentation of a product as a reference. Upon obtaining the products' weight, nutritional consumption was assessed in terms of energy, carbohydrates, fats, and sodium. Energy is measured in calories; carbohydrates, fats, and sodium, in grams. Finally, consumed food also was classified based on the food groups used in "My plate," which is part of the communication strategy of the USDA's *Dietary Guidelines for Americans, 2010*. The food groups are grains, proteins, vegetables, fruits, dairy products, and oils. An "added sugar" category was added to these groups, which includes sweetened beverages, candies, and other desserts.

Table B.1 Mean Intake of Energy and Macronutrients from Food Balance Sheets (FBS), Household Budget Surveys (HBS), and Individual Surveys (IDS), Canada, Poland, and Spain, 1990–92

	Canada			Poland			Spain		
	FBS	HBS	IDS	FBS	HBS	IDS	FBS	HBS	IDS
Energy (kcal)	3,017	2,115	2,057	3,348	2,629	2,093	3,688	2,634	2,022
Protein (g)	94.8	81.3	87.2	102.5	71.6	68.2	105.0	93.5	90.7
Carbohydrates (g)	331.0	269.4	239.7	442.0	344.0	264.9	364.3	294.0	201.7
Fat (g)	128.4	84.6	80.4	114.7	106.9	83.3	181.2	121.0	84.1

Source: Serra-Majem and others 2003.
Note: kcal = kilocalories; g = grams.

Table B.2 Countries and Surveys, Costa Rica, Guatemala, Honduras, Nicaragua, and Panama, Various Years

	Baseline	Follow up
Costa Rica	Income and Expenditures, 2004	—
Guatemala	Living Standards, 2000	Living Standards, 2005/06, 2011
Honduras	Living Standards, 2004	—
Nicaragua	Living Standards, 2001	Living Standards, 2005, 2009
Panama	Living Standards, 2003	Living Standards, 2008

Note: — = not available.

Thus, the nutrient equivalent (Ni) of the food item (i) could be given by the expression:

$$N_i = \frac{Q_i 15}{100} * \frac{p_i}{100} * \frac{f(N)_i^k}{100}$$

where

Q_i = Quantity of food item (i) bought or acquired by the household in last 15 days in grams,

p_i = Percentage of edible portion, assumed to be 100, and

$f(N)_i^k$ = Conversion factor for the relevant nutrient or proximate (k) from nutritional database per 100 grams. (k) may be calories, carbohydrates, fat, or sodium.

Notes

1. The 2005 survey involves a larger sample; it included larger samples in areas already surveyed in 2001 and also sampled newly populated areas that did not exist in the previous census (1995). The expansion of the sample was not neutral. The biggest expansion was carried out in departments with the highest poverty incidence, probably areas of difficult access or with sparsely distributed populations.

2. For example, the USDA database includes several types of tamales and bean soups, and specific items such as arepas, pupusas, empanadas, and other typical Latino meals. Finally, meals without equivalences were broken down into their components and matched by the main ingredient. For example, "prepared turkey" (pavo preparado) was coded as the item "turkey, all classes, meat & skin, cooked, roasted" in the USDA database.

Bibliography

Serra-Majem, L., D. L. MacLean, D. Brulé, W. Sekula, R. Prattala, R. Garcia-Closas, A. Yngve, M. Lalonde, and A. Petrasovits. 2003. "Comparative Analysis of Nutrition Data from National, Household, and Individual Levels: Results from a WHO-CINDI Collaborative Project in Canada, Finland, Poland and Spain." *Journal of Epidemiological Community Health* 57 (1): 74–80.

USDA (United States, Department of Agriculture) and HHS (Department of Health and Human Services). 2010. *Dietary Guidelines for Americans, 2010.* 7th ed. Washington, DC: U.S. Government Printing Office.

WHO (World Health Organization). 2004. *The Global Burden of Disease.* Geneva: WHO.

———. 2008. *The Global Burden of Disease: 2004 Update.* Geneva: WHO.

Environmental Benefits Statement

The World Bank is committed to reducing its environmental footprint. In support of this commitment, the Office of the Publisher leverages electronic publishing options and print-on-demand technology, which is located in regional hubs worldwide. Together, these initiatives enable print runs to be lowered and shipping distances decreased, resulting in reduced paper consumption, chemical use, greenhouse gas emissions, and waste.

The Office of the Publisher follows the recommended standards for paper use set by the Green Press Initiative. Whenever possible, books are printed on 50% to 100% postconsumer recycled paper, and at least 50% of the fiber in our book paper is either unbleached or bleached using Totally Chlorine Free (TCF), Processed Chlorine Free (PCF), or Enhanced Elemental Chlorine Free (EECF) processes.

More information about the Bank's environmental philosophy can be found at http://crinfo.worldbank.org/crinfo/environmental_responsibility/index.html.

green
press
INITIATIVE

www.ingramcontent.com/pod-product-compliance
Lightning Source LLC
Chambersburg PA
CBHW082353270326
41935CB00013B/1608